"THERE WILL BE BLOOD"

# NAILBITER

## VOLUME ONE

Story by
JOSHUA WILLIAMSON

Art by
MIKE HENDERSON

Colors by
ADAM GUZOWSKI

Letters & Book Design by
JOHN J. HILL

Edited by
ROB LEVIN

NAILBITER Created by
JOSHUA WILLIAMSON &
MIKE HENDERSON

## NAILBITER

VOLUME ONE: THERE WILL BE BLOOD
First printing. OCTOBER 2014.
Copyright © 2014 Joshua Williamson
and Mike Henderson. All rights reserved.
Published by Image Comics, Inc. Office of
publication: 2001 Center Street, Sixth Floor,
Berkeley, CA 94704. Originally published in
single magazine form as NAILBITER #1-5,
by Image Comics. "Nailbiter," its logos, and
the likenesses of all characters herein are
trademarks of Joshua Williamson and Mike
Henderson, unless otherwise noted. "Image"
and the Image Comics logos are registered
trademarks of Image Comics, Inc. No part
of this publication may be reproduced or
transmitted, in any form or by any means
(except for short excerpts for journalistic or
review purposes), without the express written
permission of Joshua Williamson, Mike Henderson
or Image Comics, Inc. All names, characters,
events, and locales in this publication are
entirely fictional. Any resemblance to actual
persons (living or dead), events, or places, without
satiric intent, is coincidental. Printed in the USA.
For information regarding the CPSIA on
this printed material call: 203-595-3636
and provide reference #RICH−585453.
For international rights, contact:
foreignlicensing@imagecomics.com.
ISBN: 978-1632151124

# ISSUE ONE

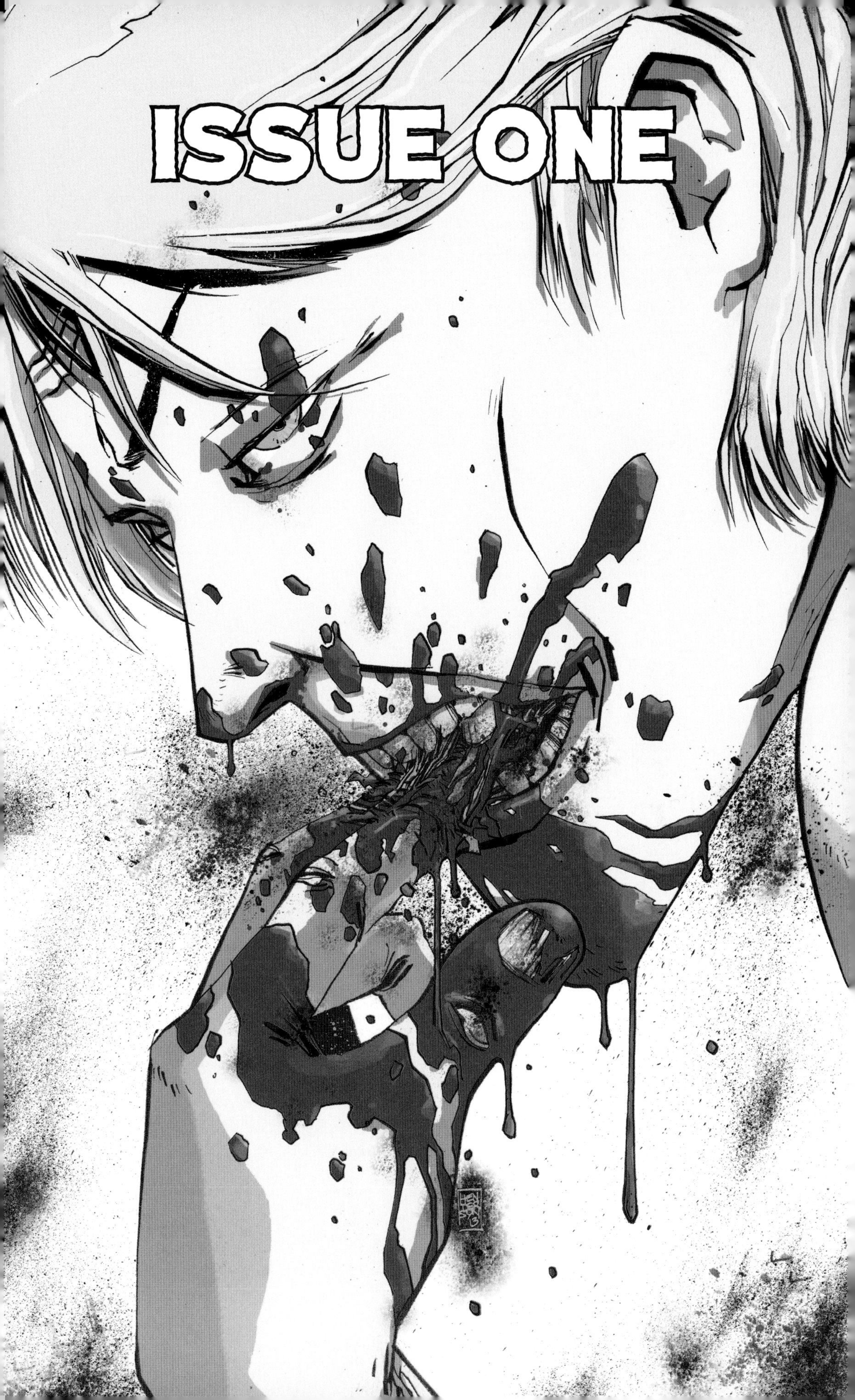

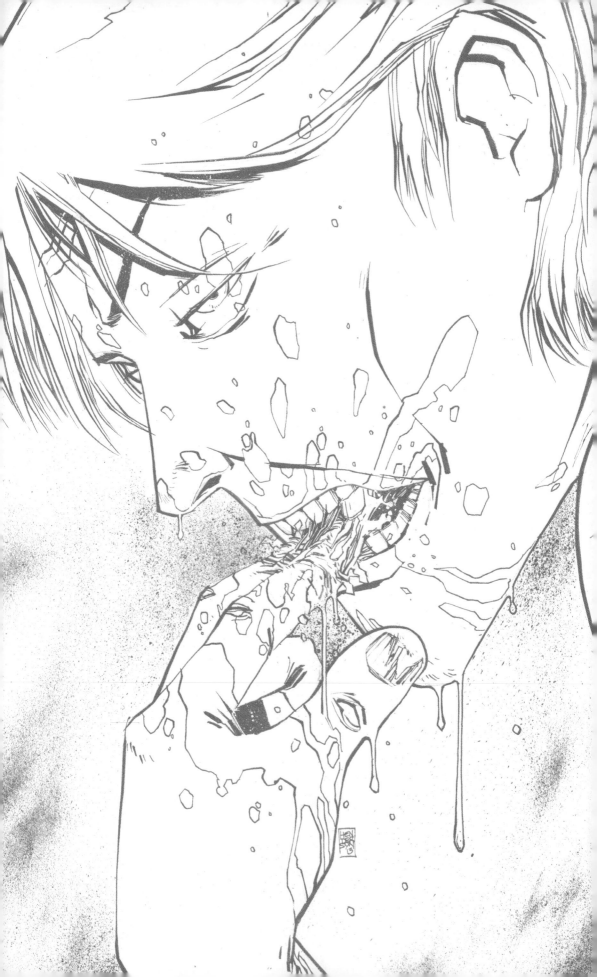

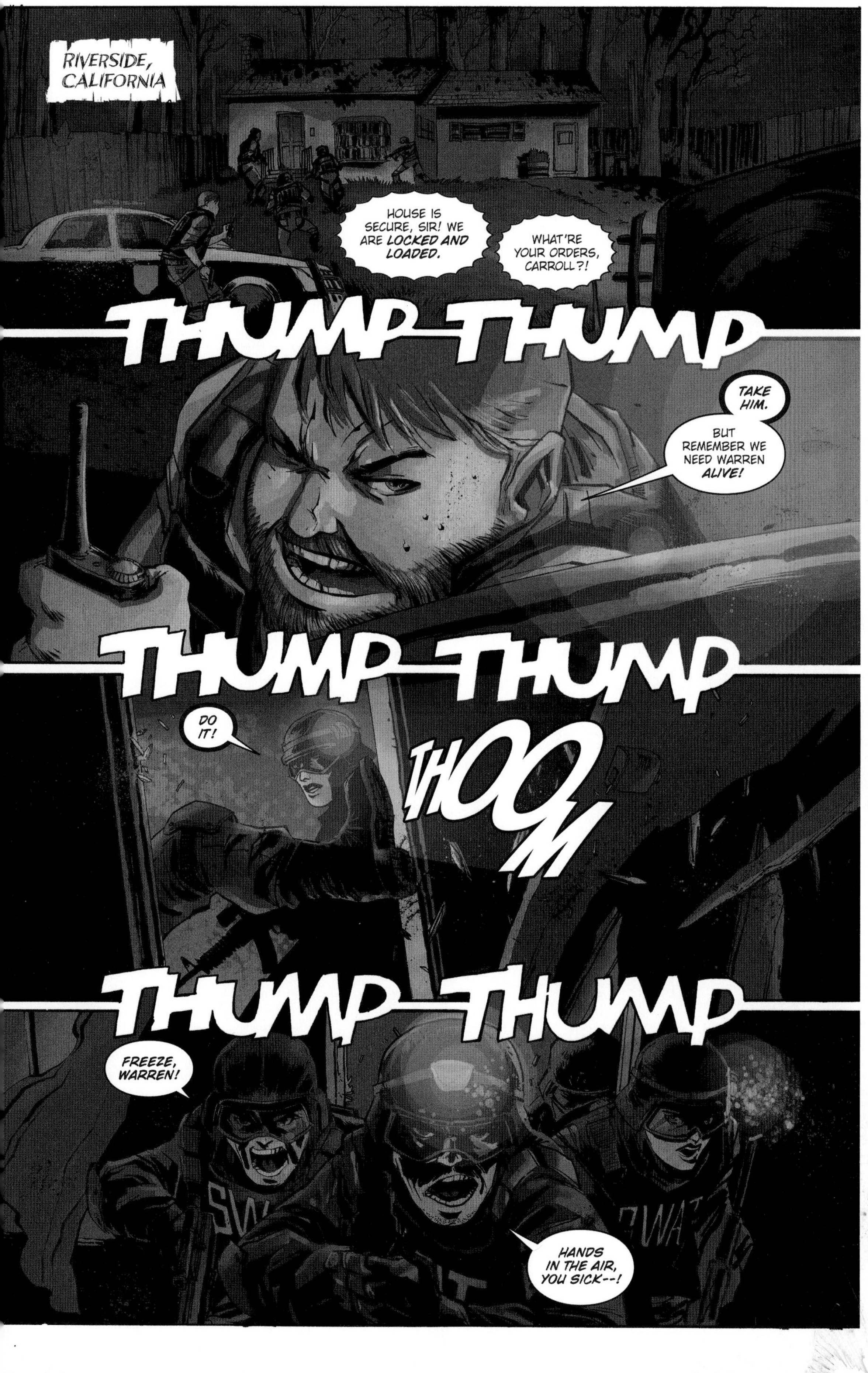
RIVERSIDE, CALIFORNIA
HOUSE IS SECURE, SIR! WE ARE LOCKED AND LOADED.
WHAT'RE YOUR ORDERS, CARROLL?!
THUMP THUMP
TAKE HIM.
BUT REMEMBER WE NEED WARREN ALIVE!
THUMP THUMP
DO IT!
THOOM
THUMP THUMP
FREEZE, WARREN!
HANDS IN THE AIR, YOU SICK--!

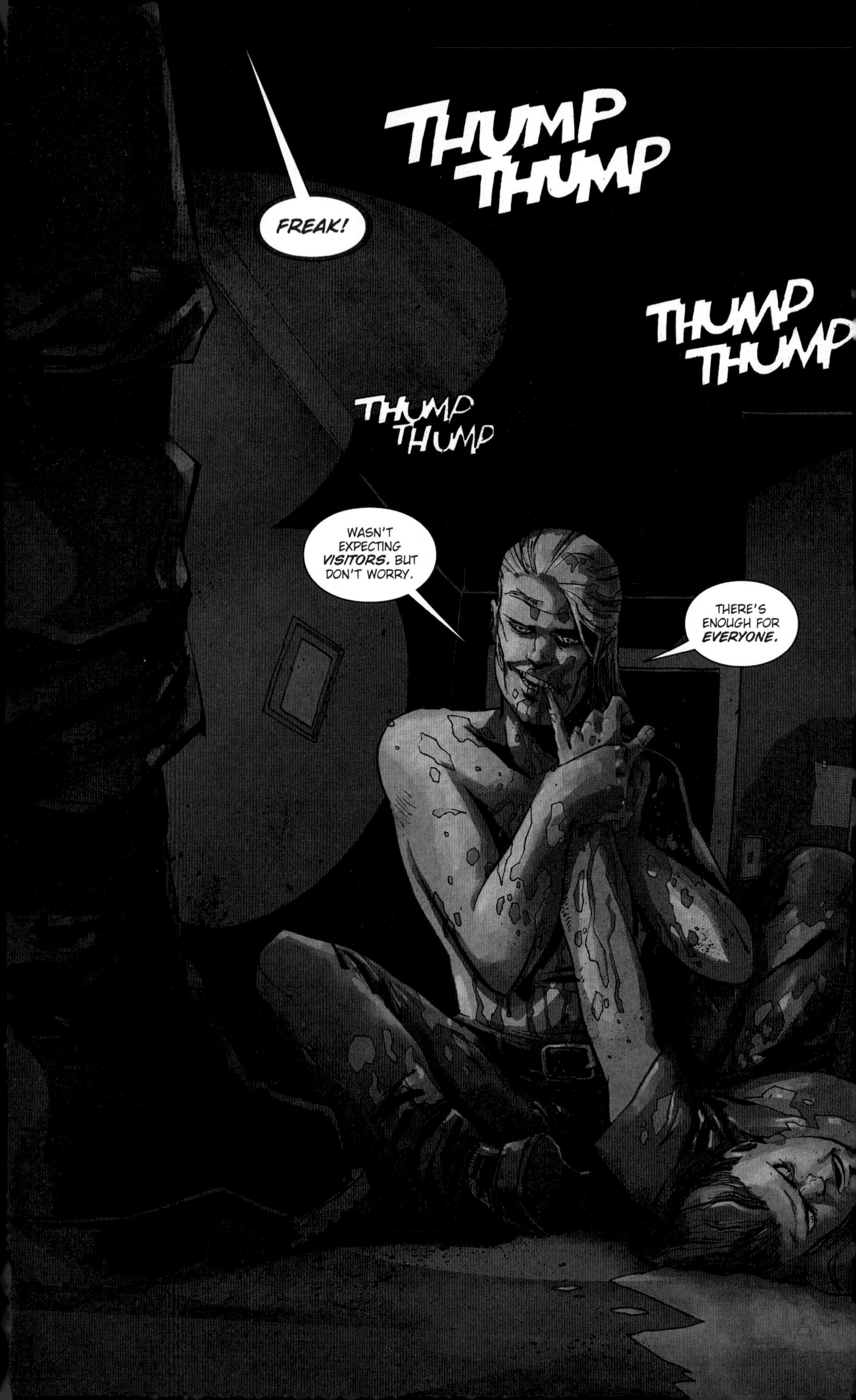
FREAK!
THUMP THUMP
THUMP THUMP
THUMP THUMP
WASN'T EXPECTING VISITORS. BUT DON'T WORRY.
THERE'S ENOUGH FOR EVERYONE.

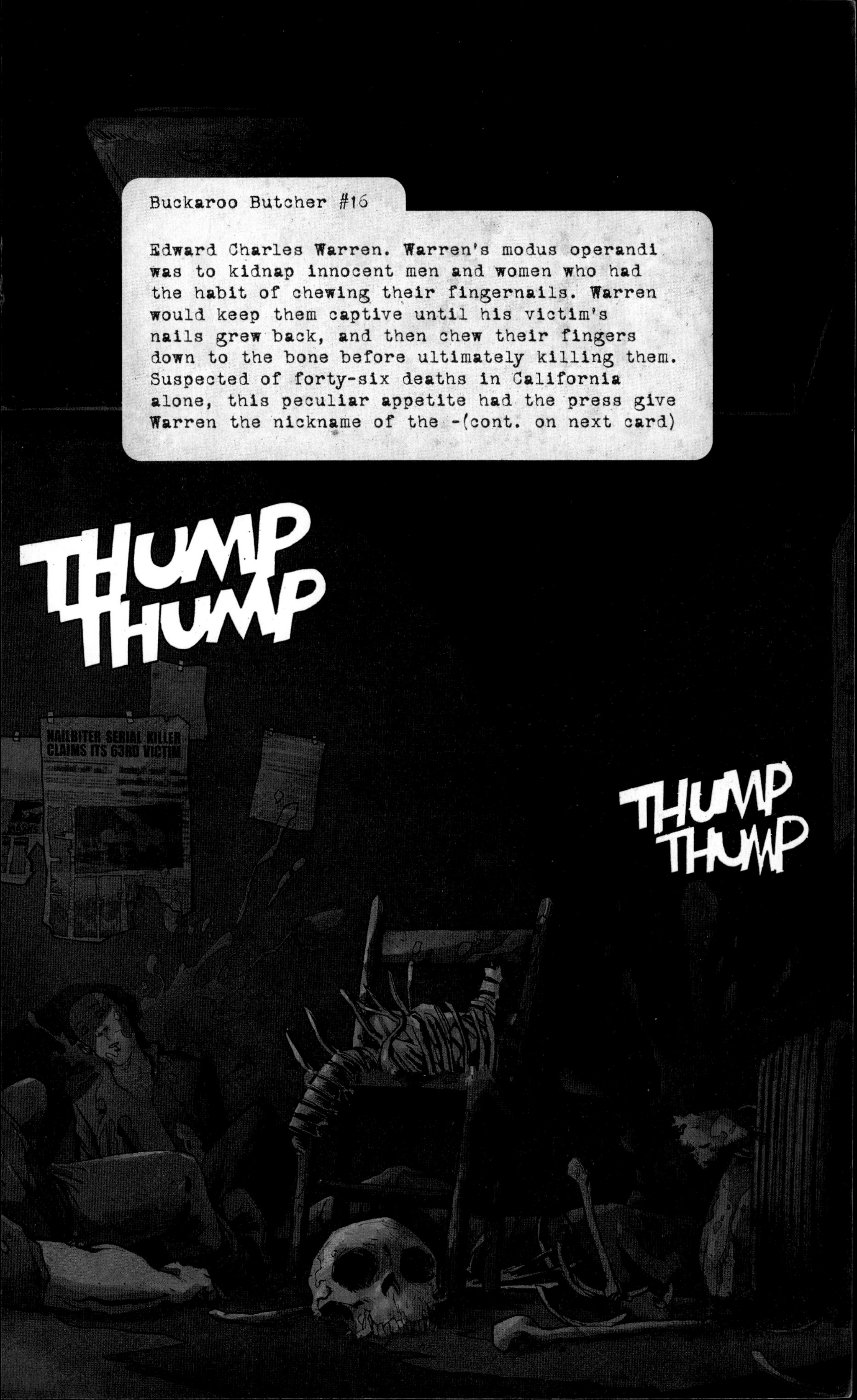
Buckaroo Butcher #16
Edward Charles Warren. Warren's modus operandi was to kidnap innocent men and women who had the habit of chewing their fingernails. Warren would keep them captive until his victim's nails grew back, and then chew their fingers down to the bone before ultimately killing them. Suspected of forty-six deaths in California alone, this peculiar appetite had the press give Warren the nickname of the -(cont. on next card)
THUMP THUMP
NAILBITER SERIAL KILLER CLAIMS ITS 63RD VICTIM
THUMP THUMP

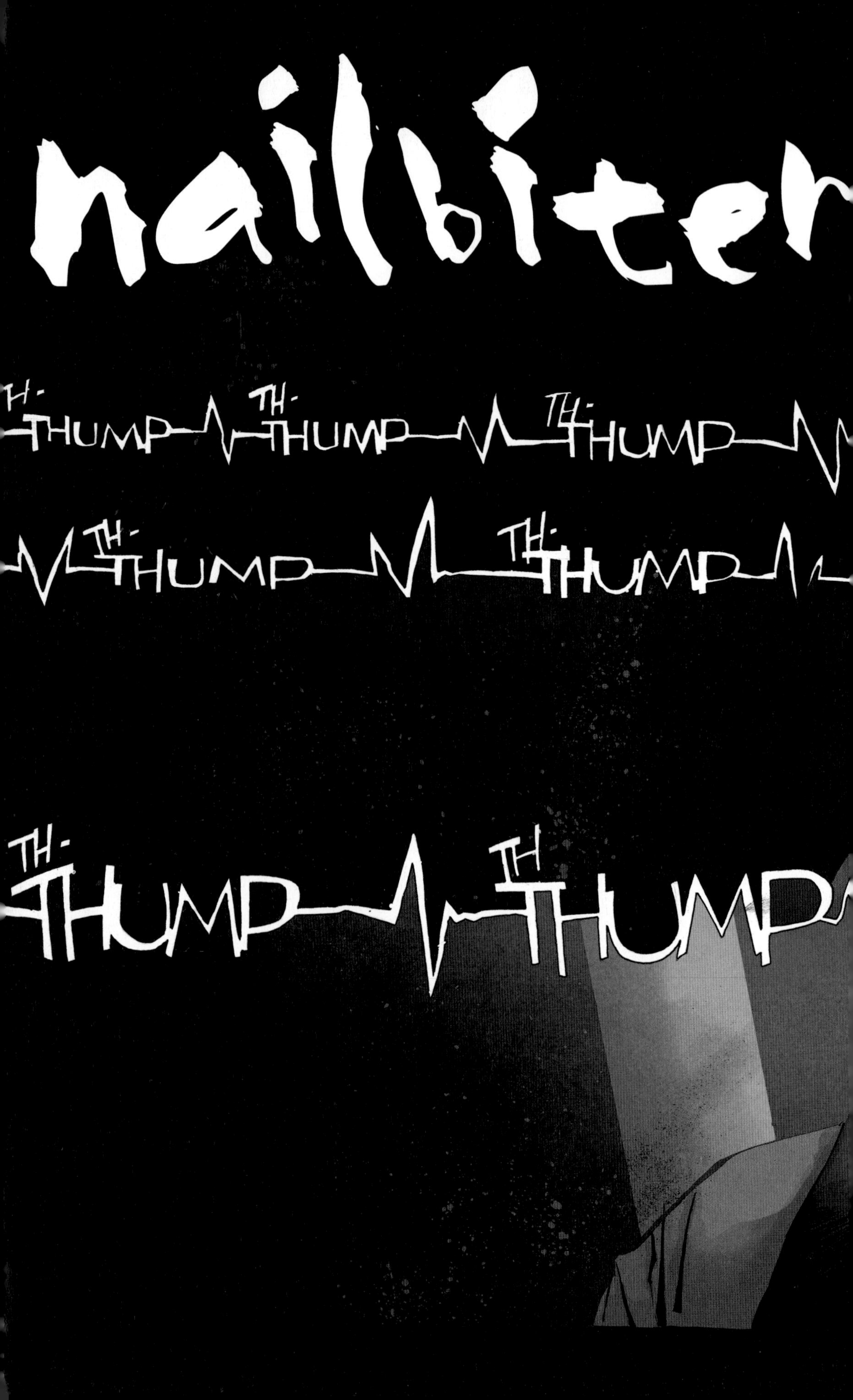
nailbiter
TH-THUMP
TH-THUMP
TH-THUMP
TH-THUMP
TH-THUMP
TH-THUMP
TH THUMP

# chapter One

## "there will be blood"

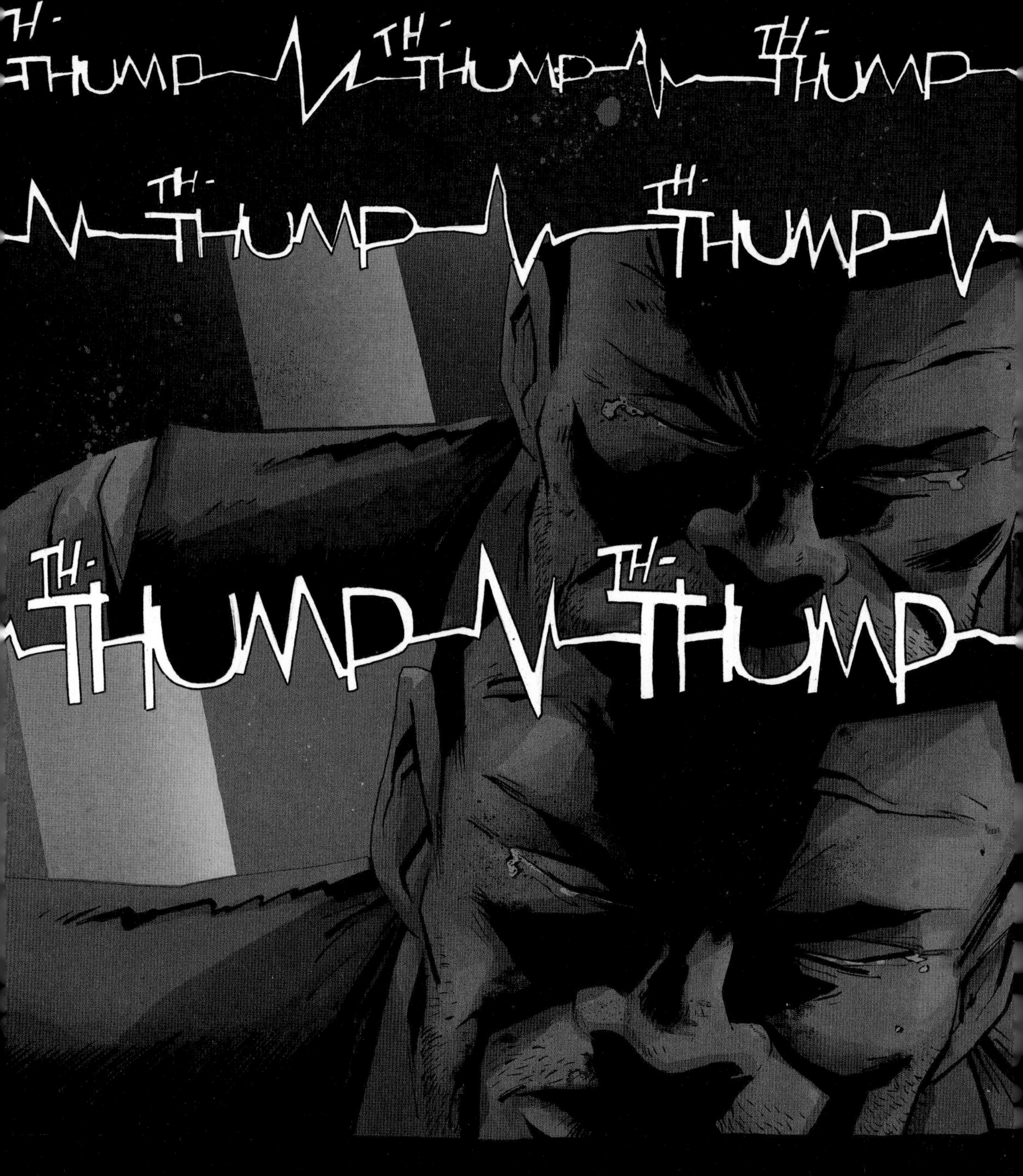

TH-THUMP
TH-THUMP
TH-THUMP
TH-THUMP
TH-THUMP
TH-THUMP
TH-THUMP

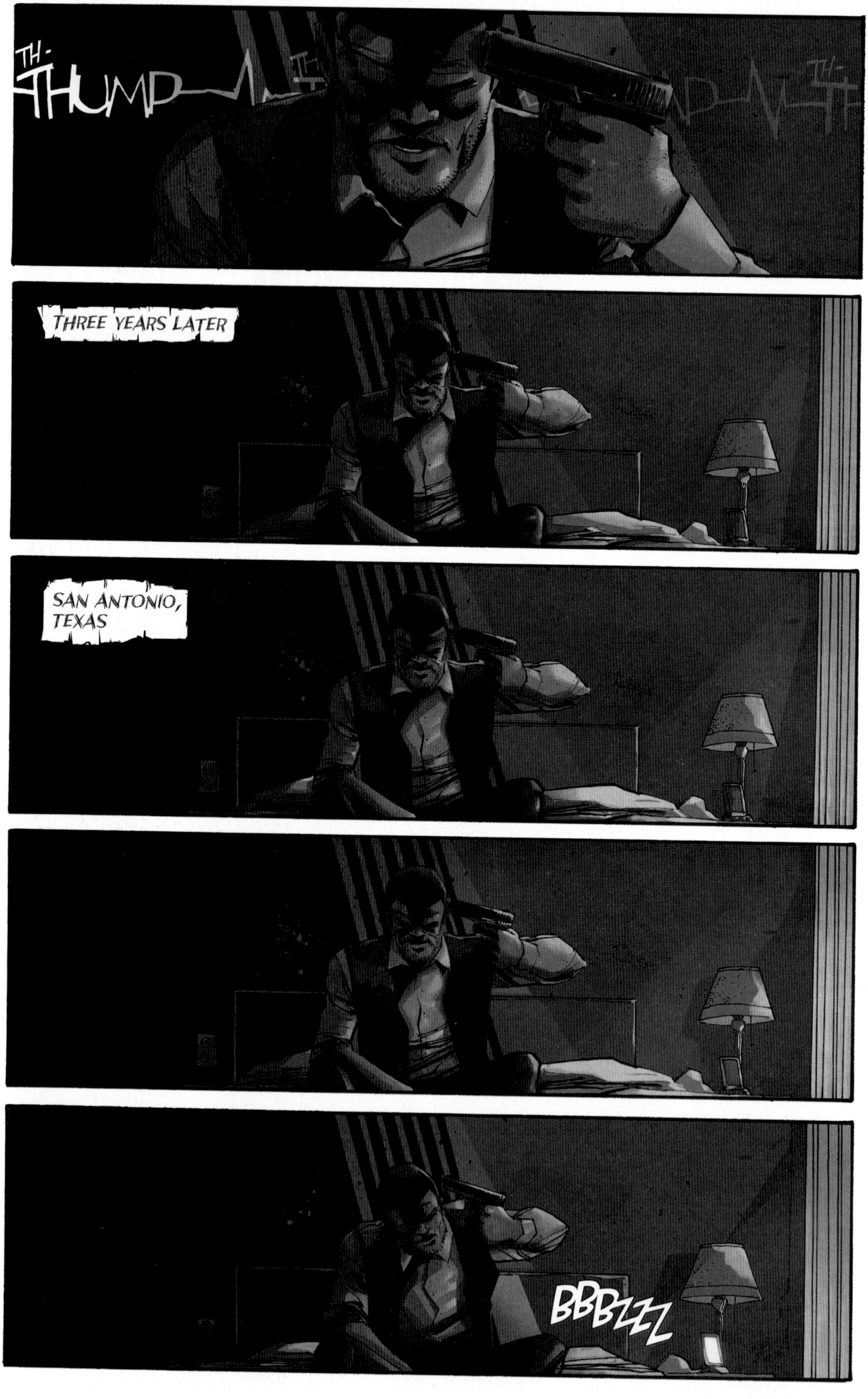
TH-THUMP
TH-
THREE YEARS LATER
SAN ANTONIO, TEXAS
BBBZZZ

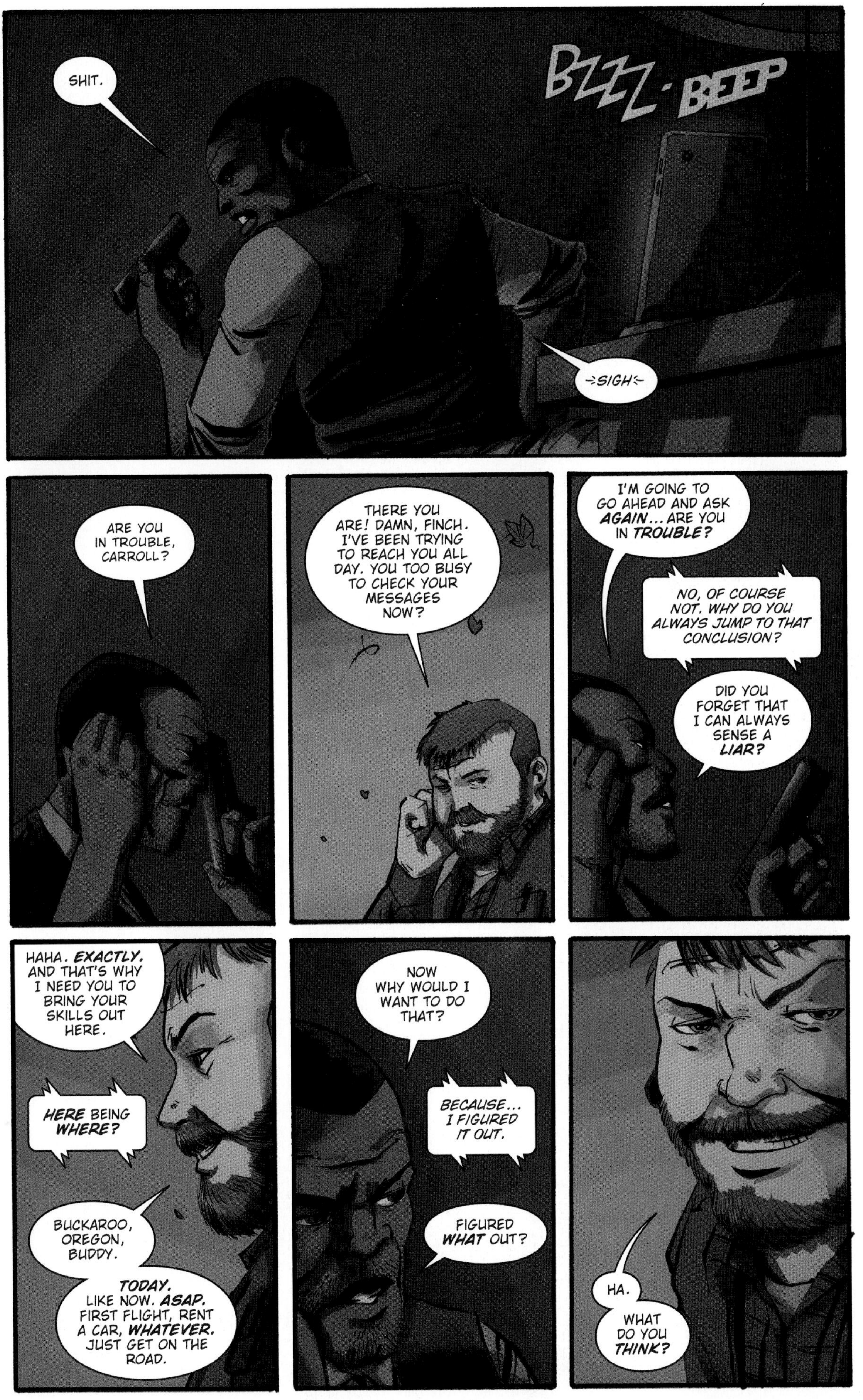
SHIT.
BZZZ-BEEP
~SIGH~
ARE YOU IN TROUBLE, CARROLL?
THERE YOU ARE! DAMN, FINCH. I'VE BEEN TRYING TO REACH YOU ALL DAY. YOU TOO BUSY TO CHECK YOUR MESSAGES NOW?
I'M GOING TO GO AHEAD AND ASK AGAIN... ARE YOU IN TROUBLE?
NO, OF COURSE NOT. WHY DO YOU ALWAYS JUMP TO THAT CONCLUSION?
DID YOU FORGET THAT I CAN ALWAYS SENSE A LIAR?
HAHA. EXACTLY. AND THAT'S WHY I NEED YOU TO BRING YOUR SKILLS OUT HERE.
HERE BEING WHERE?
BUCKAROO, OREGON, BUDDY.
TODAY. LIKE NOW. ASAP. FIRST FLIGHT, RENT A CAR, WHATEVER. JUST GET ON THE ROAD.
NOW WHY WOULD I WANT TO DO THAT?
BECAUSE... I FIGURED IT OUT.
FIGURED WHAT OUT?
HA.
WHAT DO YOU THINK?

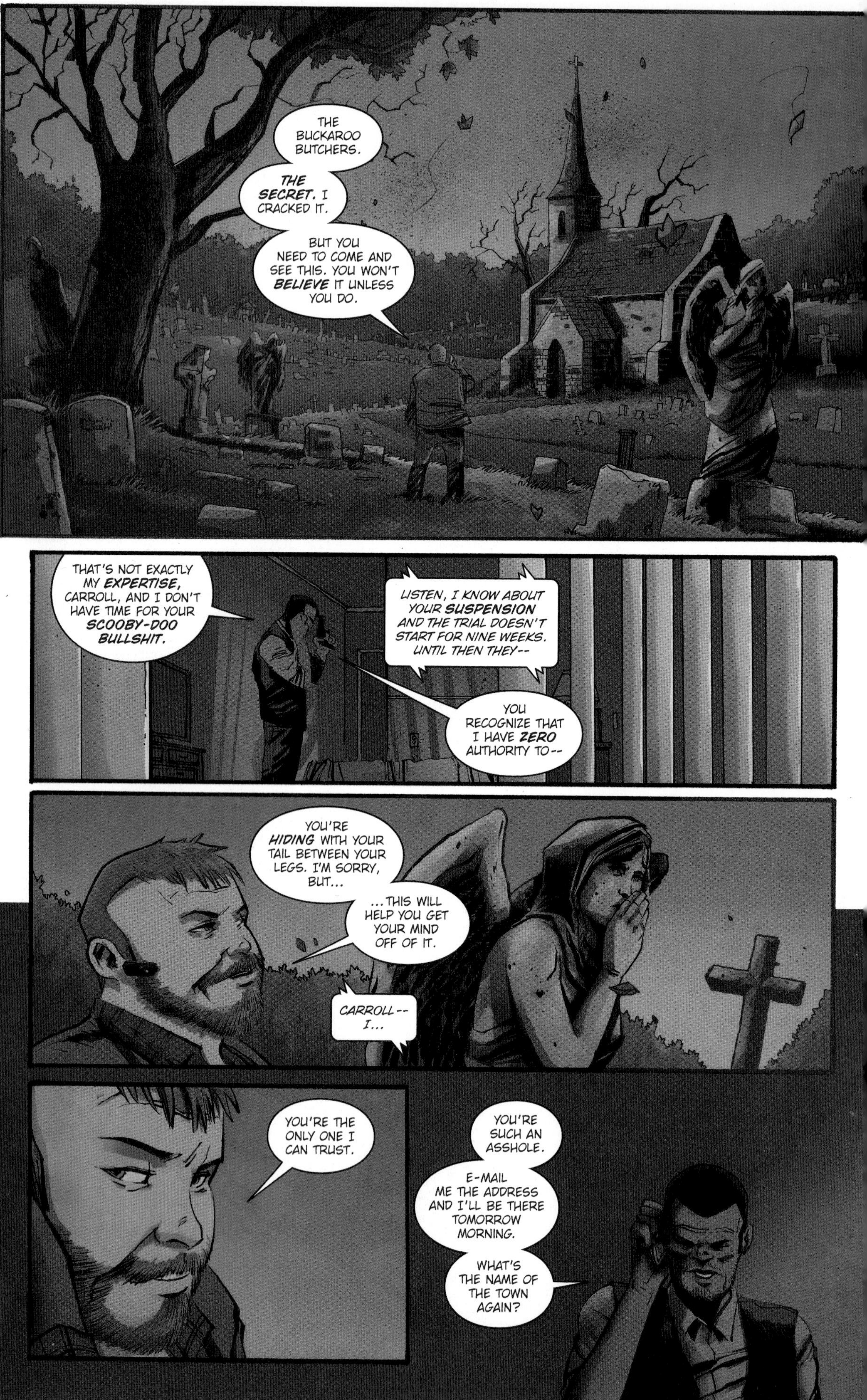
THE BUCKAROO BUTCHERS.
THE SECRET. I CRACKED IT.
BUT YOU NEED TO COME AND SEE THIS. YOU WON'T BELIEVE IT UNLESS YOU DO.
THAT'S NOT EXACTLY MY EXPERTISE, CARROLL, AND I DON'T HAVE TIME FOR YOUR SCOOBY-DOO BULLSHIT.
LISTEN, I KNOW ABOUT YOUR SUSPENSION AND THE TRIAL DOESN'T START FOR NINE WEEKS. UNTIL THEN THEY--
YOU RECOGNIZE THAT I HAVE ZERO AUTHORITY TO--
YOU'RE HIDING WITH YOUR TAIL BETWEEN YOUR LEGS. I'M SORRY, BUT...
...THIS WILL HELP YOU GET YOUR MIND OFF OF IT.
CARROLL-- I...
YOU'RE THE ONLY ONE I CAN TRUST.
YOU'RE SUCH AN ASSHOLE.
E-MAIL ME THE ADDRESS AND I'LL BE THERE TOMORROW MORNING.
WHAT'S THE NAME OF THE TOWN AGAIN?

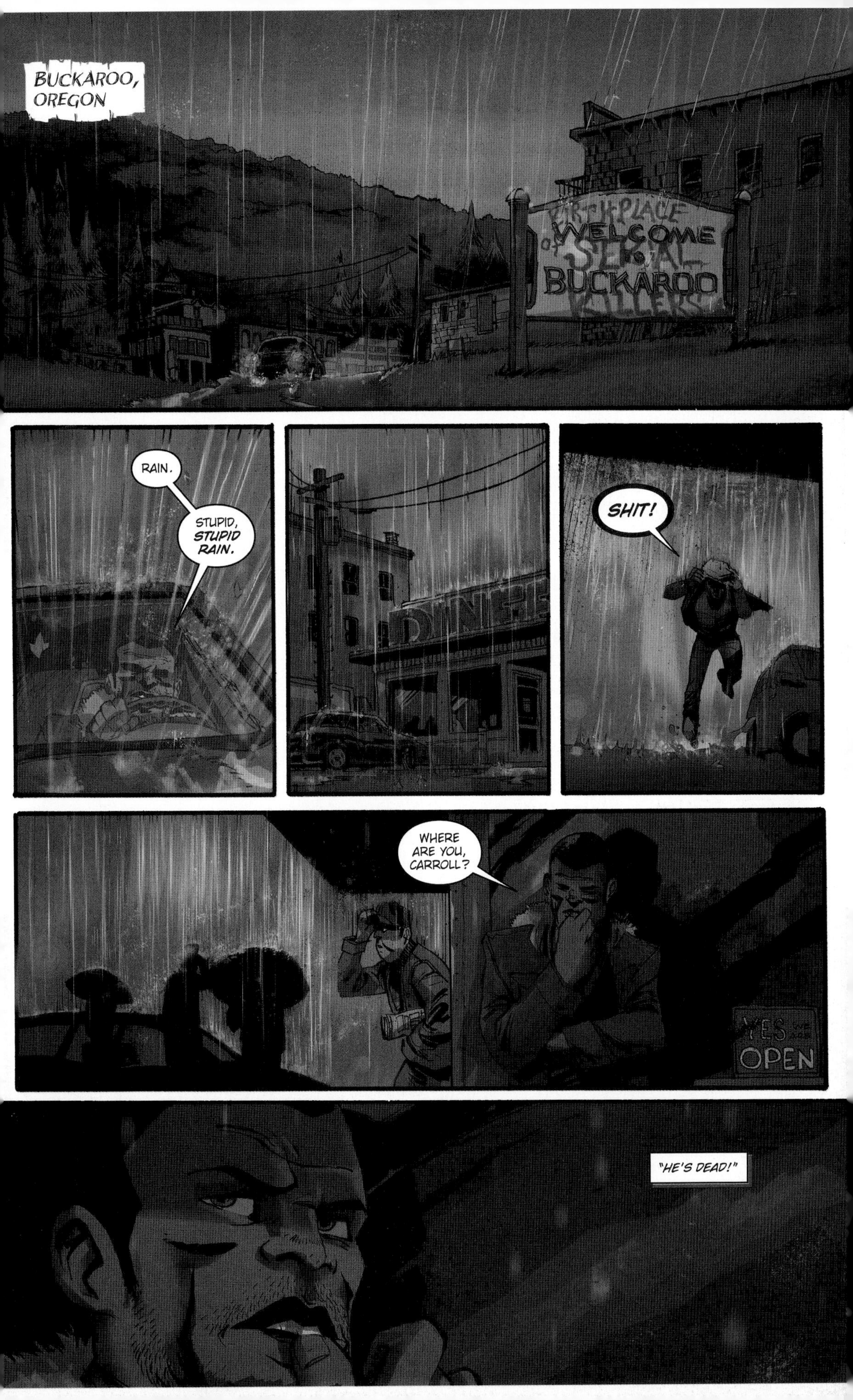
BUCKAROO, OREGON
WELCOME
BUCKAROO
RAIN.
STUPID, STUPID RAIN.
SHIT!
WHERE ARE YOU, CARROLL?
YES
OPEN
"HE'S DEAD!"

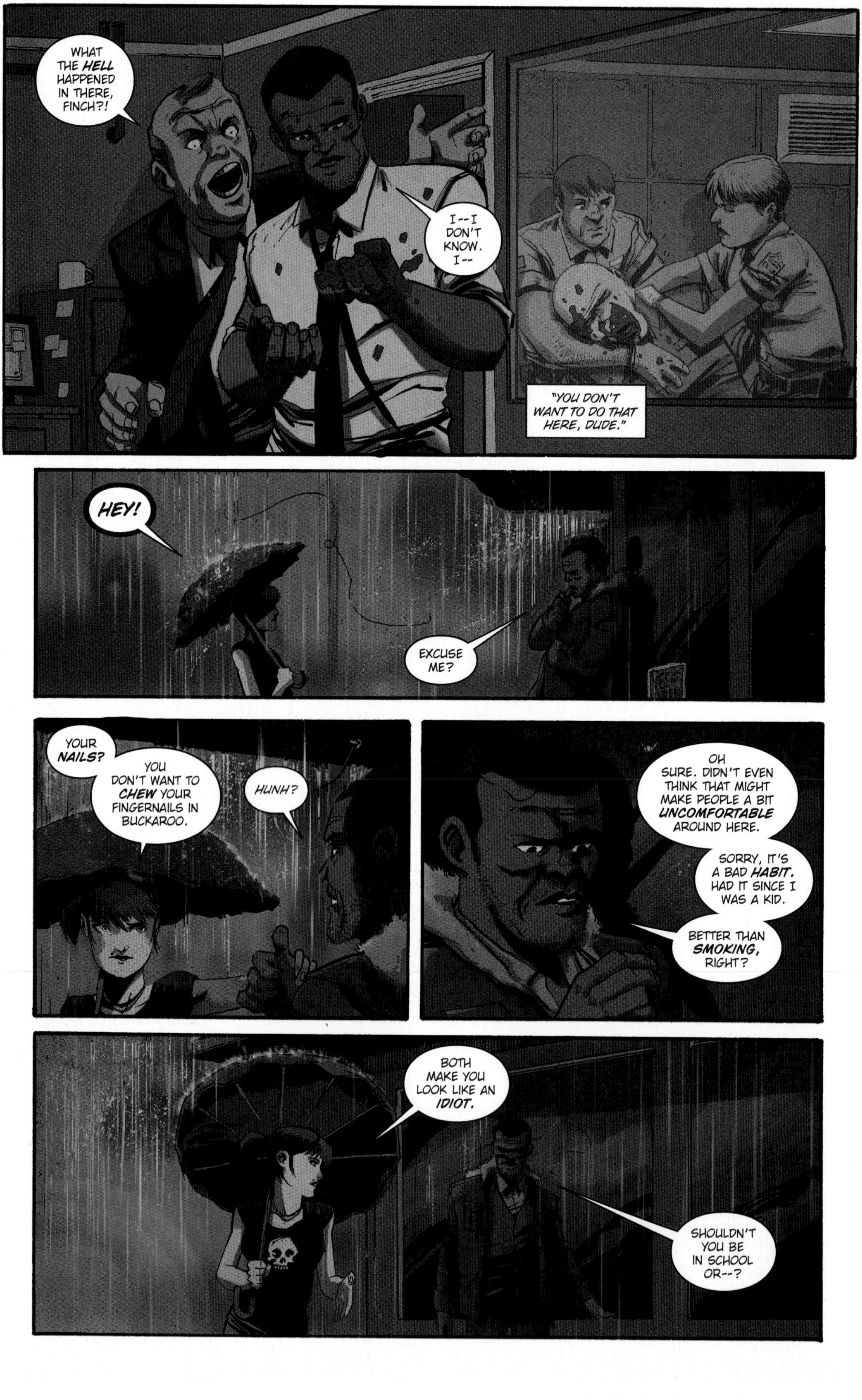

WHAT THE HELL HAPPENED IN THERE, FINCH?!
I--I DON'T KNOW. I--
"YOU DON'T WANT TO DO THAT HERE, DUDE."
HEY!
EXCUSE ME?
YOUR NAILS?
YOU DON'T WANT TO CHEW YOUR FINGERNAILS IN BUCKAROO.
HUNH?
OH SURE. DIDN'T EVEN THINK THAT MIGHT MAKE PEOPLE A BIT UNCOMFORTABLE AROUND HERE.
SORRY, IT'S A BAD HABIT. HAD IT SINCE I WAS A KID.
BETTER THAN SMOKING, RIGHT?
BOTH MAKE YOU LOOK LIKE AN IDIOT.
SHOULDN'T YOU BE IN SCHOOL OR--?

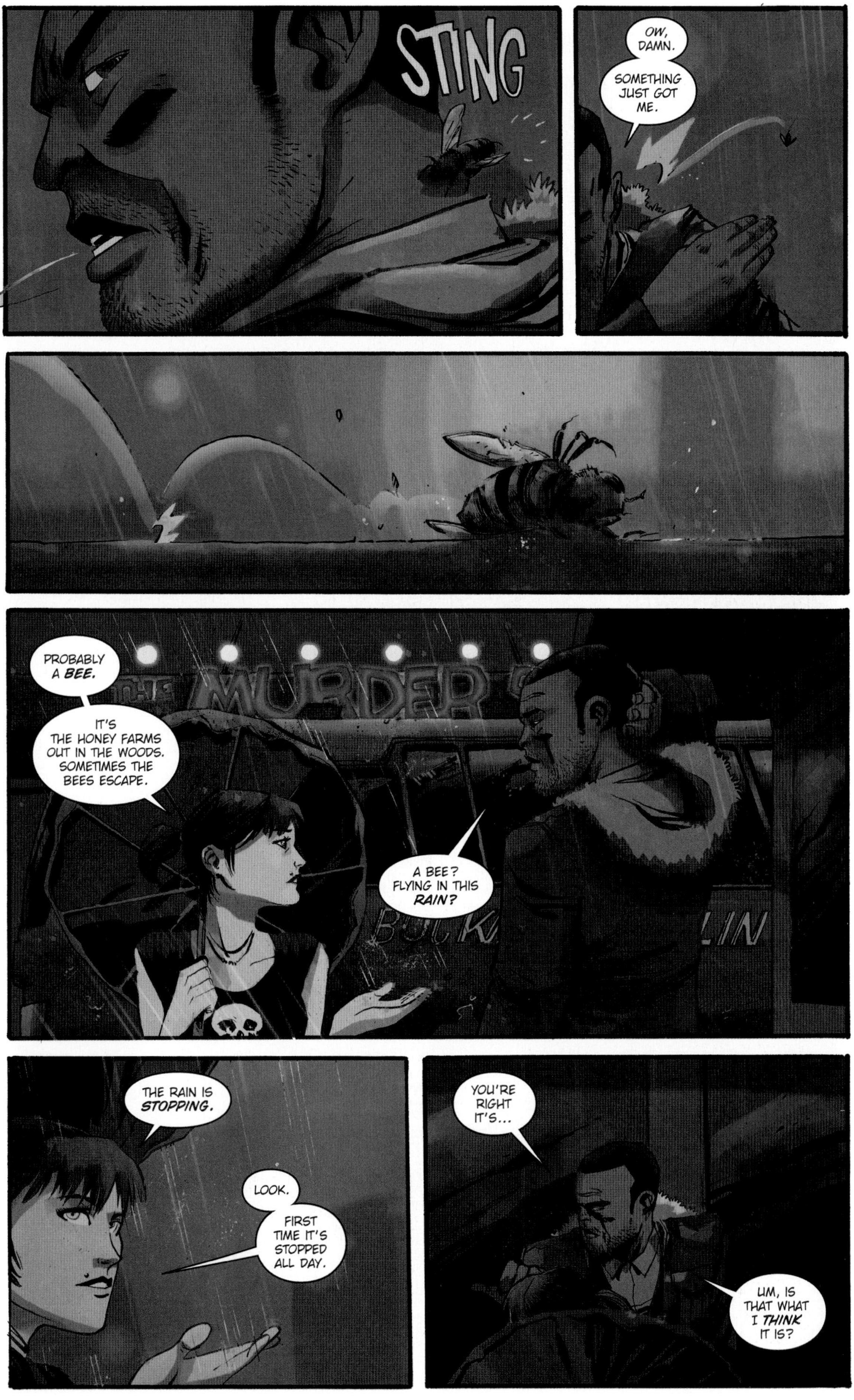
STING
OW, DAMN.
SOMETHING JUST GOT ME.
PROBABLY A BEE.
IT'S THE HONEY FARMS OUT IN THE WOODS. SOMETIMES THE BEES ESCAPE.
A BEE? FLYING IN THIS RAIN?
THE RAIN IS STOPPING.
LOOK.
FIRST TIME IT'S STOPPED ALL DAY.
YOU'RE RIGHT IT'S...
UM, IS THAT WHAT I THINK IT IS?

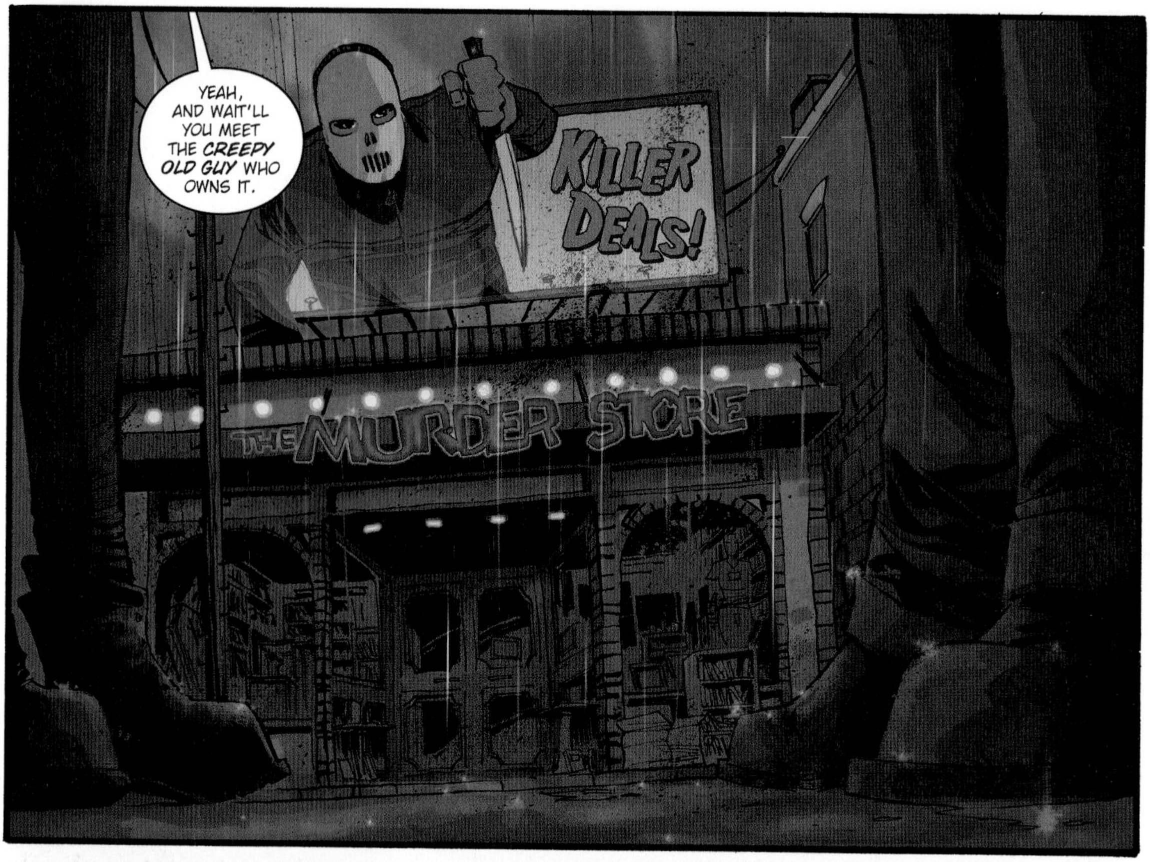
YEAH, AND WAIT'LL YOU MEET THE **CREEPY OLD GUY** WHO OWNS IT.
KILLER DEALS!
THE MURDER STORE

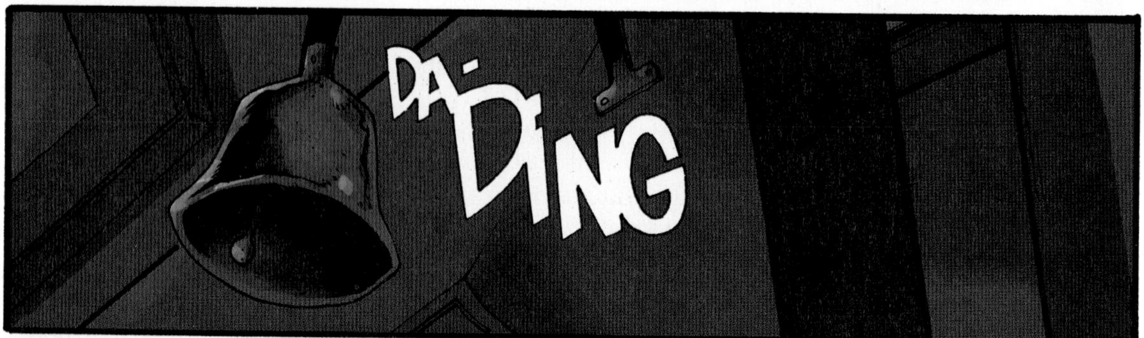
DA-DING

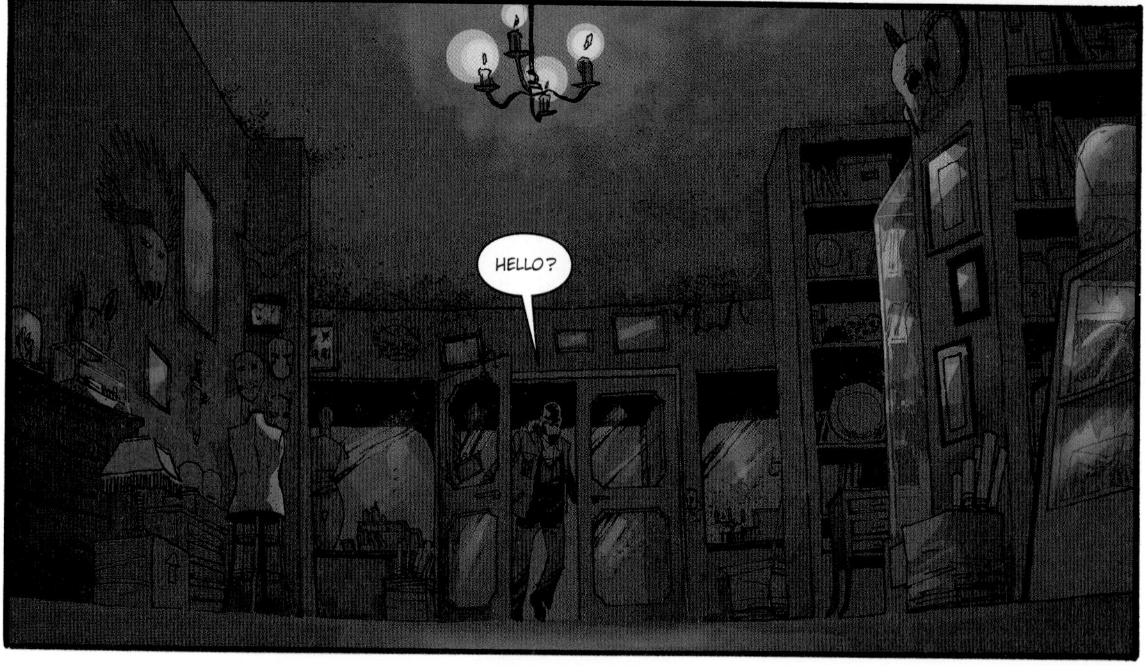
HELLO?

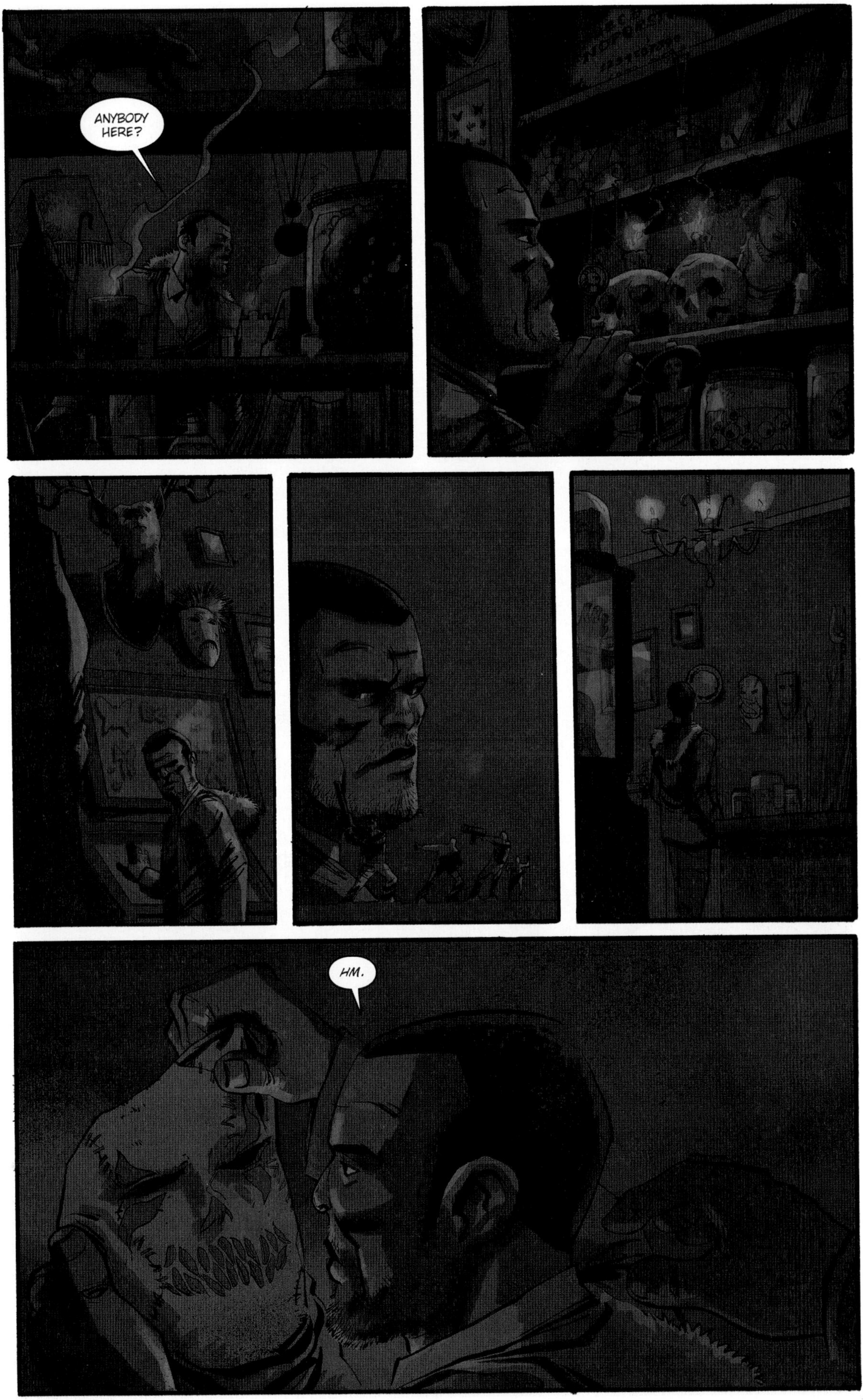
ANYBODY HERE?
HM.

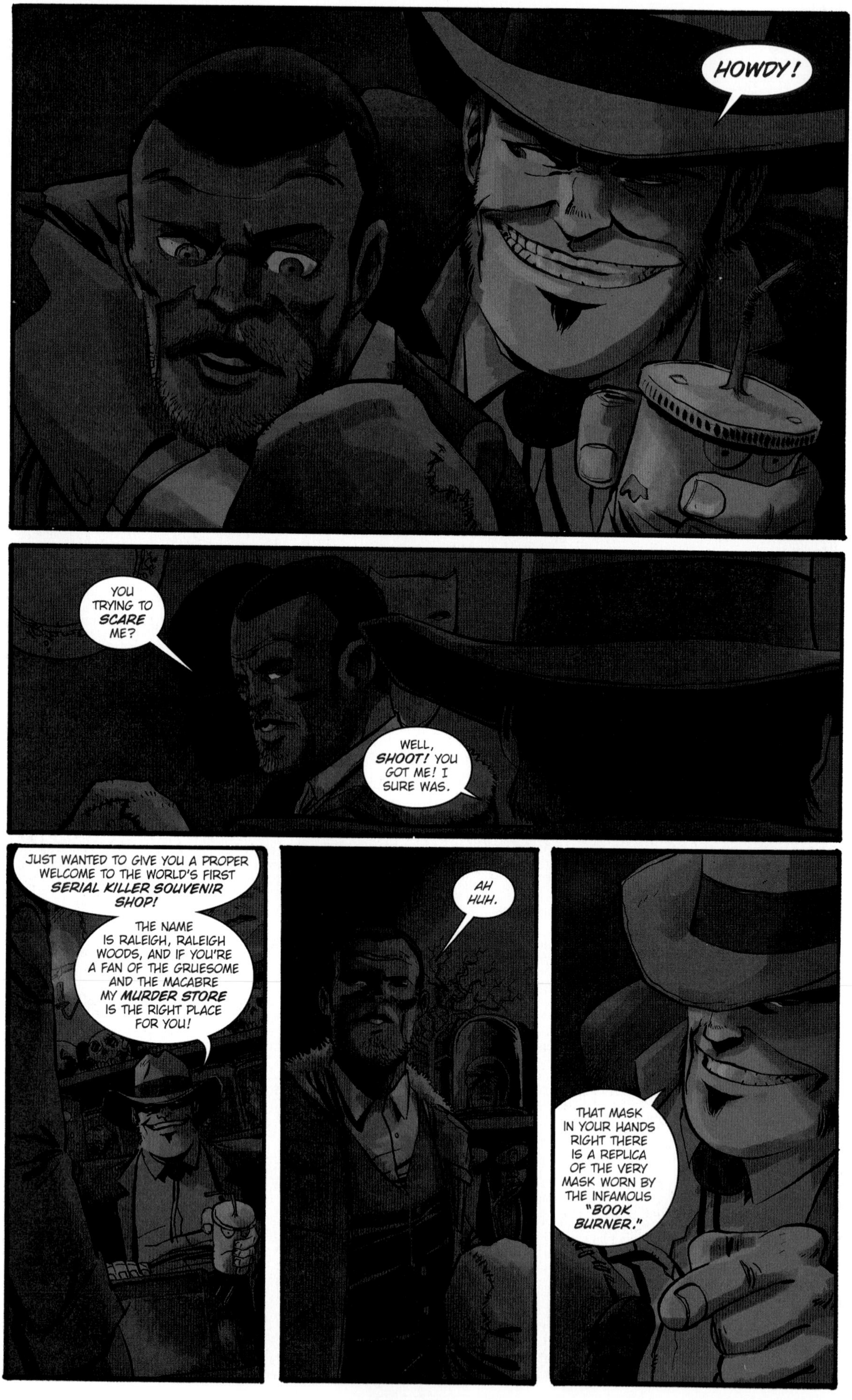
HOWDY!
YOU TRYING TO SCARE ME?
WELL, SHOOT! YOU GOT ME! I SURE WAS.
JUST WANTED TO GIVE YOU A PROPER WELCOME TO THE WORLD'S FIRST SERIAL KILLER SOUVENIR SHOP!
THE NAME IS RALEIGH, RALEIGH WOODS, AND IF YOU'RE A FAN OF THE GRUESOME AND THE MACABRE MY MURDER STORE IS THE RIGHT PLACE FOR YOU!
AH HUH.
THAT MASK IN YOUR HANDS RIGHT THERE IS A REPLICA OF THE VERY MASK WORN BY THE INFAMOUS "BOOK BURNER."

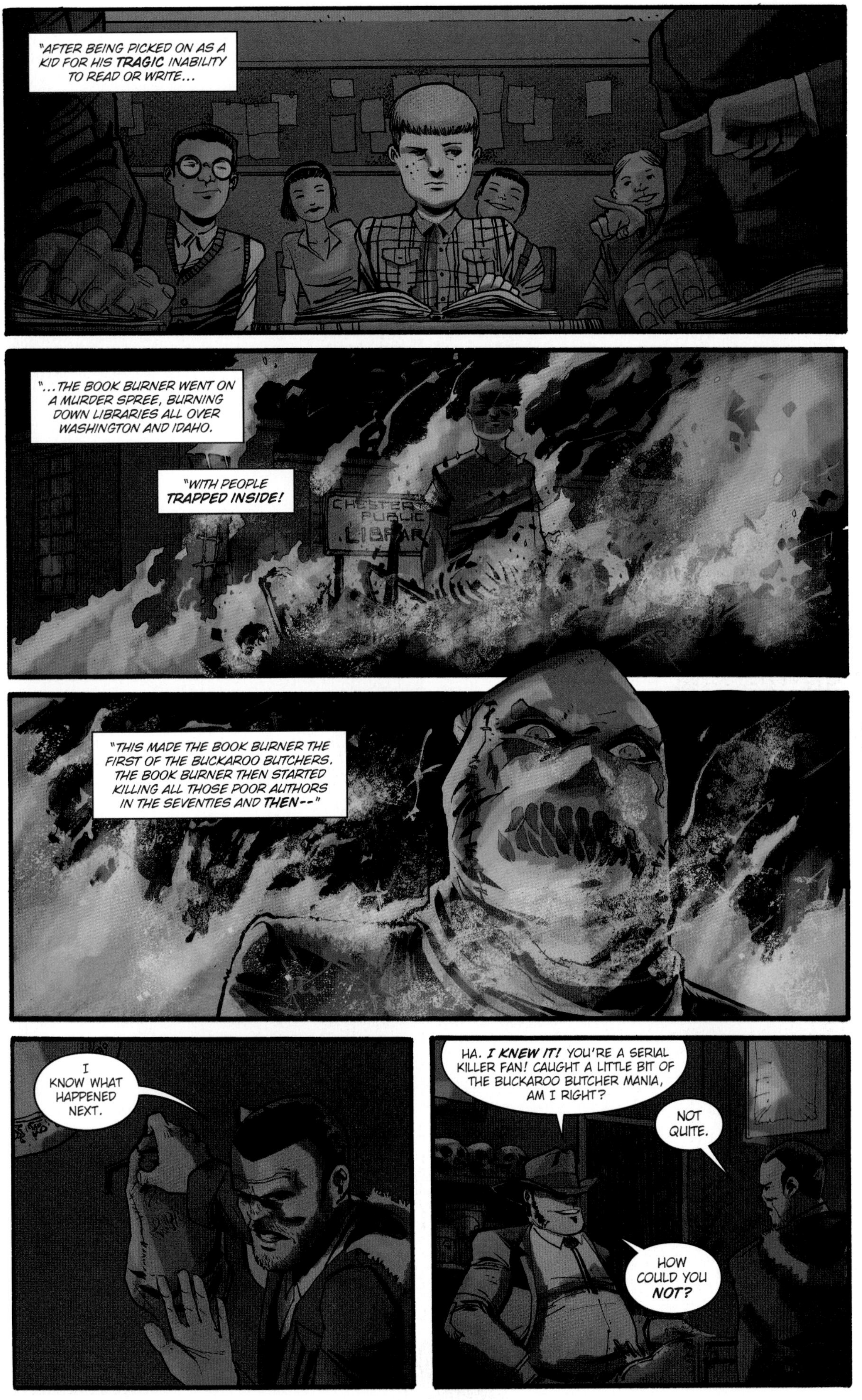
"AFTER BEING PICKED ON AS A KID FOR HIS TRAGIC INABILITY TO READ OR WRITE...
"...THE BOOK BURNER WENT ON A MURDER SPREE, BURNING DOWN LIBRARIES ALL OVER WASHINGTON AND IDAHO.
"WITH PEOPLE TRAPPED INSIDE!
CHESTER PUBLIC LIBRAR
"THIS MADE THE BOOK BURNER THE FIRST OF THE BUCKAROO BUTCHERS. THE BOOK BURNER THEN STARTED KILLING ALL THOSE POOR AUTHORS IN THE SEVENTIES AND THEN--"
I KNOW WHAT HAPPENED NEXT.
HA. I KNEW IT! YOU'RE A SERIAL KILLER FAN! CAUGHT A LITTLE BIT OF THE BUCKAROO BUTCHER MANIA, AM I RIGHT?
NOT QUITE.
HOW COULD YOU NOT?

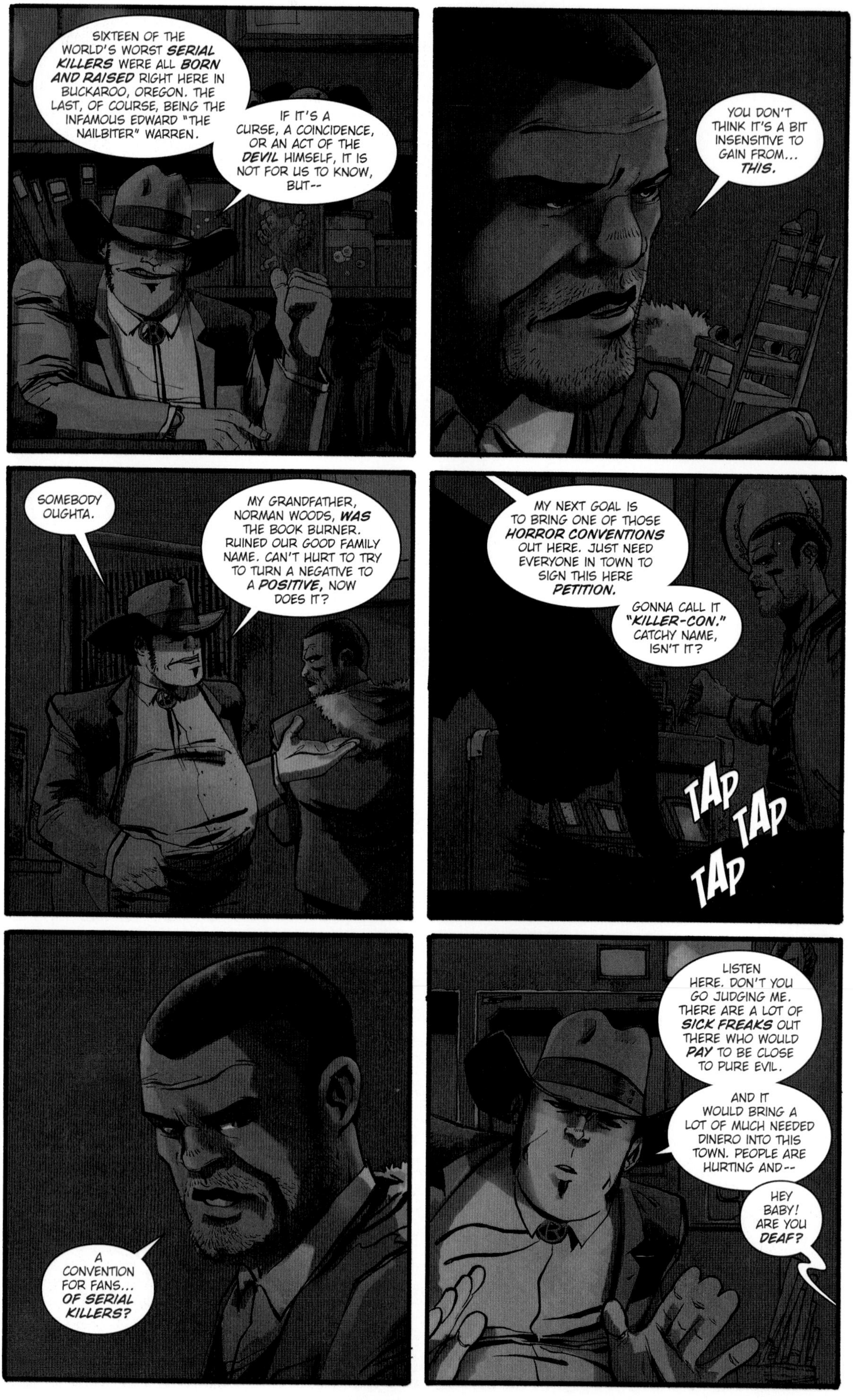
SIXTEEN OF THE WORLD'S WORST SERIAL KILLERS WERE ALL BORN AND RAISED RIGHT HERE IN BUCKAROO, OREGON. THE LAST, OF COURSE, BEING THE INFAMOUS EDWARD "THE NAILBITER" WARREN.
IF IT'S A CURSE, A COINCIDENCE, OR AN ACT OF THE DEVIL HIMSELF, IT IS NOT FOR US TO KNOW, BUT--
YOU DON'T THINK IT'S A BIT INSENSITIVE TO GAIN FROM... THIS.
SOMEBODY OUGHTA.
MY GRANDFATHER, NORMAN WOODS, WAS THE BOOK BURNER. RUINED OUR GOOD FAMILY NAME. CAN'T HURT TO TRY TO TURN A NEGATIVE TO A POSITIVE, NOW DOES IT?
MY NEXT GOAL IS TO BRING ONE OF THOSE HORROR CONVENTIONS OUT HERE. JUST NEED EVERYONE IN TOWN TO SIGN THIS HERE PETITION.
GONNA CALL IT "KILLER-CON." CATCHY NAME, ISN'T IT?
TAP TAP TAP
A CONVENTION FOR FANS... OF SERIAL KILLERS?
LISTEN HERE. DON'T YOU GO JUDGING ME. THERE ARE A LOT OF SICK FREAKS OUT THERE WHO WOULD PAY TO BE CLOSE TO PURE EVIL.
AND IT WOULD BRING A LOT OF MUCH NEEDED DINERO INTO THIS TOWN. PEOPLE ARE HURTING AND--
HEY BABY! ARE YOU DEAF?

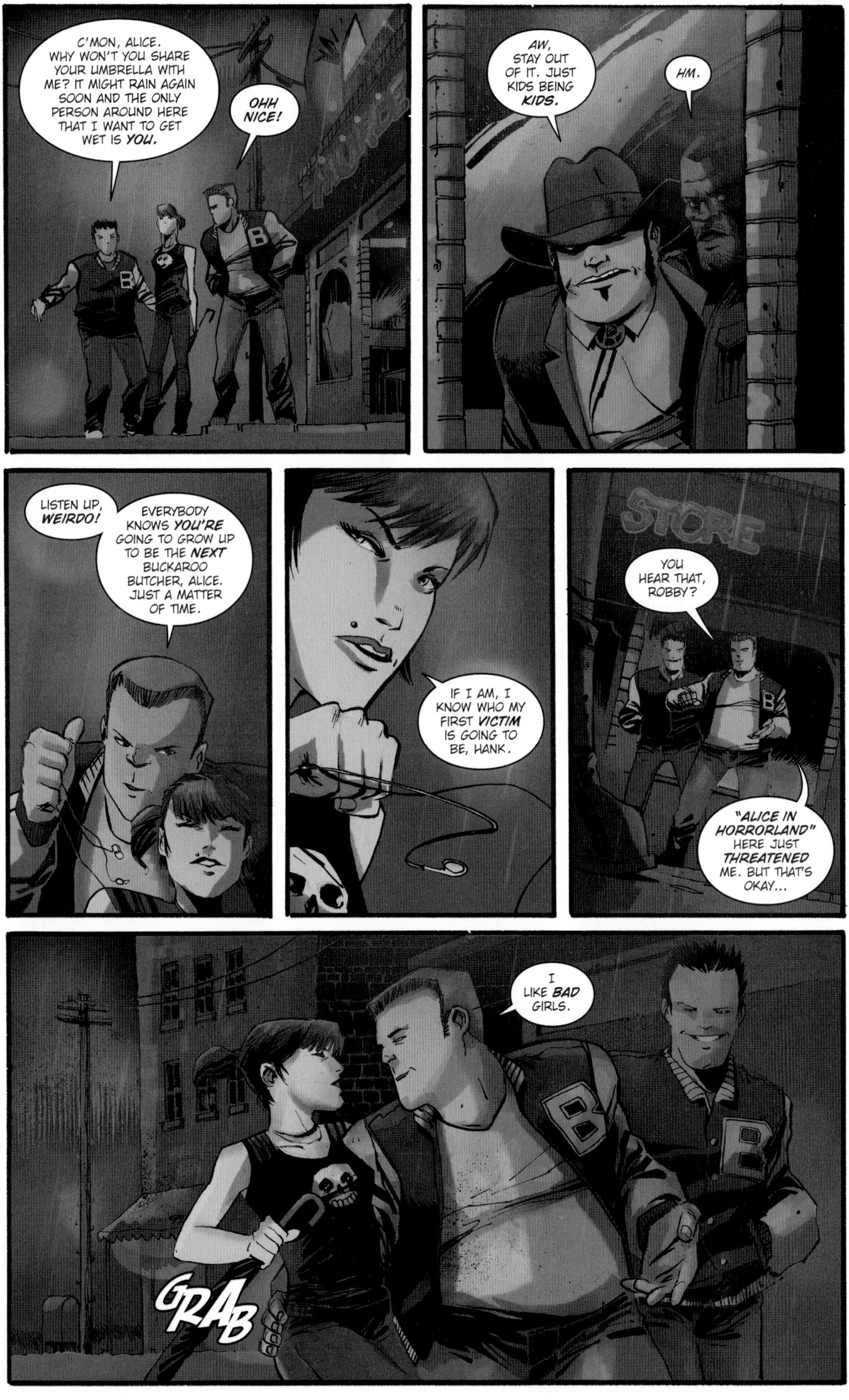
C'MON, ALICE. WHY WON'T YOU SHARE YOUR UMBRELLA WITH ME? IT MIGHT RAIN AGAIN SOON AND THE ONLY PERSON AROUND HERE THAT I WANT TO GET WET IS YOU.
OHH NICE!
AW, STAY OUT OF IT. JUST KIDS BEING KIDS.
HM.
LISTEN UP, WEIRDO!
EVERYBODY KNOWS YOU'RE GOING TO GROW UP TO BE THE NEXT BUCKAROO BUTCHER, ALICE. JUST A MATTER OF TIME.
IF I AM, I KNOW WHO MY FIRST VICTIM IS GOING TO BE, HANK.
STORE
YOU HEAR THAT, ROBBY?
"ALICE IN HORRORLAND" HERE JUST THREATENED ME. BUT THAT'S OKAY...
I LIKE BAD GIRLS.
GRAB

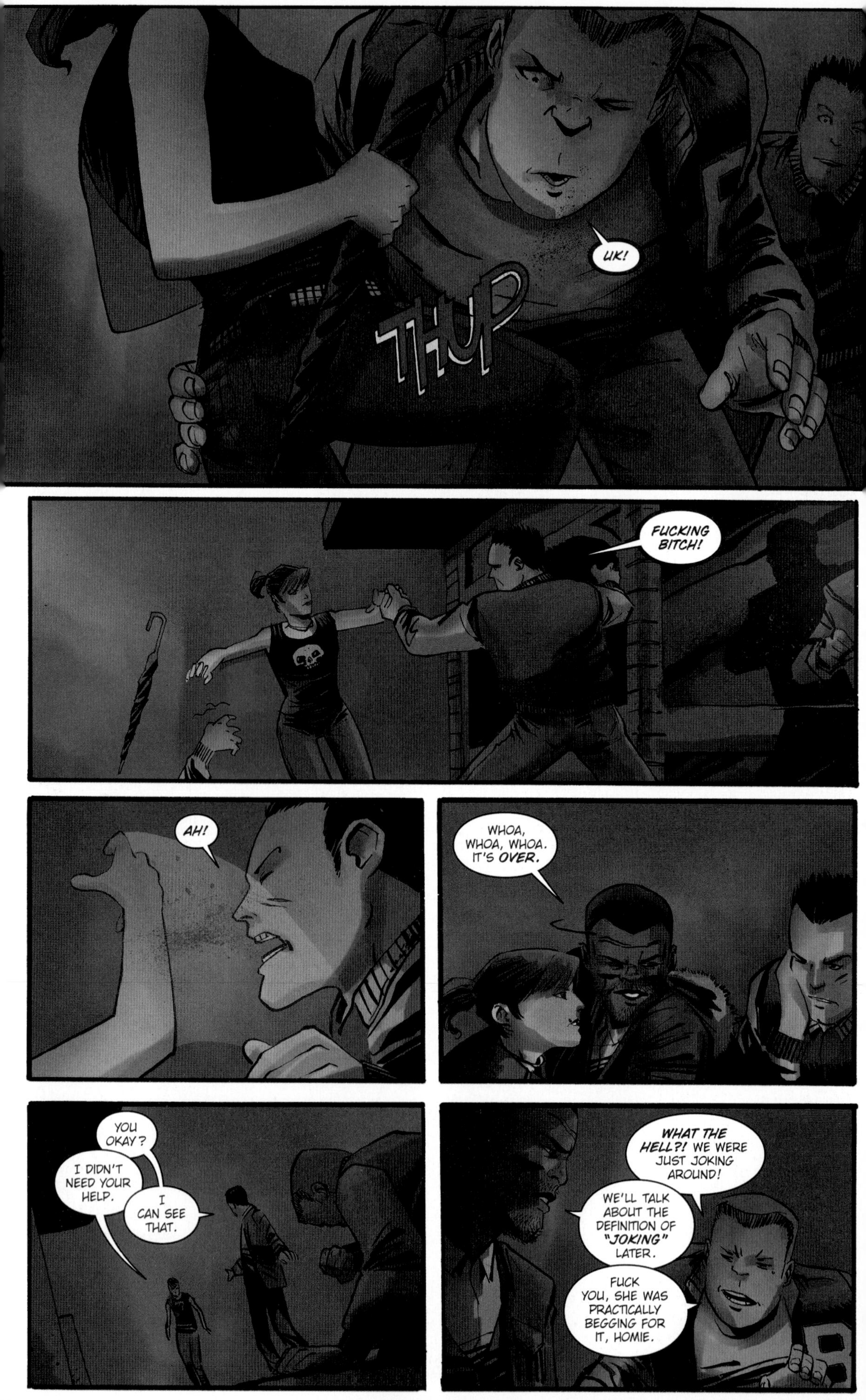
UK!
THUP
FUCKING BITCH!
AH!
WHOA, WHOA, WHOA. IT'S OVER.
YOU OKAY?
I DIDN'T NEED YOUR HELP.
I CAN SEE THAT.
WHAT THE HELL?! WE WERE JUST JOKING AROUND!
WE'LL TALK ABOUT THE DEFINITION OF "JOKING" LATER.
FUCK YOU, SHE WAS PRACTICALLY BEGGING FOR IT, HOMIE.

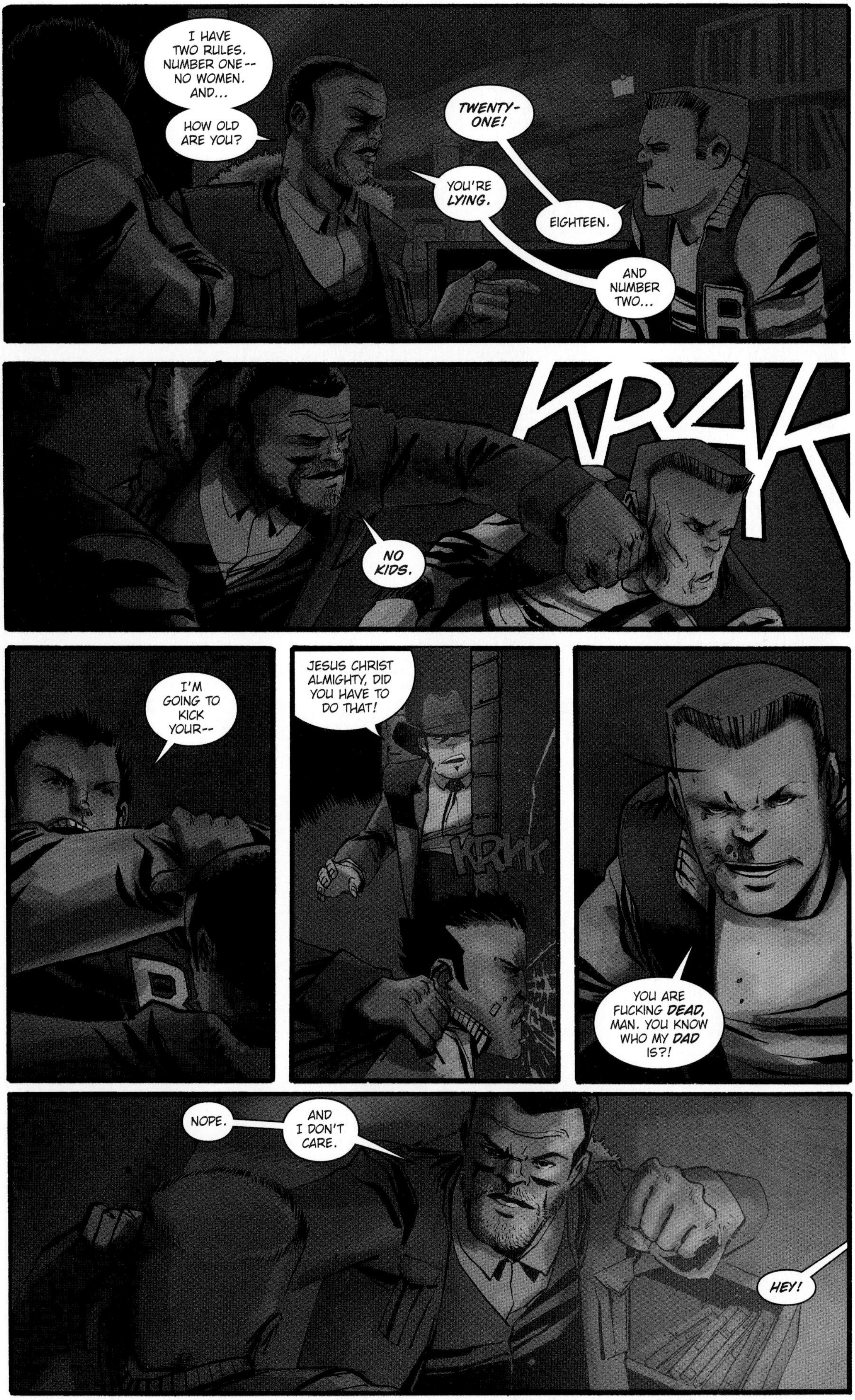
I HAVE TWO RULES. NUMBER ONE-- NO WOMEN. AND...
HOW OLD ARE YOU?
TWENTY-ONE!
YOU'RE LYING.
EIGHTEEN.
AND NUMBER TWO...
KRAK
NO KIDS.
I'M GOING TO KICK YOUR--
JESUS CHRIST ALMIGHTY, DID YOU HAVE TO DO THAT!
KRKK
YOU ARE FUCKING DEAD, MAN. YOU KNOW WHO MY DAD IS?!
NOPE.
AND I DON'T CARE.
HEY!

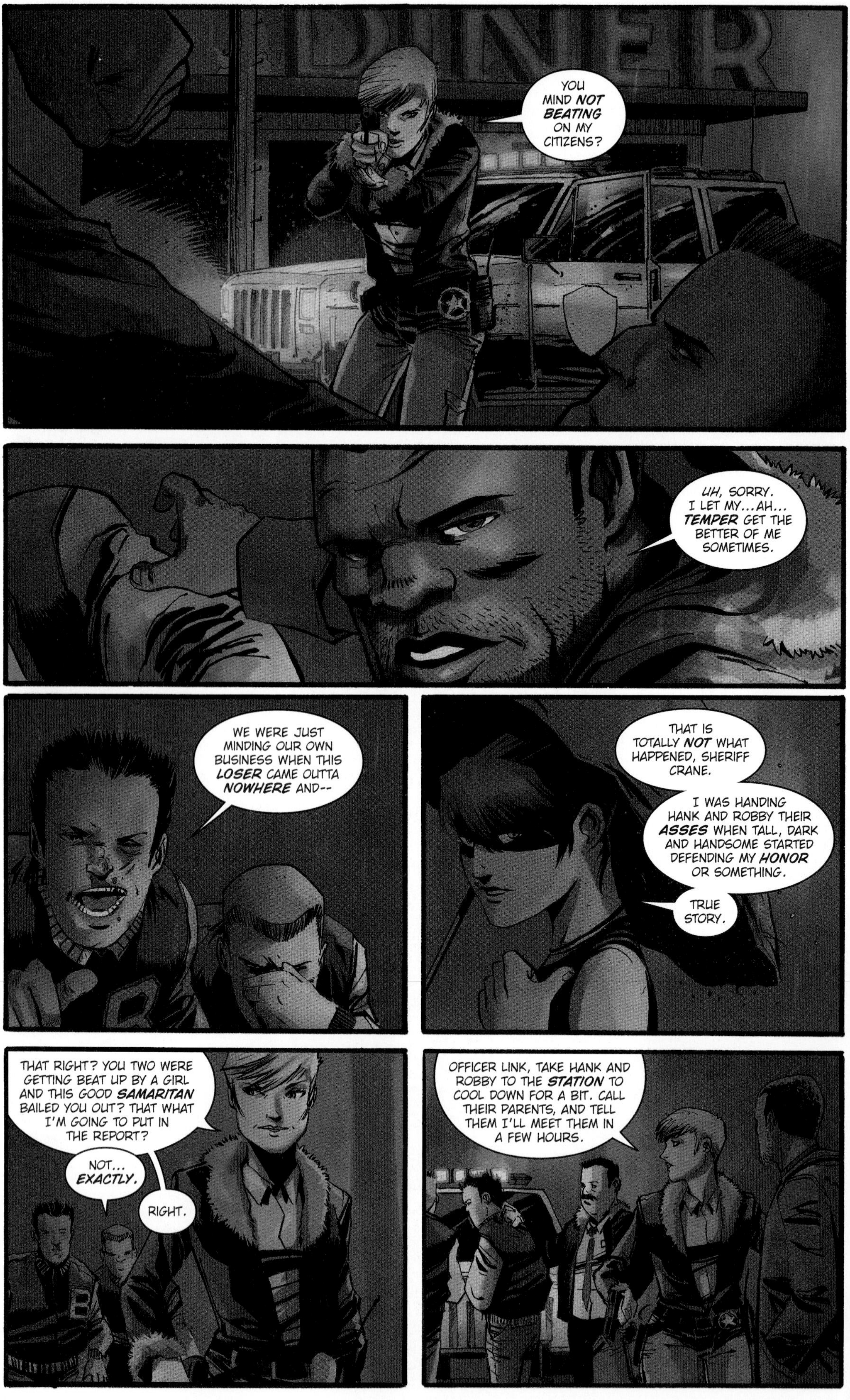
DINER
YOU MIND NOT BEATING ON MY CITIZENS?
UH, SORRY. I LET MY...AH... TEMPER GET THE BETTER OF ME SOMETIMES.
WE WERE JUST MINDING OUR OWN BUSINESS WHEN THIS LOSER CAME OUTTA NOWHERE AND--
THAT IS TOTALLY NOT WHAT HAPPENED, SHERIFF CRANE.
I WAS HANDING HANK AND ROBBY THEIR ASSES WHEN TALL, DARK AND HANDSOME STARTED DEFENDING MY HONOR OR SOMETHING.
TRUE STORY.
THAT RIGHT? YOU TWO WERE GETTING BEAT UP BY A GIRL AND THIS GOOD SAMARITAN BAILED YOU OUT? THAT WHAT I'M GOING TO PUT IN THE REPORT?
NOT... EXACTLY.
RIGHT.
OFFICER LINK, TAKE HANK AND ROBBY TO THE STATION TO COOL DOWN FOR A BIT. CALL THEIR PARENTS, AND TELL THEM I'LL MEET THEM IN A FEW HOURS.

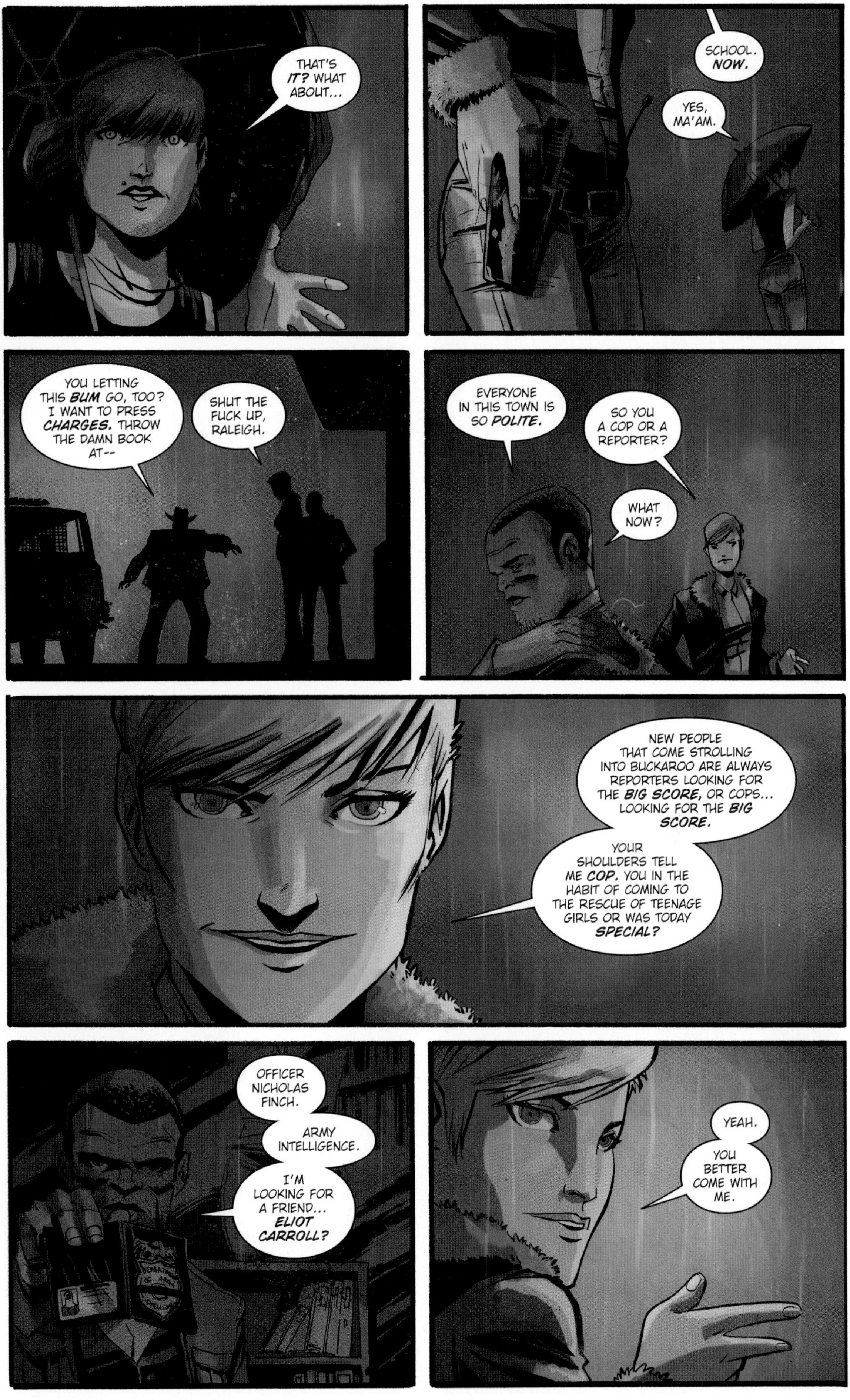
THAT'S IT? WHAT ABOUT...
SCHOOL. NOW.
YES, MA'AM.
YOU LETTING THIS BUM GO, TOO? I WANT TO PRESS CHARGES. THROW THE DAMN BOOK AT--
SHUT THE FUCK UP, RALEIGH.
EVERYONE IN THIS TOWN IS SO POLITE.
SO YOU A COP OR A REPORTER?
WHAT NOW?
NEW PEOPLE THAT COME STROLLING INTO BUCKAROO ARE ALWAYS REPORTERS LOOKING FOR THE BIG SCORE, OR COPS... LOOKING FOR THE BIG SCORE.
YOUR SHOULDERS TELL ME COP. YOU IN THE HABIT OF COMING TO THE RESCUE OF TEENAGE GIRLS OR WAS TODAY SPECIAL?
OFFICER NICHOLAS FINCH.
ARMY INTELLIGENCE.
I'M LOOKING FOR A FRIEND... ELIOT CARROLL?
YEAH.
YOU BETTER COME WITH ME.

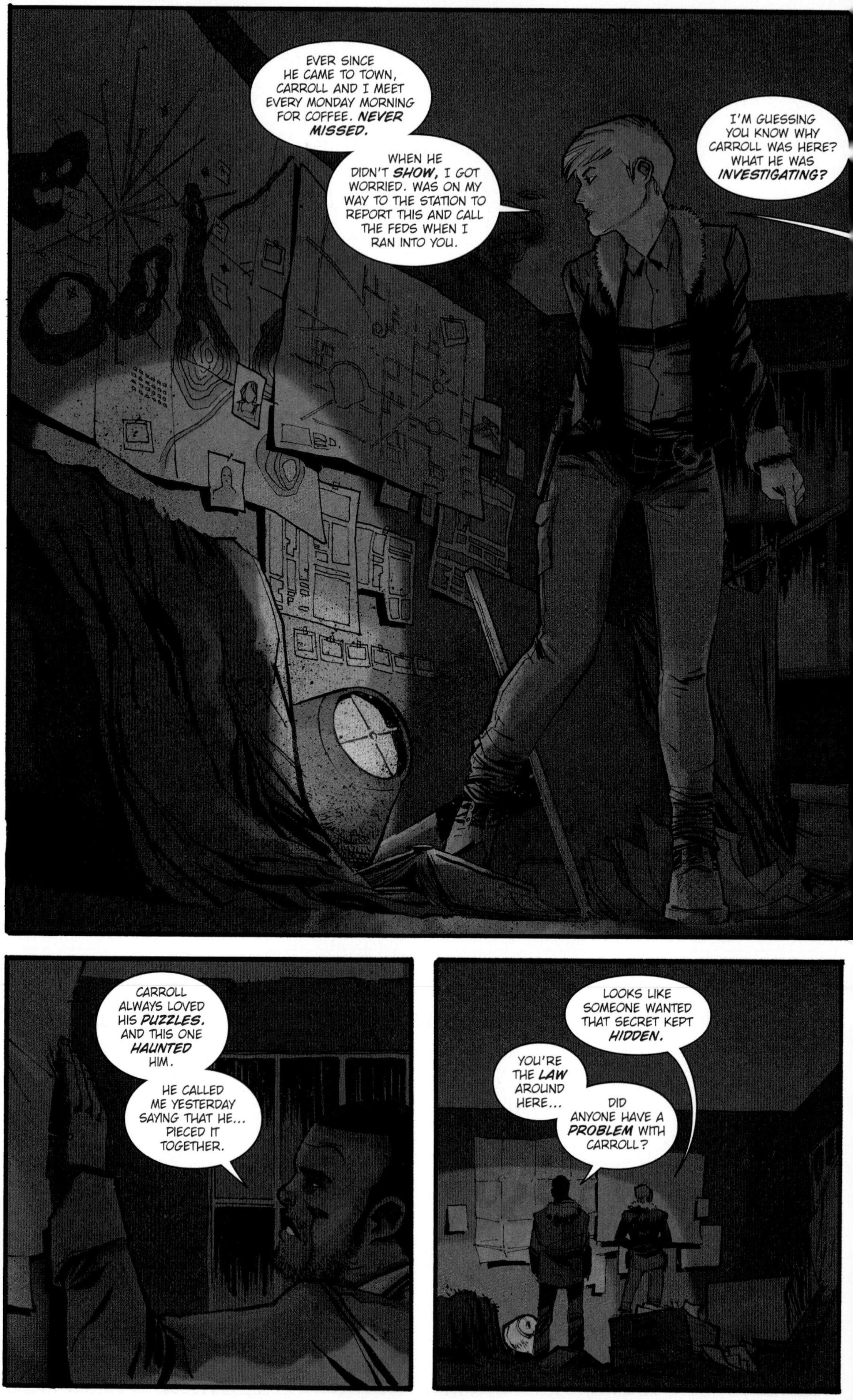

EVER SINCE HE CAME TO TOWN, CARROLL AND I MEET EVERY MONDAY MORNING FOR COFFEE. **NEVER MISSED.**
WHEN HE DIDN'T **SHOW,** I GOT WORRIED. WAS ON MY WAY TO THE STATION TO REPORT THIS AND CALL THE FEDS WHEN I RAN INTO YOU.
I'M GUESSING YOU KNOW WHY CARROLL WAS HERE? WHAT HE WAS ***INVESTIGATING?***
CARROLL ALWAYS LOVED HIS ***PUZZLES.*** AND THIS ONE ***HAUNTED*** HIM.
HE CALLED ME YESTERDAY SAYING THAT HE... PIECED IT TOGETHER.
LOOKS LIKE SOMEONE WANTED THAT SECRET KEPT ***HIDDEN.***
YOU'RE THE ***LAW*** AROUND HERE...
DID ANYONE HAVE A ***PROBLEM*** WITH CARROLL?

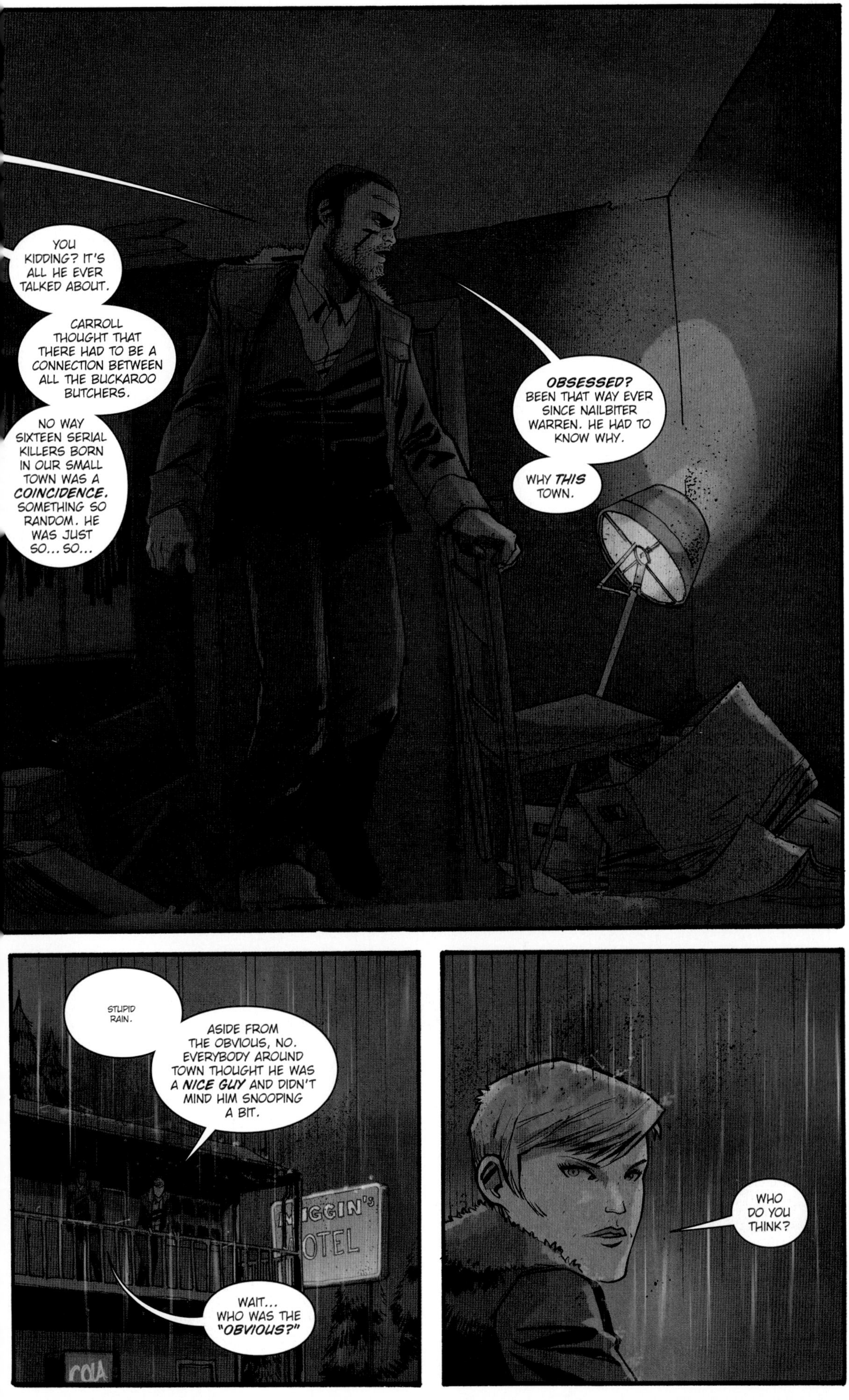
YOU KIDDING? IT'S ALL HE EVER TALKED ABOUT.
CARROLL THOUGHT THAT THERE HAD TO BE A CONNECTION BETWEEN ALL THE BUCKAROO BUTCHERS.
NO WAY SIXTEEN SERIAL KILLERS BORN IN OUR SMALL TOWN WAS A COINCIDENCE. SOMETHING SO RANDOM. HE WAS JUST SO... SO...
OBSESSED? BEEN THAT WAY EVER SINCE NAILBITER WARREN. HE HAD TO KNOW WHY.
WHY THIS TOWN.
STUPID RAIN.
ASIDE FROM THE OBVIOUS, NO. EVERYBODY AROUND TOWN THOUGHT HE WAS A NICE GUY AND DIDN'T MIND HIM SNOOPING A BIT.
WAIT... WHO WAS THE "OBVIOUS?"
COLA
WHO DO YOU THINK?

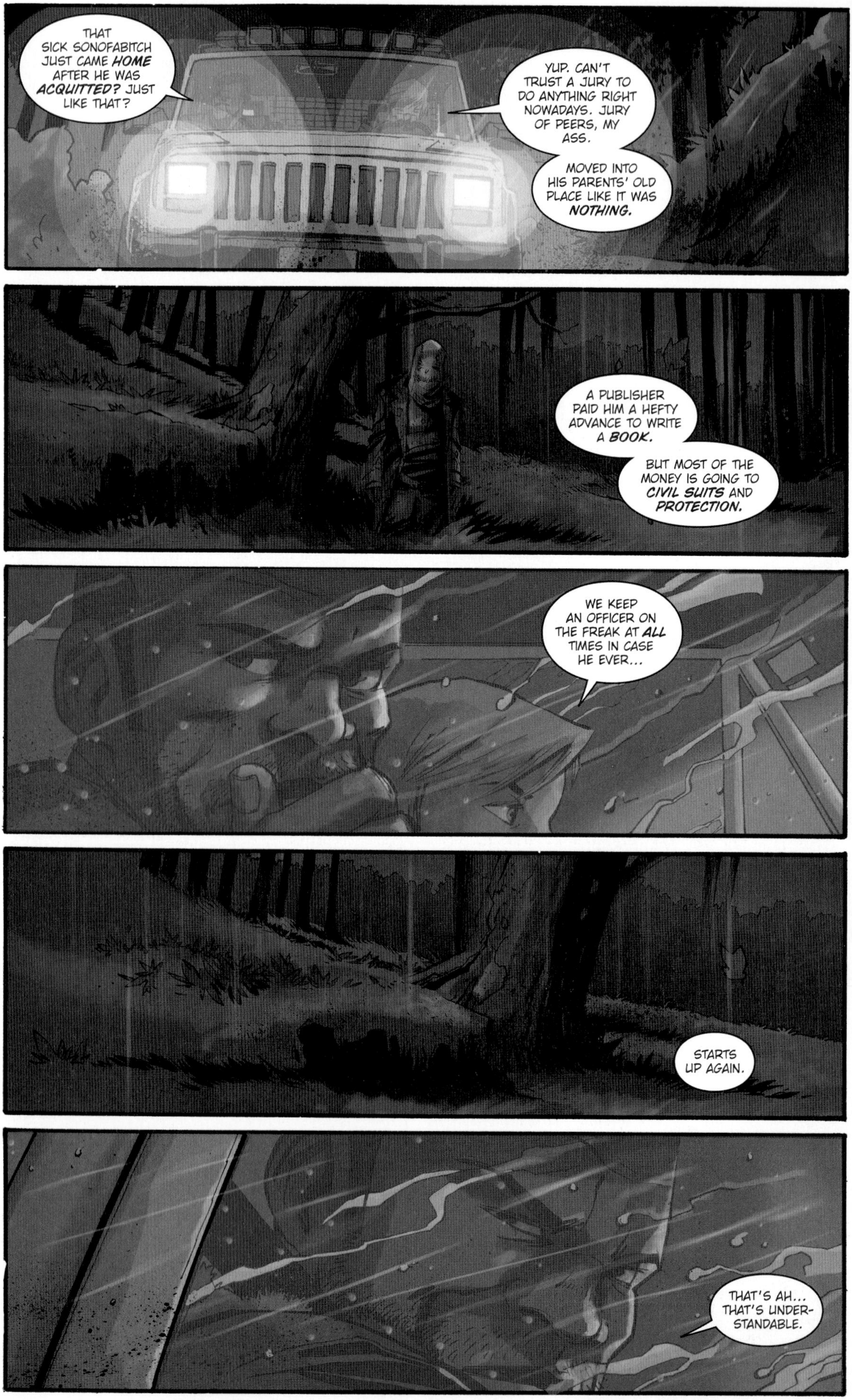
THAT SICK SONOFABITCH JUST CAME **HOME** AFTER HE WAS **ACQUITTED?** JUST LIKE THAT?
YUP. CAN'T TRUST A JURY TO DO ANYTHING RIGHT NOWADAYS. JURY OF PEERS, MY ASS.
MOVED INTO HIS PARENTS' OLD PLACE LIKE IT WAS **NOTHING.**
A PUBLISHER PAID HIM A HEFTY ADVANCE TO WRITE A **BOOK.**
BUT MOST OF THE MONEY IS GOING TO **CIVIL SUITS** AND **PROTECTION.**
WE KEEP AN OFFICER ON THE FREAK AT **ALL** TIMES IN CASE HE EVER...
STARTS UP AGAIN.
THAT'S AH... THAT'S UNDER-STANDABLE.

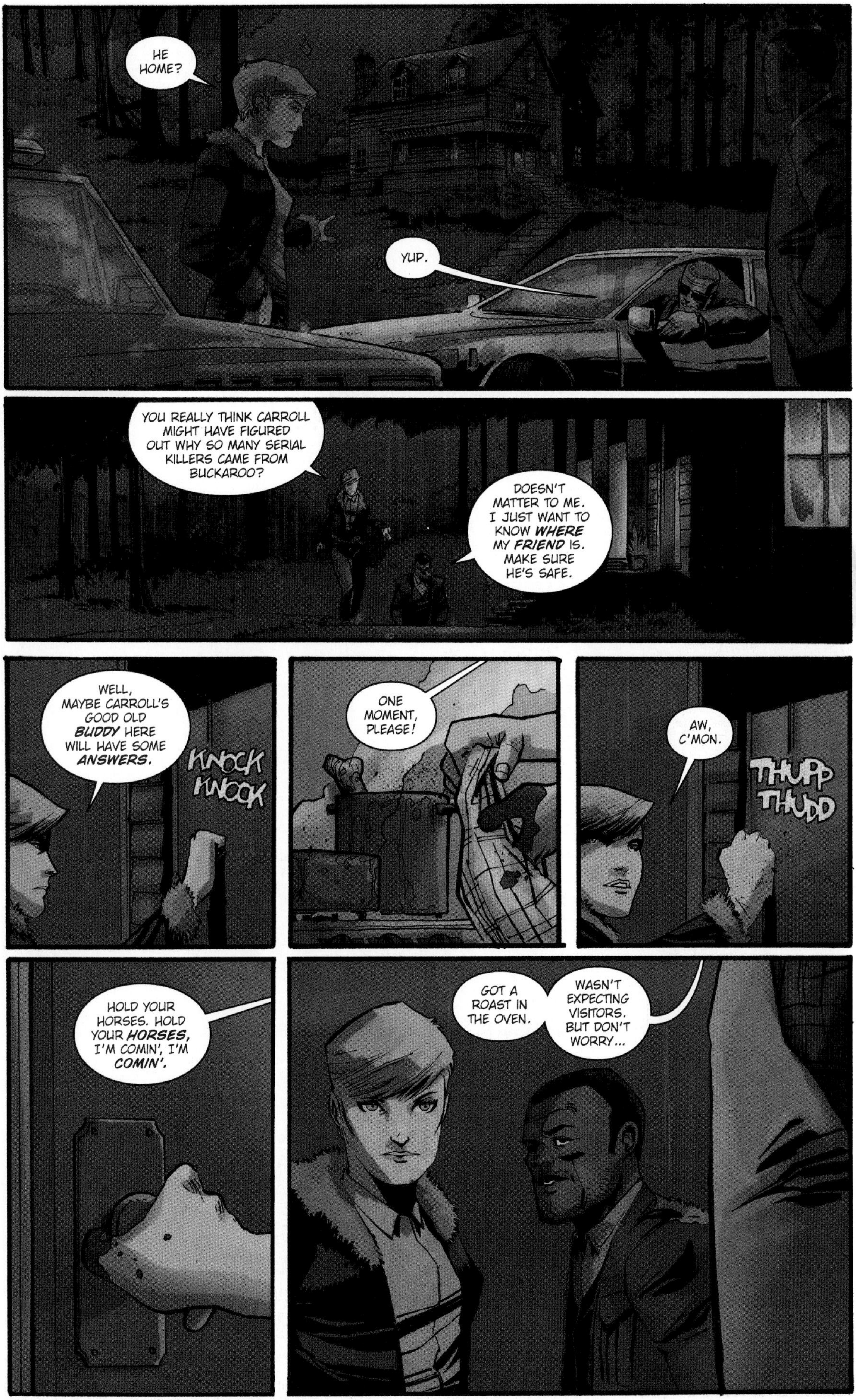
HE HOME?
YUP.
YOU REALLY THINK CARROLL MIGHT HAVE FIGURED OUT WHY SO MANY SERIAL KILLERS CAME FROM BUCKAROO?
DOESN'T MATTER TO ME. I JUST WANT TO KNOW WHERE MY FRIEND IS. MAKE SURE HE'S SAFE.
WELL, MAYBE CARROLL'S GOOD OLD BUDDY HERE WILL HAVE SOME ANSWERS.
KNOCK KNOCK
ONE MOMENT, PLEASE!
AW, C'MON.
THUPP THUDD
HOLD YOUR HORSES. HOLD YOUR HORSES, I'M COMIN', I'M COMIN'.
GOT A ROAST IN THE OVEN.
WASN'T EXPECTING VISITORS. BUT DON'T WORRY...

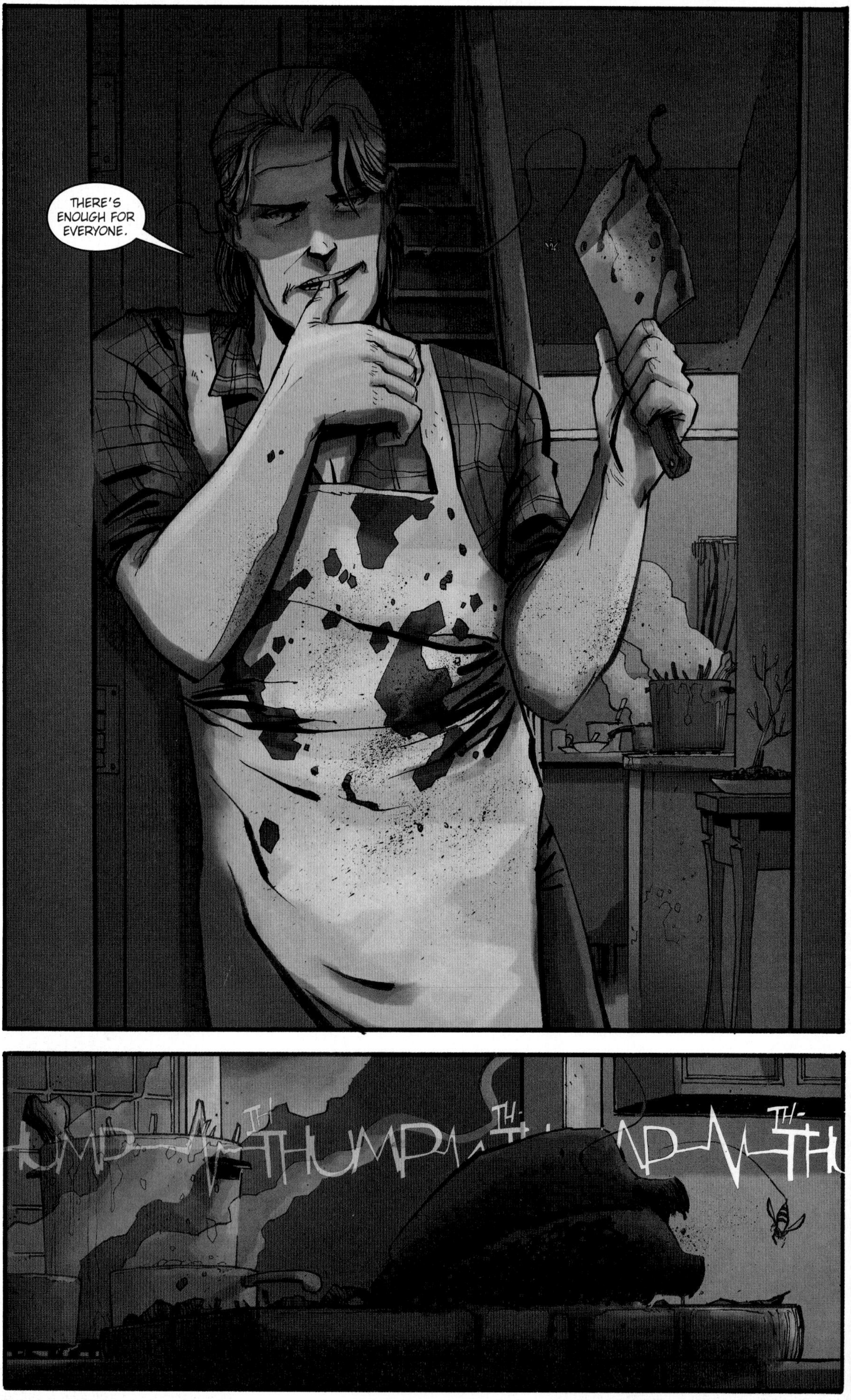
THERE'S ENOUGH FOR EVERYONE.
TH-THUMP

# ISSUE TWO

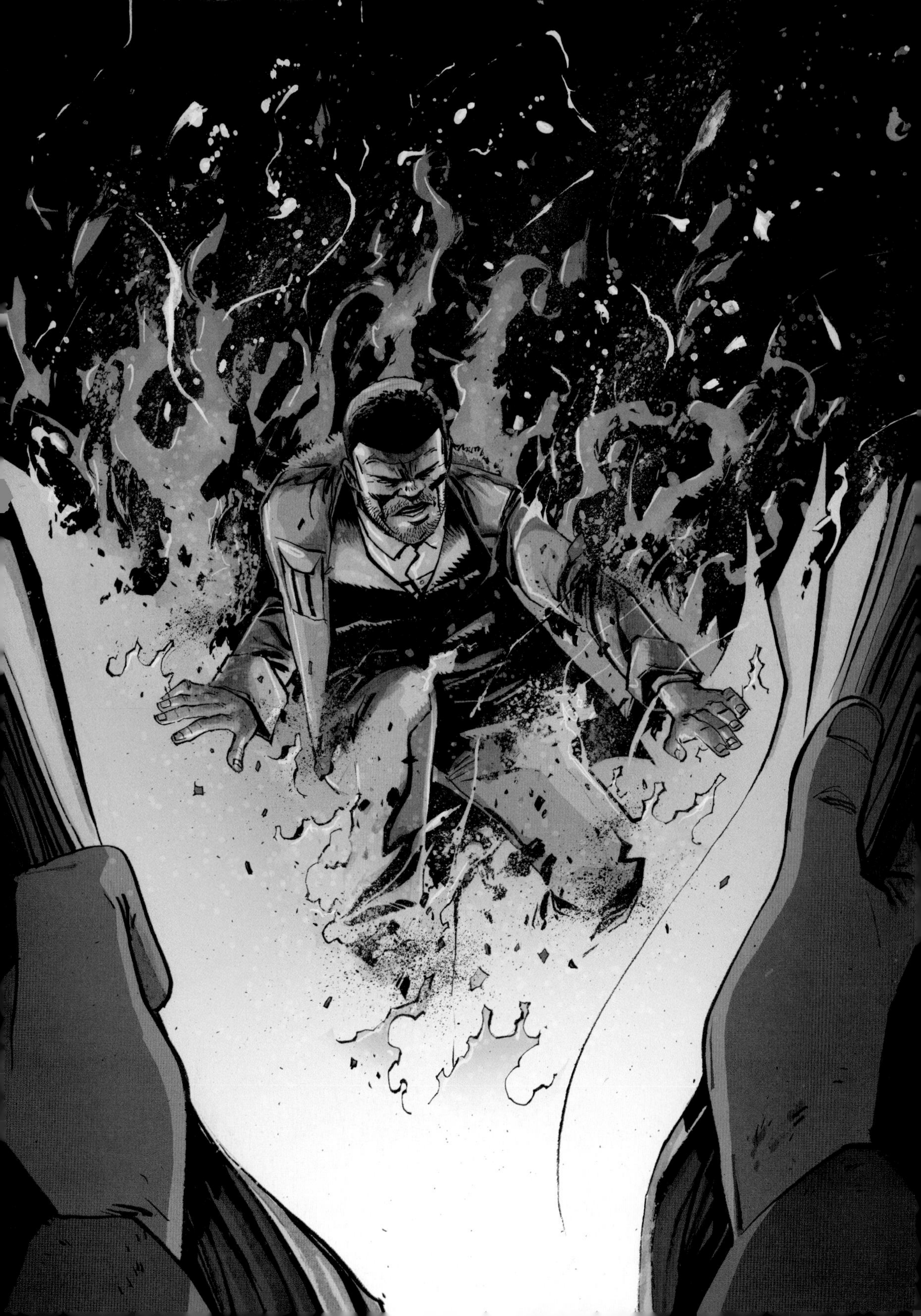

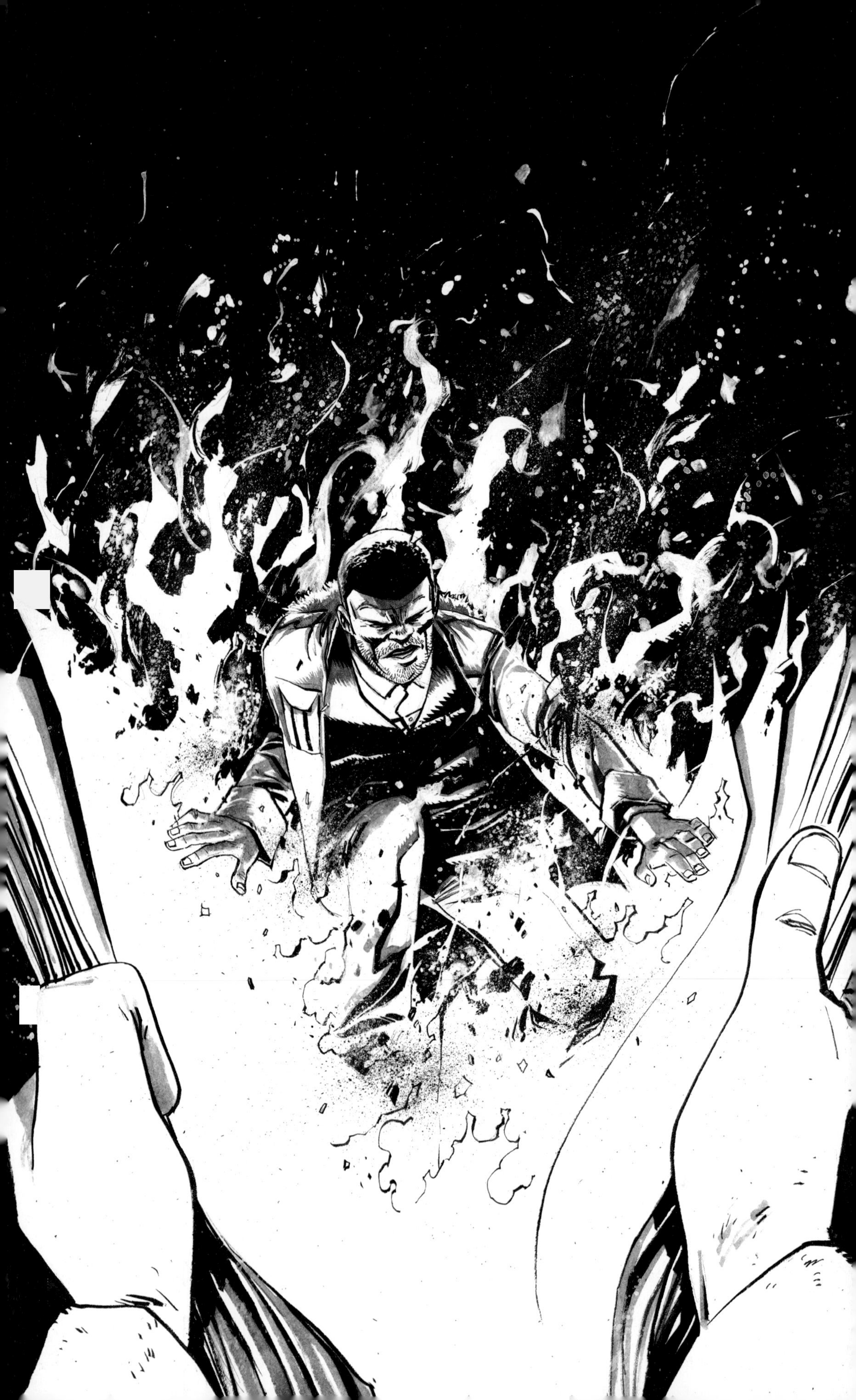

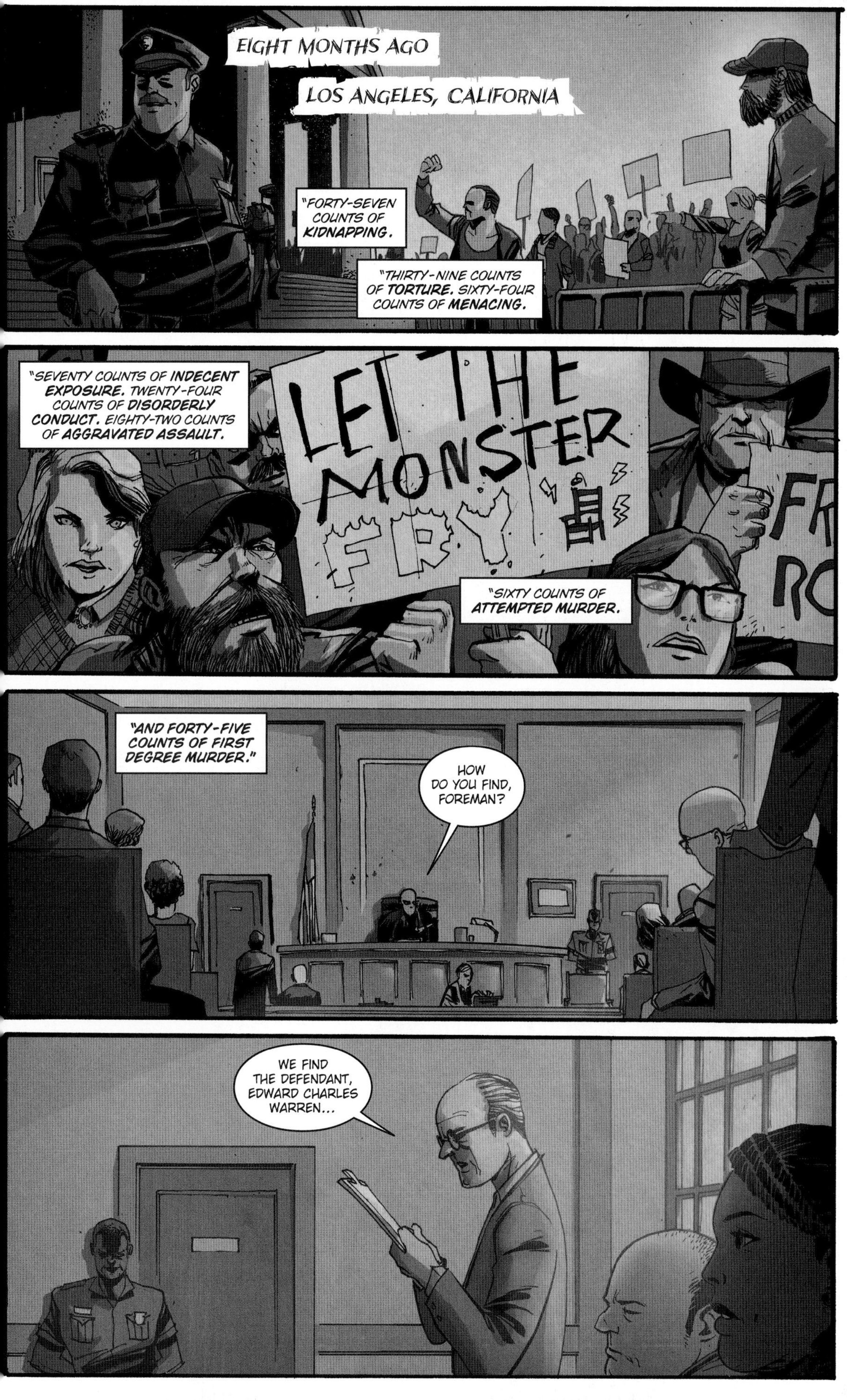
EIGHT MONTHS AGO
LOS ANGELES, CALIFORNIA
"FORTY-SEVEN COUNTS OF KIDNAPPING.
"THIRTY-NINE COUNTS OF TORTURE. SIXTY-FOUR COUNTS OF MENACING.
"SEVENTY COUNTS OF INDECENT EXPOSURE. TWENTY-FOUR COUNTS OF DISORDERLY CONDUCT. EIGHTY-TWO COUNTS OF AGGRAVATED ASSAULT.
LET THE MONSTER FRY
"SIXTY COUNTS OF ATTEMPTED MURDER.
"AND FORTY-FIVE COUNTS OF FIRST DEGREE MURDER."
HOW DO YOU FIND, FOREMAN?
WE FIND THE DEFENDANT, EDWARD CHARLES WARREN...

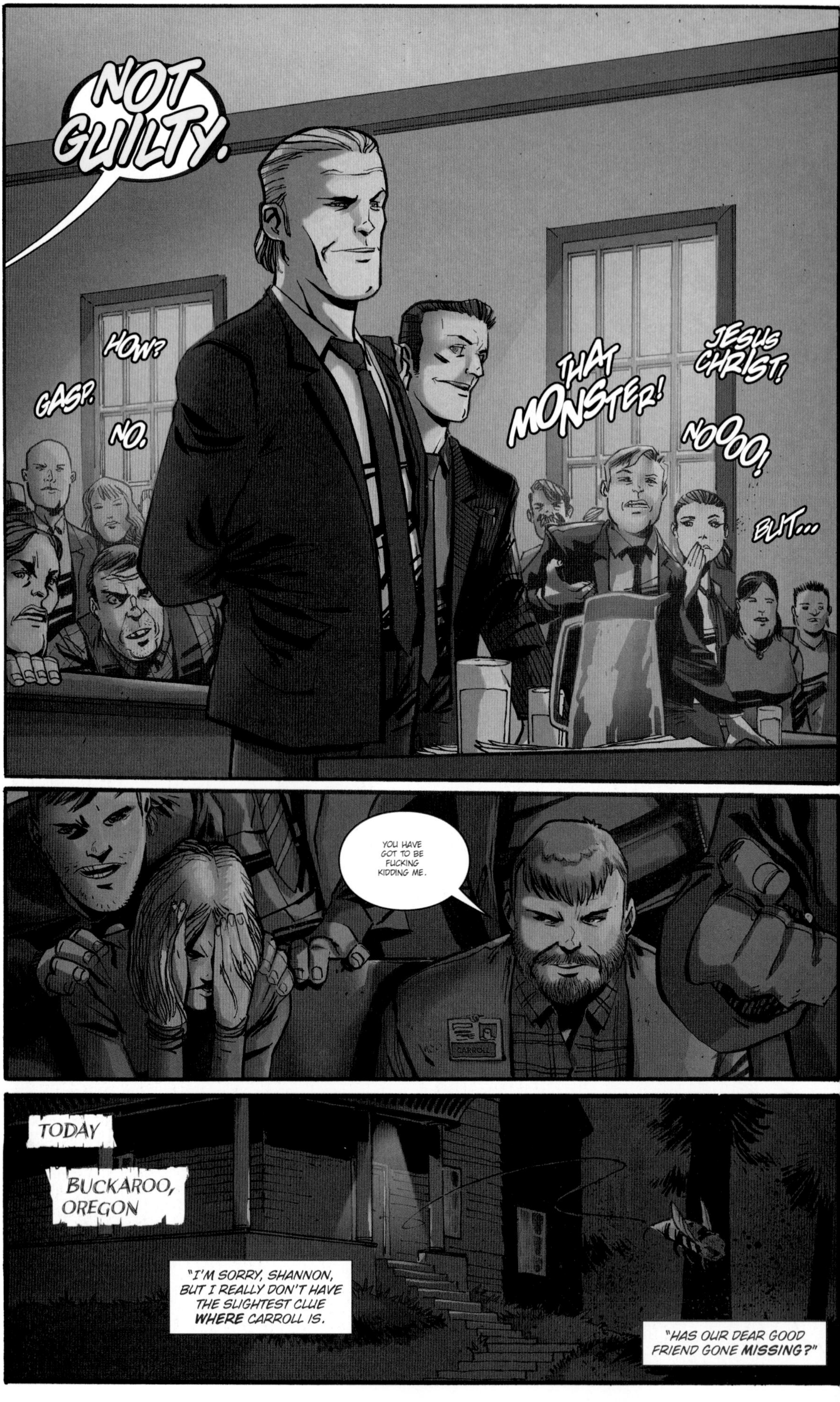
NOT GUILTY.
HOW?
GASP.
NO.
THAT MONSTER!
JESUS CHRIST!
NOOOO!
BUT...
YOU HAVE GOT TO BE FUCKING KIDDING ME.
CARROLL
TODAY
BUCKAROO, OREGON
"I'M SORRY, SHANNON, BUT I REALLY DON'T HAVE THE SLIGHTEST CLUE WHERE CARROLL IS.
"HAS OUR DEAR GOOD FRIEND GONE MISSING?"

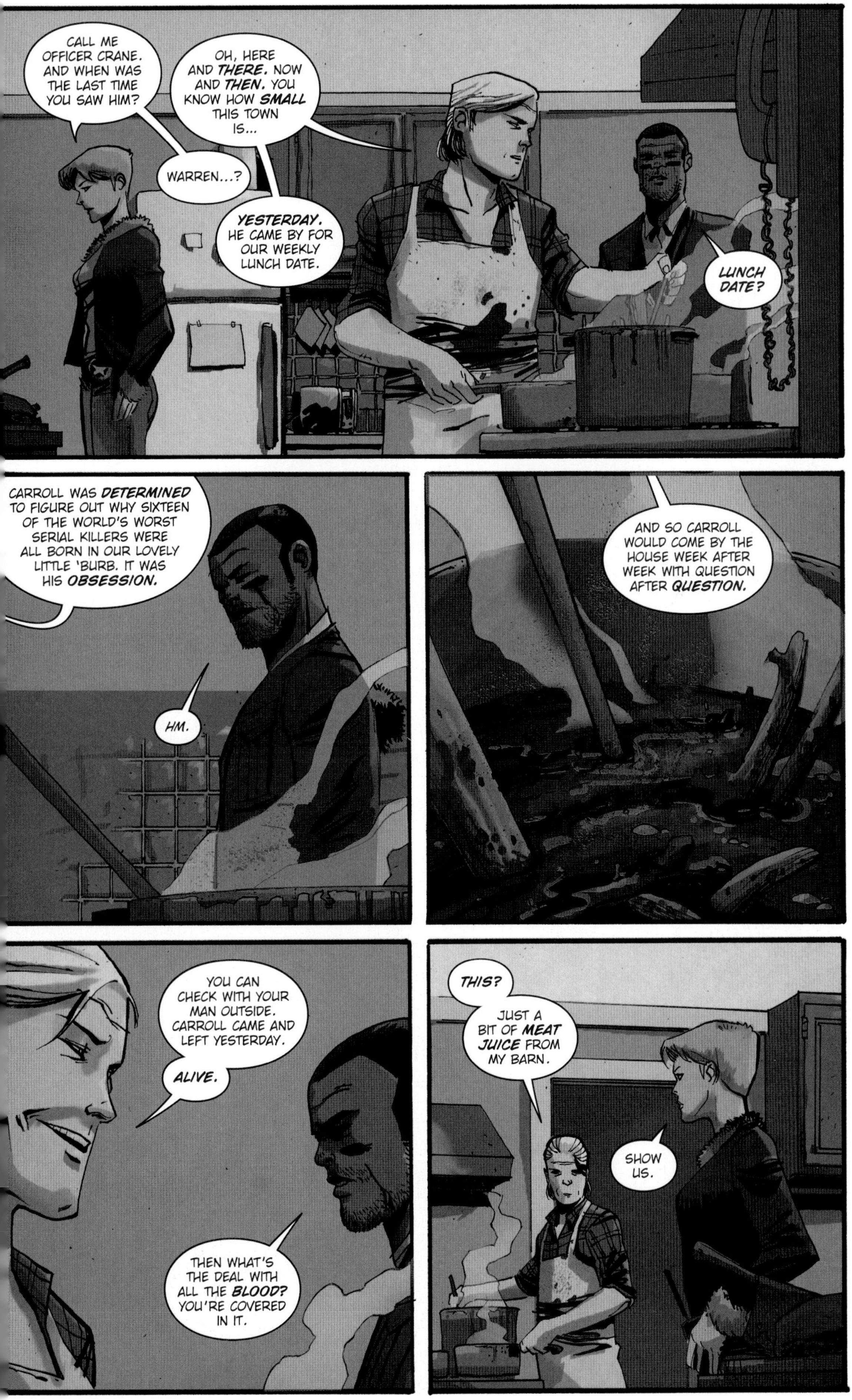
CALL ME OFFICER CRANE. AND WHEN WAS THE LAST TIME YOU SAW HIM?
OH, HERE AND THERE. NOW AND THEN. YOU KNOW HOW SMALL THIS TOWN IS...
WARREN...?
YESTERDAY. HE CAME BY FOR OUR WEEKLY LUNCH DATE.
LUNCH DATE?
CARROLL WAS DETERMINED TO FIGURE OUT WHY SIXTEEN OF THE WORLD'S WORST SERIAL KILLERS WERE ALL BORN IN OUR LOVELY LITTLE 'BURB. IT WAS HIS OBSESSION.
HM.
AND SO CARROLL WOULD COME BY THE HOUSE WEEK AFTER WEEK WITH QUESTION AFTER QUESTION.
YOU CAN CHECK WITH YOUR MAN OUTSIDE. CARROLL CAME AND LEFT YESTERDAY.
ALIVE.
THEN WHAT'S THE DEAL WITH ALL THE BLOOD? YOU'RE COVERED IN IT.
THIS?
JUST A BIT OF MEAT JUICE FROM MY BARN.
SHOW US.

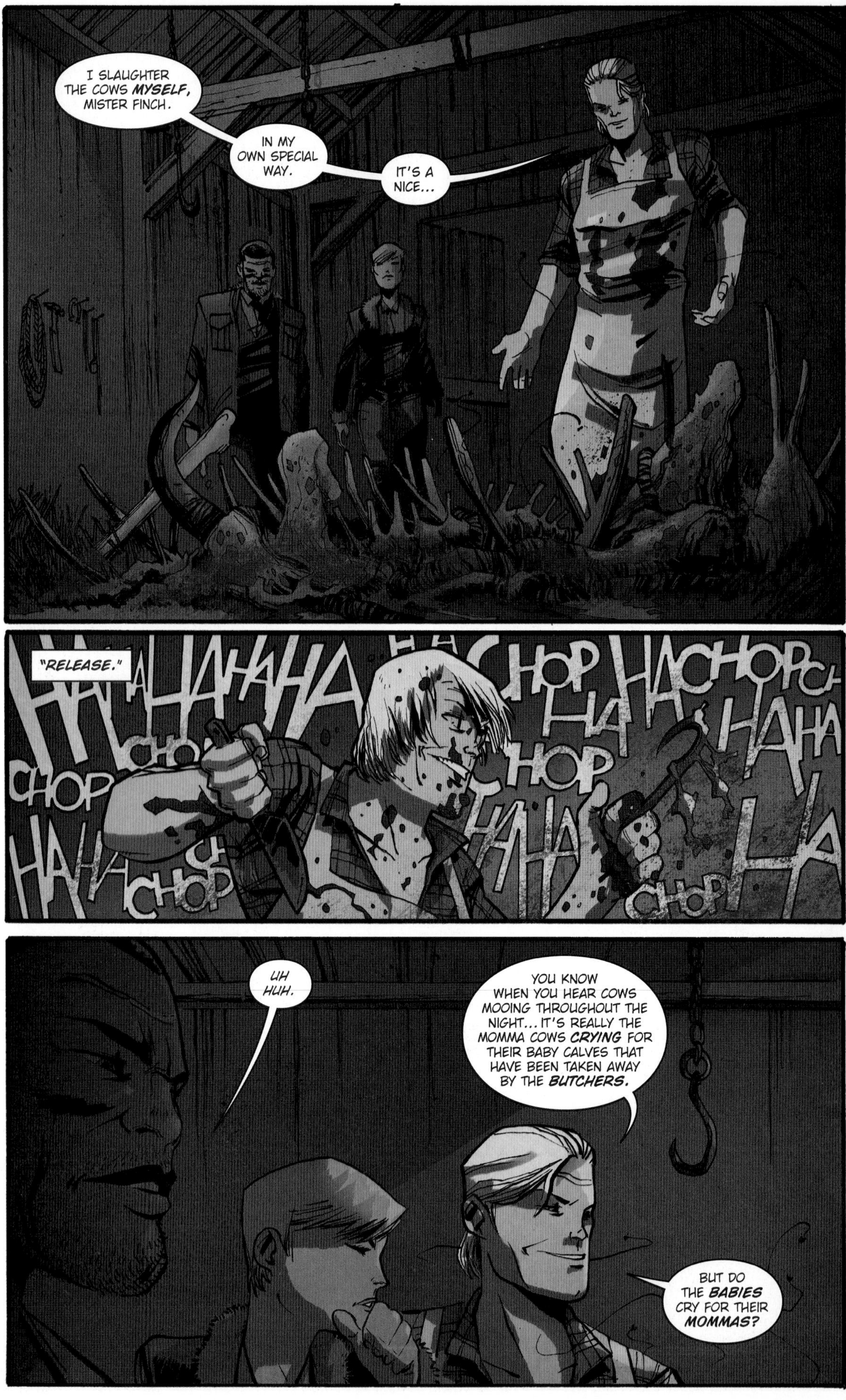
I SLAUGHTER THE COWS MYSELF, MISTER FINCH.
IN MY OWN SPECIAL WAY.
IT'S A NICE...
"RELEASE."
HAHAHAHAHA
HA
CHOP HACHOP
HA
HAHA
CHOP
CHOP
CHOP
HAHA
HAHACHOP
CHOP
HA
UH HUH.
YOU KNOW WHEN YOU HEAR COWS MOOING THROUGHOUT THE NIGHT... IT'S REALLY THE MOMMA COWS CRYING FOR THEIR BABY CALVES THAT HAVE BEEN TAKEN AWAY BY THE BUTCHERS.
BUT DO THE BABIES CRY FOR THEIR MOMMAS?

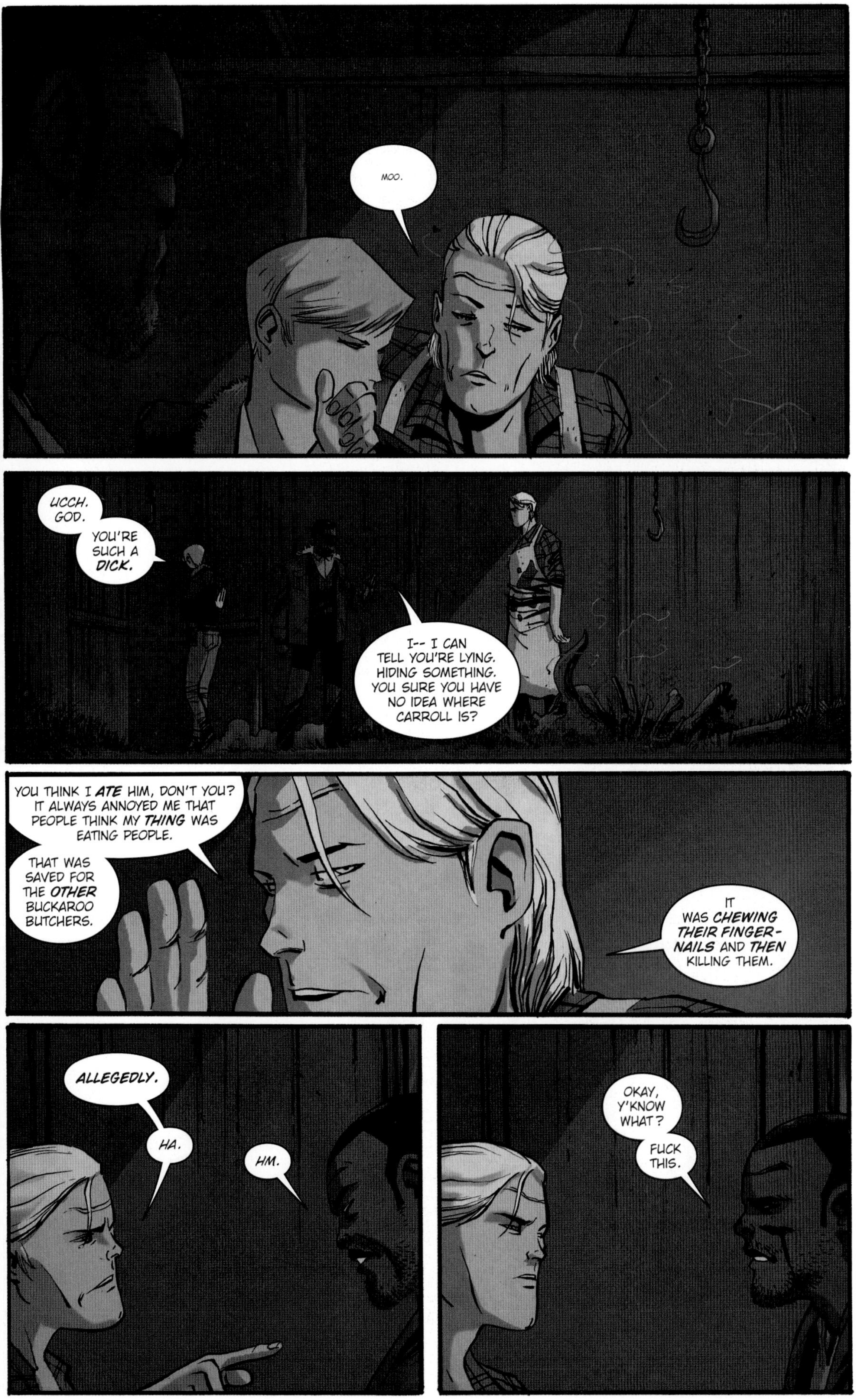
MOO.
UCCH. GOD.
YOU'RE SUCH A DICK.
I-- I CAN TELL YOU'RE LYING. HIDING SOMETHING. YOU SURE YOU HAVE NO IDEA WHERE CARROLL IS?
YOU THINK I ATE HIM, DON'T YOU? IT ALWAYS ANNOYED ME THAT PEOPLE THINK MY THING WAS EATING PEOPLE.
THAT WAS SAVED FOR THE OTHER BUCKAROO BUTCHERS.
IT WAS CHEWING THEIR FINGER-NAILS AND THEN KILLING THEM.
ALLEGEDLY.
HA.
HM.
OKAY, Y'KNOW WHAT?
FUCK THIS.

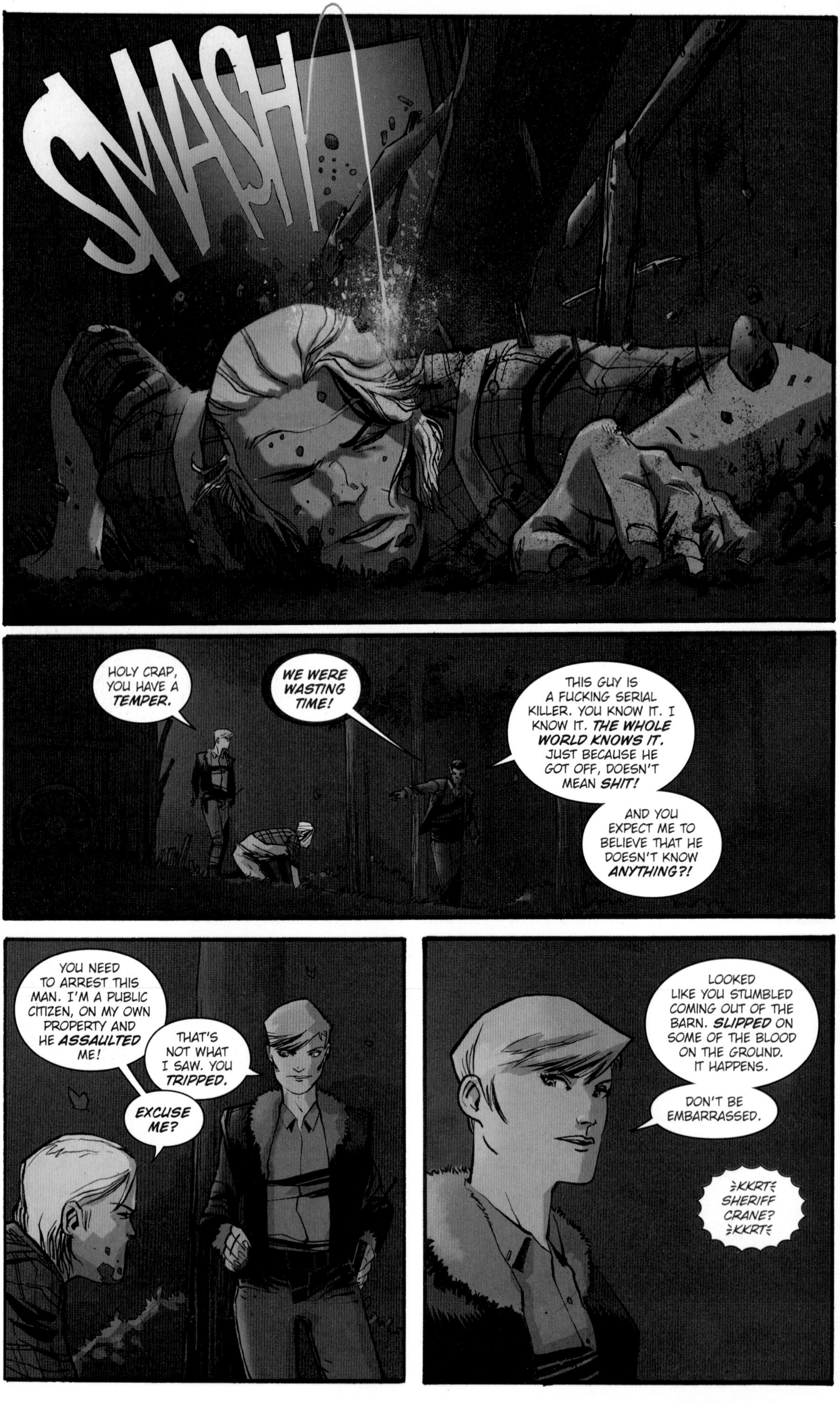
SMASH
HOLY CRAP, YOU HAVE A TEMPER.
WE WERE WASTING TIME!
THIS GUY IS A FUCKING SERIAL KILLER. YOU KNOW IT. I KNOW IT. THE WHOLE WORLD KNOWS IT. JUST BECAUSE HE GOT OFF, DOESN'T MEAN SHIT!
AND YOU EXPECT ME TO BELIEVE THAT HE DOESN'T KNOW ANYTHING?!
YOU NEED TO ARREST THIS MAN. I'M A PUBLIC CITIZEN, ON MY OWN PROPERTY AND HE ASSAULTED ME!
THAT'S NOT WHAT I SAW. YOU TRIPPED.
EXCUSE ME?
LOOKED LIKE YOU STUMBLED COMING OUT OF THE BARN. SLIPPED ON SOME OF THE BLOOD ON THE GROUND. IT HAPPENS.
DON'T BE EMBARRASSED.
KKRT SHERIFF CRANE? KKRT

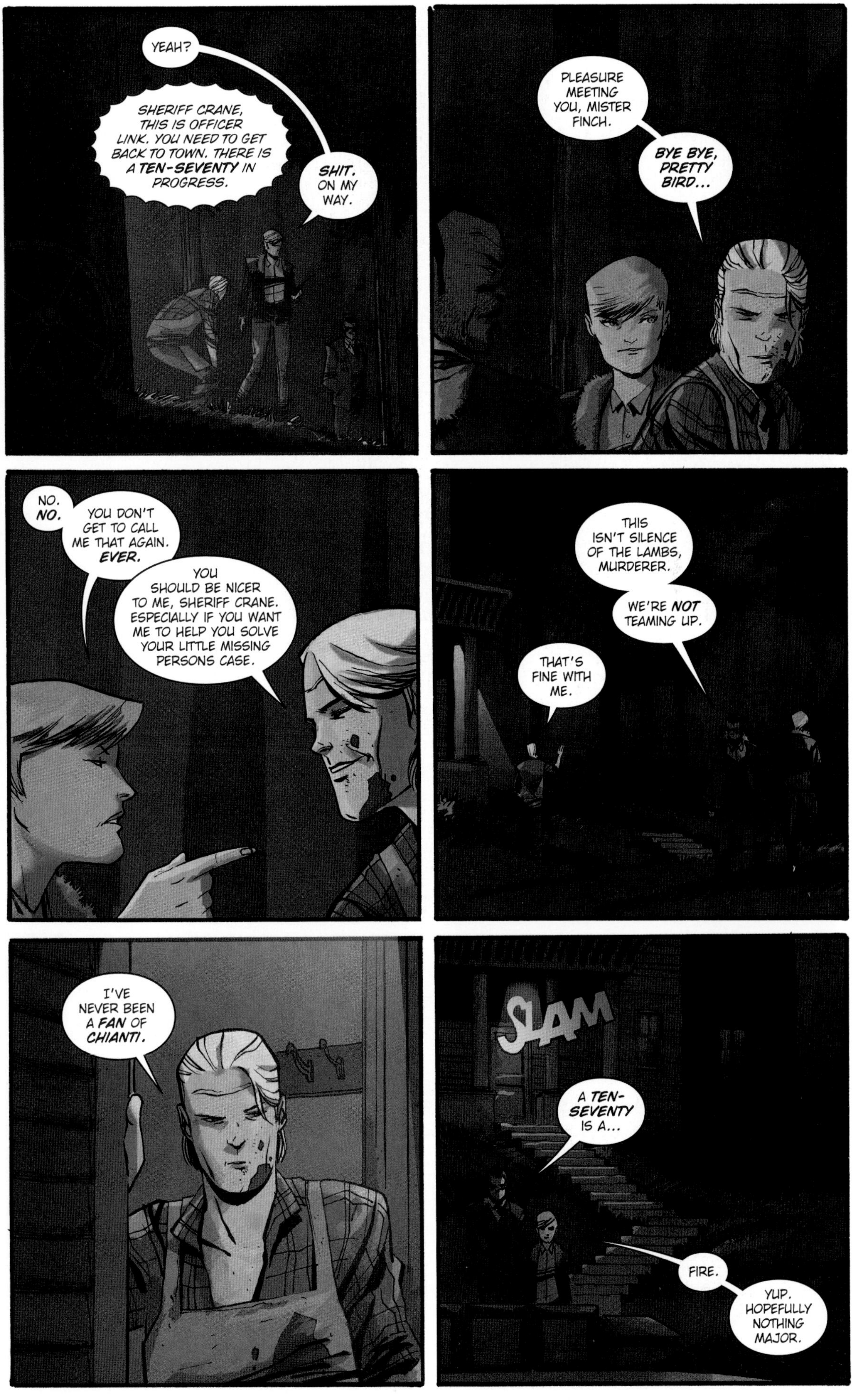
YEAH?
SHERIFF CRANE, THIS IS OFFICER LINK. YOU NEED TO GET BACK TO TOWN. THERE IS A TEN-SEVENTY IN PROGRESS.
SHIT. ON MY WAY.
PLEASURE MEETING YOU, MISTER FINCH.
BYE BYE, PRETTY BIRD...
NO. NO.
YOU DON'T GET TO CALL ME THAT AGAIN. EVER.
YOU SHOULD BE NICER TO ME, SHERIFF CRANE. ESPECIALLY IF YOU WANT ME TO HELP YOU SOLVE YOUR LITTLE MISSING PERSONS CASE.
THIS ISN'T SILENCE OF THE LAMBS, MURDERER.
WE'RE NOT TEAMING UP.
THAT'S FINE WITH ME.
I'VE NEVER BEEN A FAN OF CHIANTI.
SLAM
A TEN-SEVENTY IS A...
FIRE.
YUP. HOPEFULLY NOTHING MAJOR.

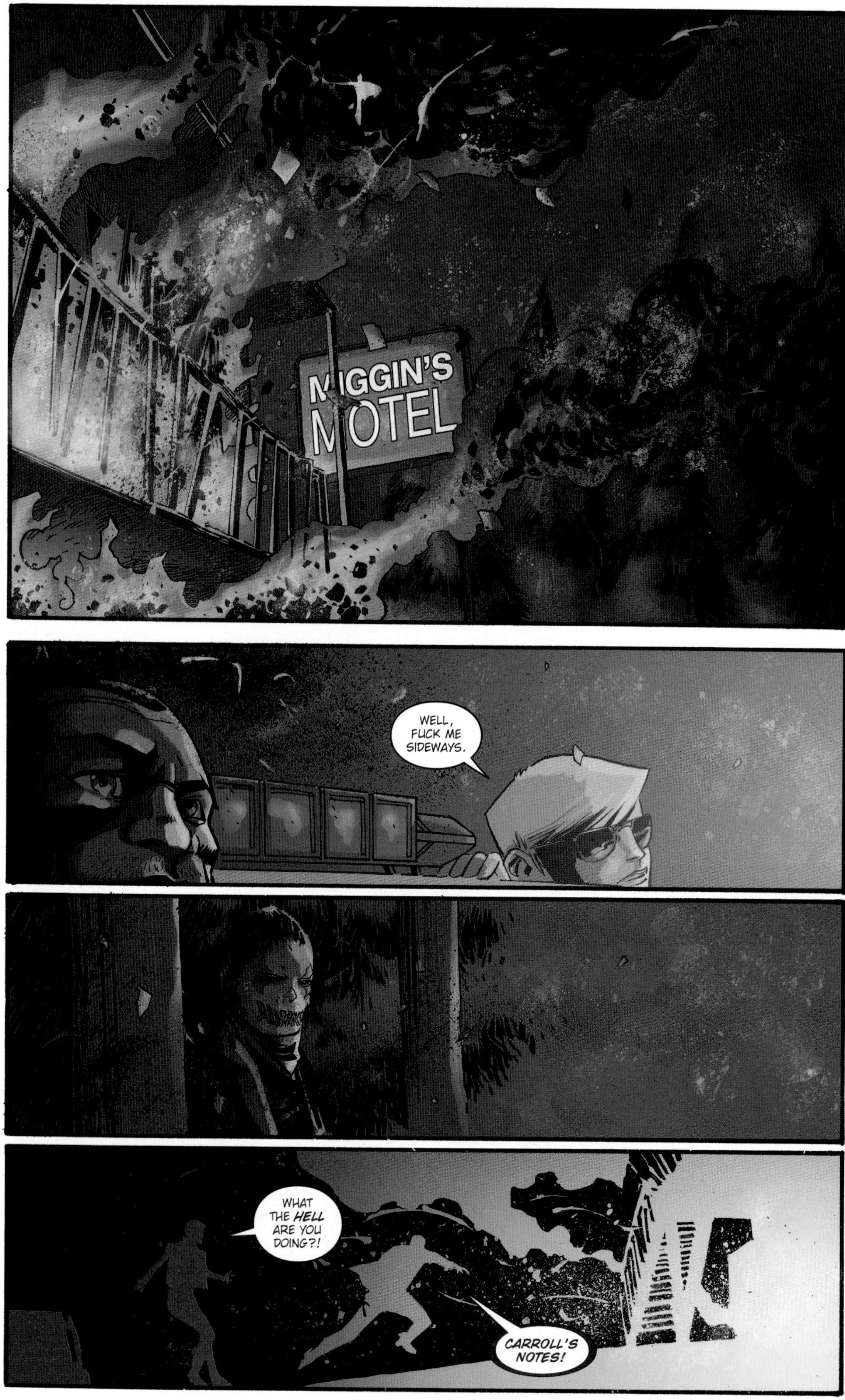

MIGGIN'S MOTEL
WELL, FUCK ME SIDEWAYS.
WHAT THE *HELL* ARE YOU DOING?!
*CARROLL'S NOTES!*

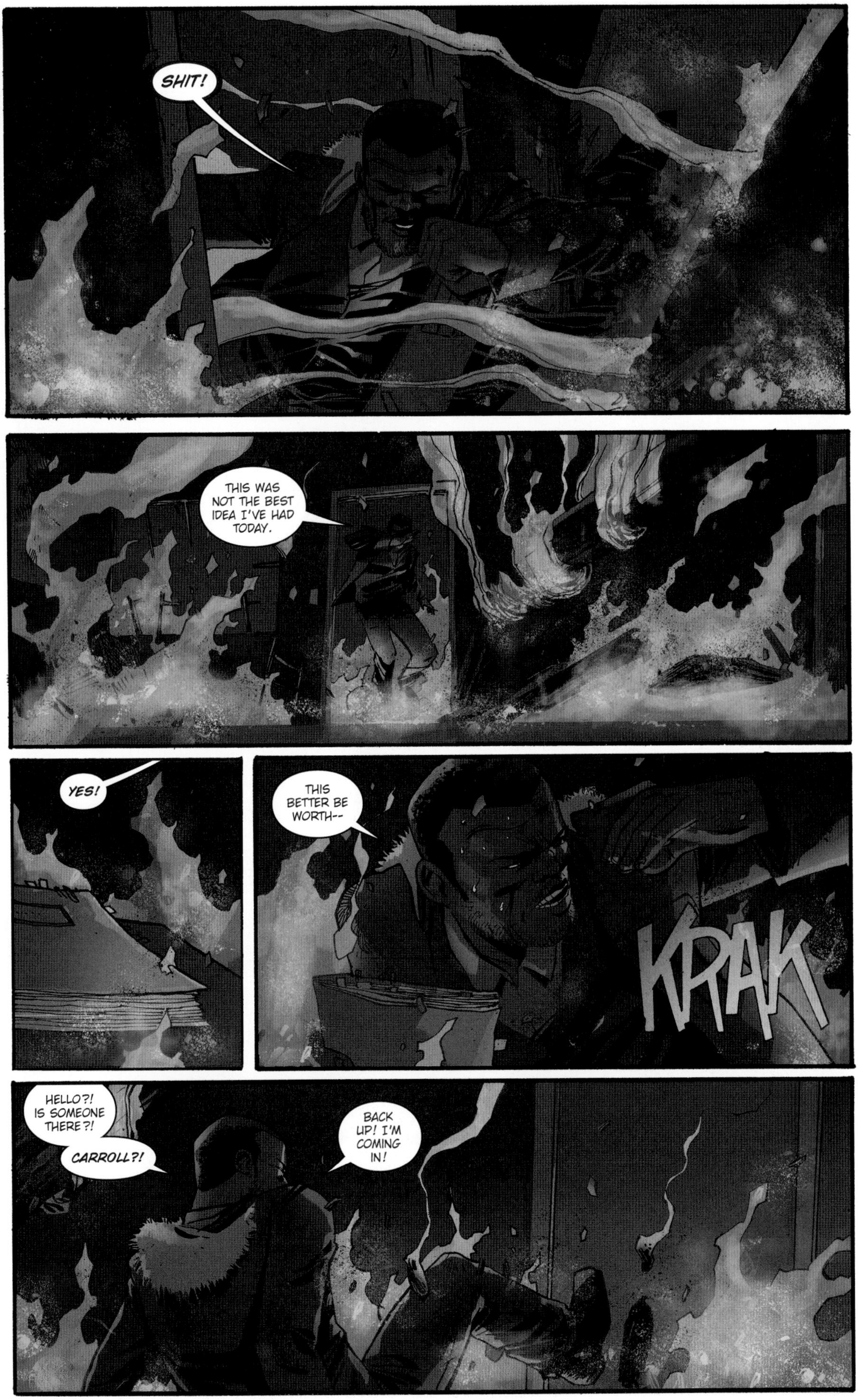
SHIT!
THIS WAS NOT THE BEST IDEA I'VE HAD TODAY.
YES!
THIS BETTER BE WORTH--
KRAK
HELLO?! IS SOMEONE THERE?!
CARROLL?!
BACK UP! I'M COMING IN!

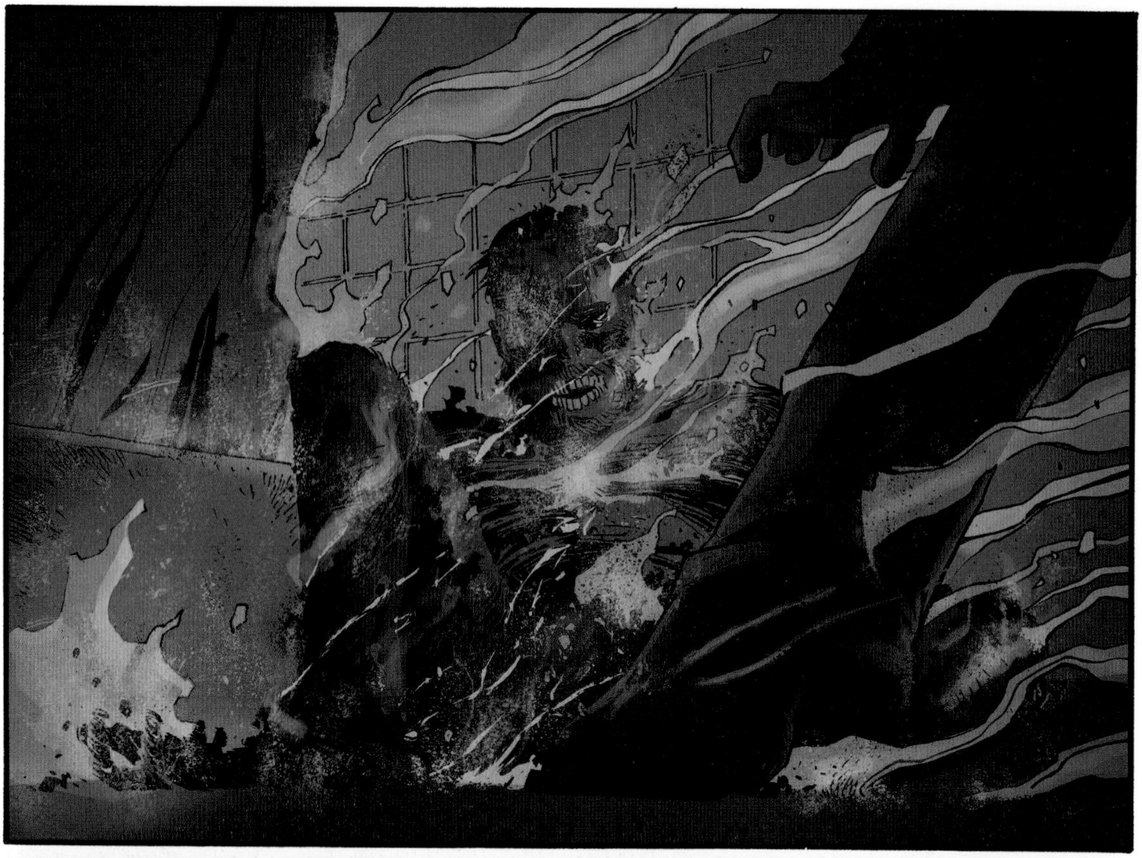

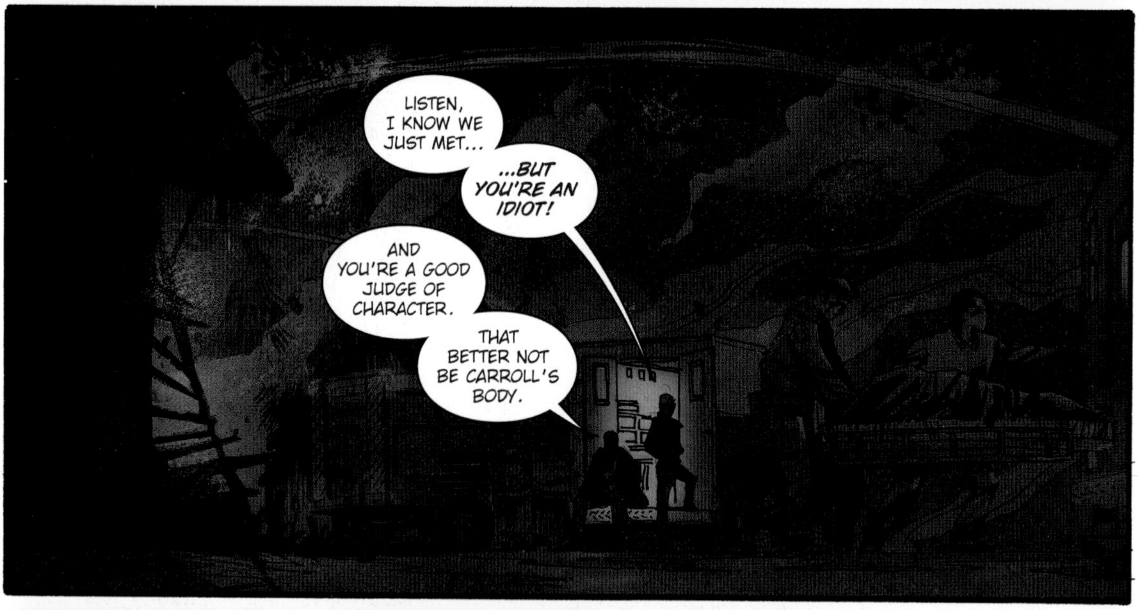
LISTEN, I KNOW WE JUST MET...
...BUT YOU'RE AN IDIOT!
AND YOU'RE A GOOD JUDGE OF CHARACTER.
THAT BETTER NOT BE CARROLL'S BODY.

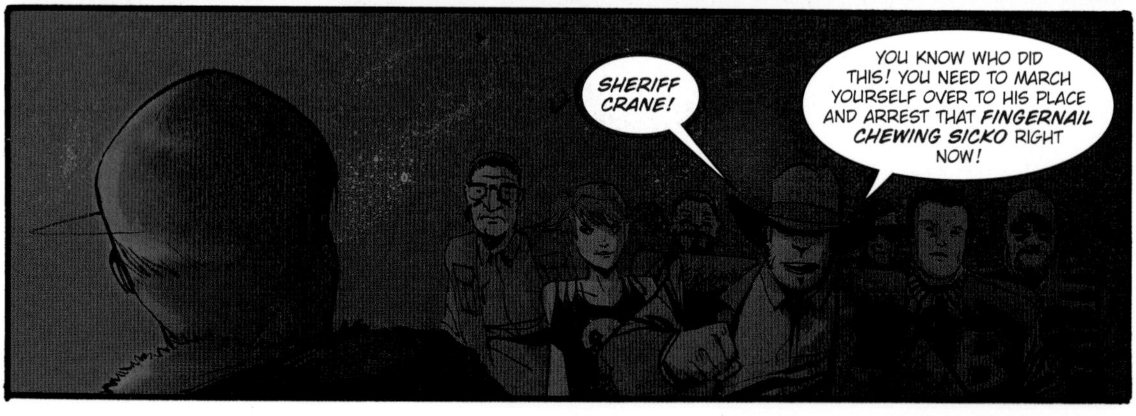
SHERIFF CRANE!
YOU KNOW WHO DID THIS! YOU NEED TO MARCH YOURSELF OVER TO HIS PLACE AND ARREST THAT FINGERNAIL CHEWING SICKO RIGHT NOW!

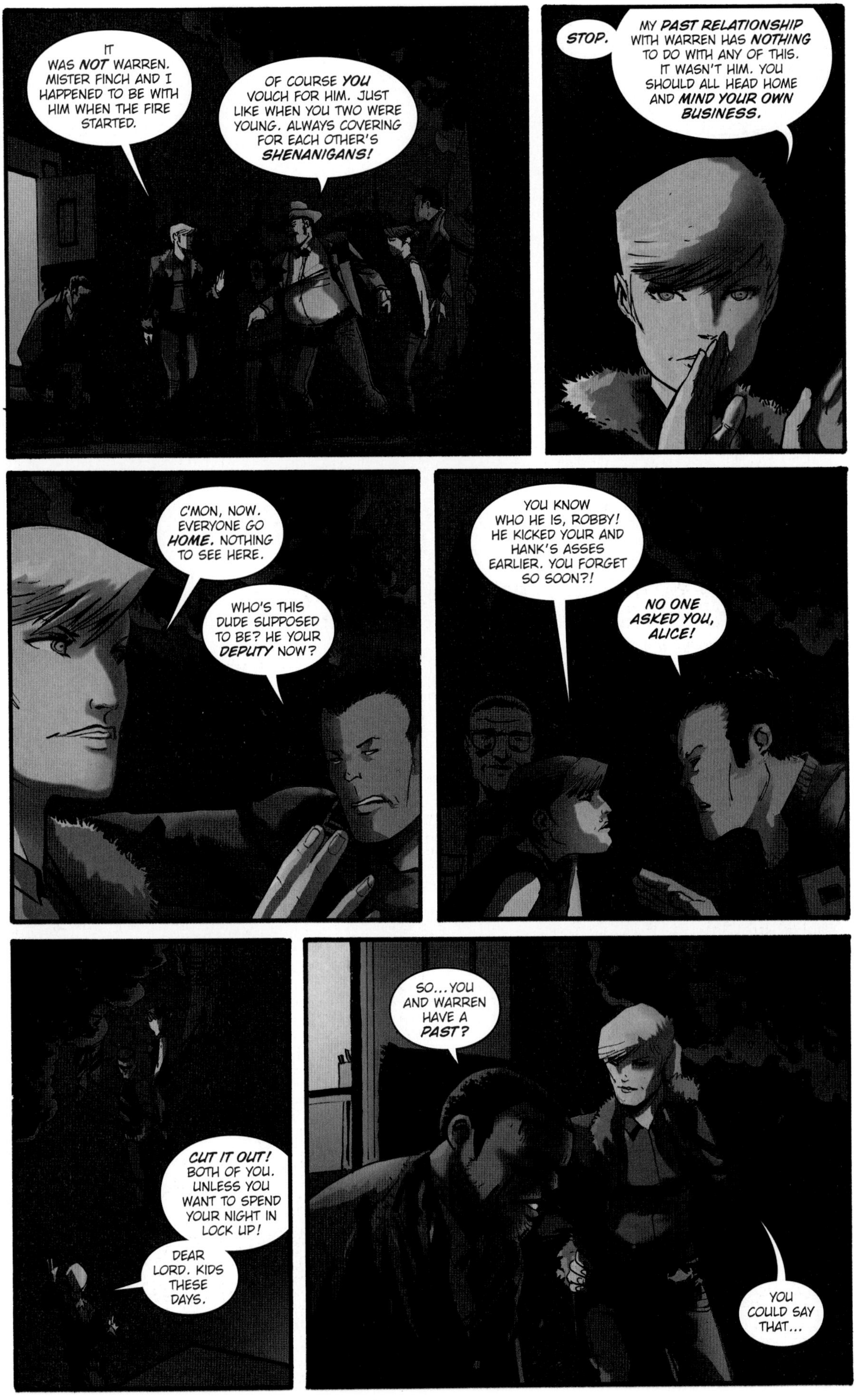
IT WAS NOT WARREN. MISTER FINCH AND I HAPPENED TO BE WITH HIM WHEN THE FIRE STARTED.
OF COURSE YOU VOUCH FOR HIM. JUST LIKE WHEN YOU TWO WERE YOUNG. ALWAYS COVERING FOR EACH OTHER'S SHENANIGANS!
STOP.
MY PAST RELATIONSHIP WITH WARREN HAS NOTHING TO DO WITH ANY OF THIS. IT WASN'T HIM. YOU SHOULD ALL HEAD HOME AND MIND YOUR OWN BUSINESS.
C'MON, NOW. EVERYONE GO HOME. NOTHING TO SEE HERE.
WHO'S THIS DUDE SUPPOSED TO BE? HE YOUR DEPUTY NOW?
YOU KNOW WHO HE IS, ROBBY! HE KICKED YOUR AND HANK'S ASSES EARLIER. YOU FORGET SO SOON?!
NO ONE ASKED YOU, ALICE!
CUT IT OUT! BOTH OF YOU. UNLESS YOU WANT TO SPEND YOUR NIGHT IN LOCK UP!
DEAR LORD. KIDS THESE DAYS.
SO...YOU AND WARREN HAVE A PAST?
YOU COULD SAY THAT...

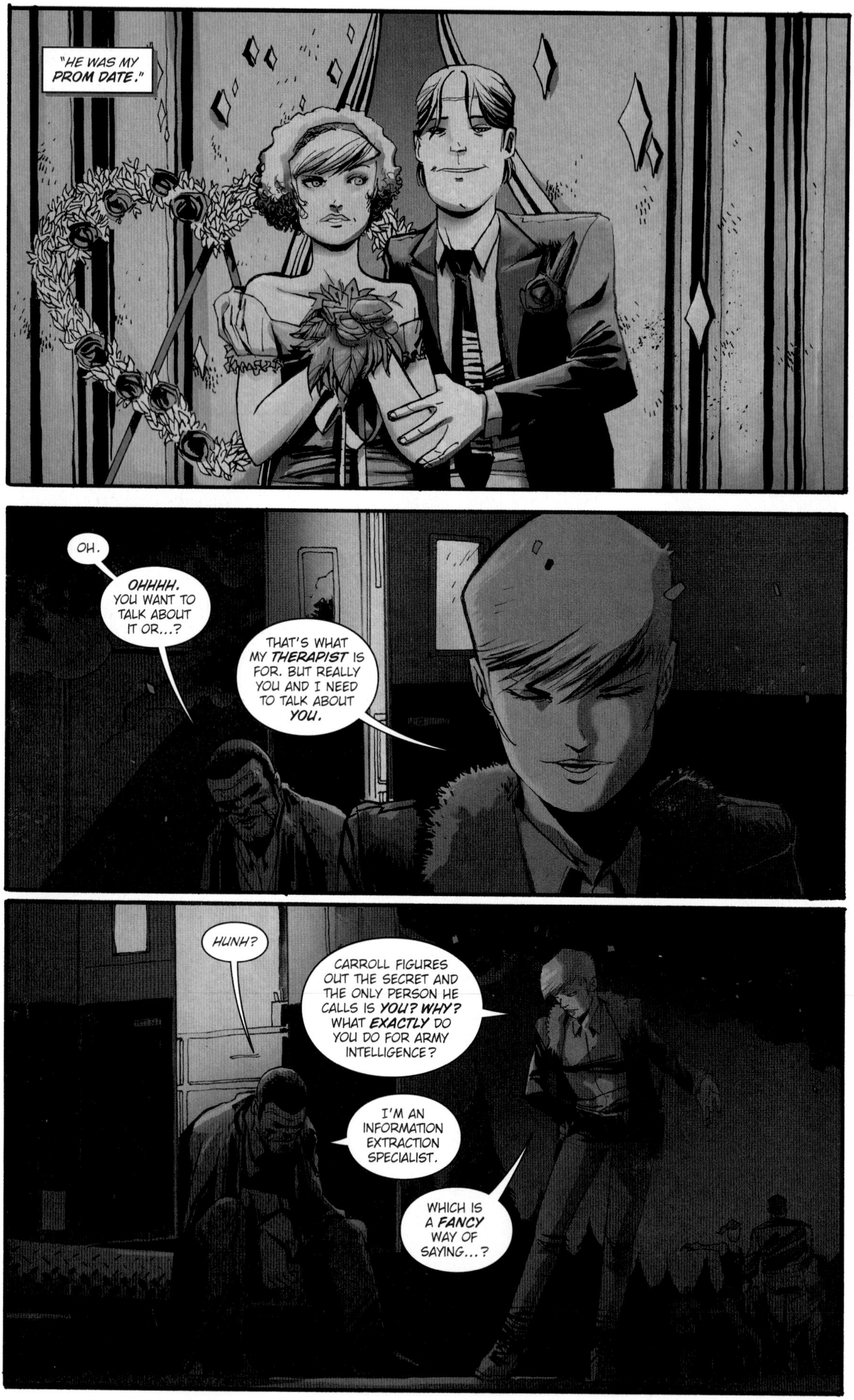
"HE WAS MY PROM DATE."
OH.
OHHHH. YOU WANT TO TALK ABOUT IT OR...?
THAT'S WHAT MY THERAPIST IS FOR. BUT REALLY YOU AND I NEED TO TALK ABOUT YOU.
HUNH?
CARROLL FIGURES OUT THE SECRET AND THE ONLY PERSON HE CALLS IS YOU? WHY? WHAT EXACTLY DO YOU DO FOR ARMY INTELLIGENCE?
I'M AN INFORMATION EXTRACTION SPECIALIST.
WHICH IS A FANCY WAY OF SAYING...?

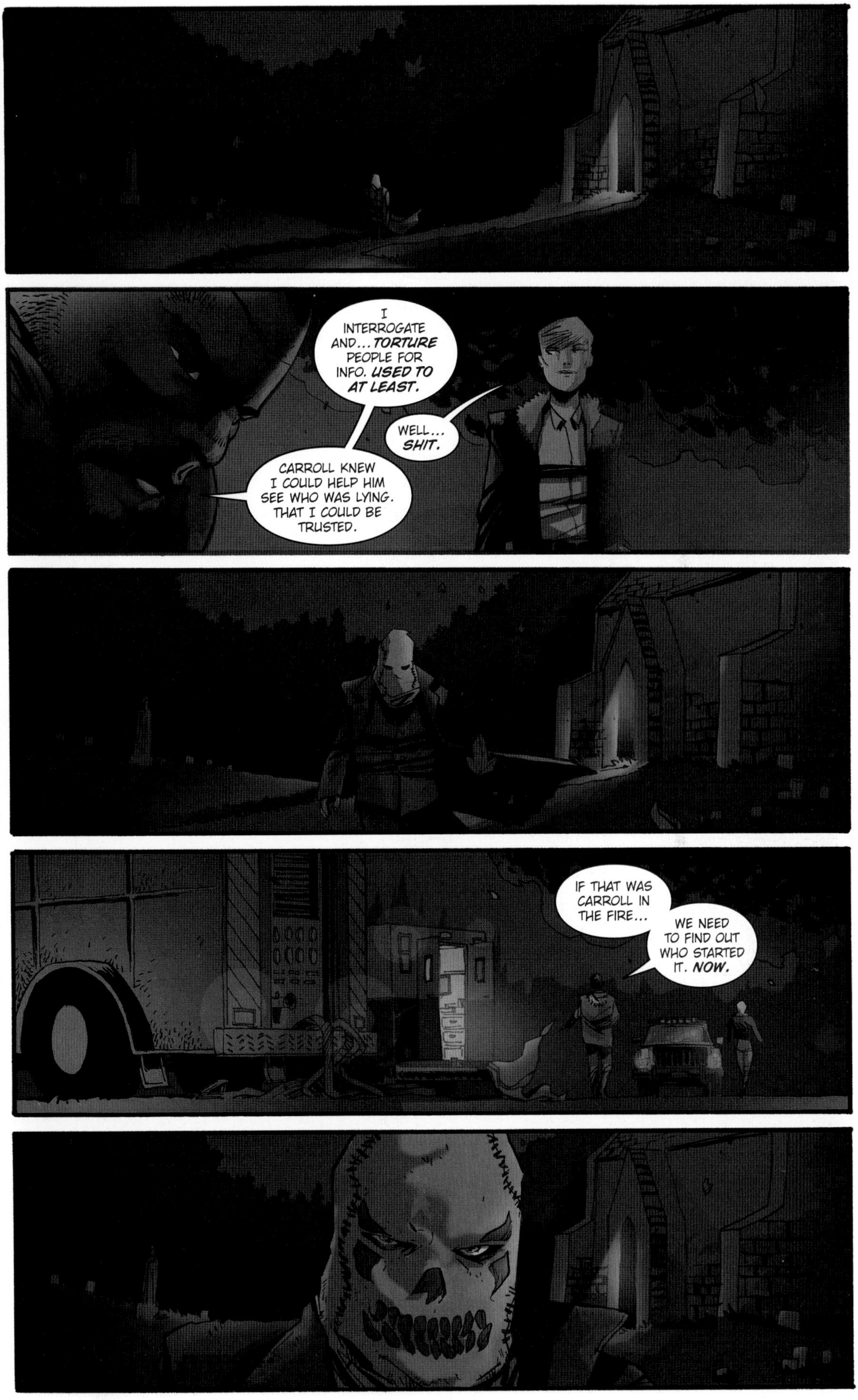
I INTERROGATE AND... TORTURE PEOPLE FOR INFO. USED TO AT LEAST.
WELL... SHIT.
CARROLL KNEW I COULD HELP HIM SEE WHO WAS LYING. THAT I COULD BE TRUSTED.
IF THAT WAS CARROLL IN THE FIRE...
WE NEED TO FIND OUT WHO STARTED IT. NOW.

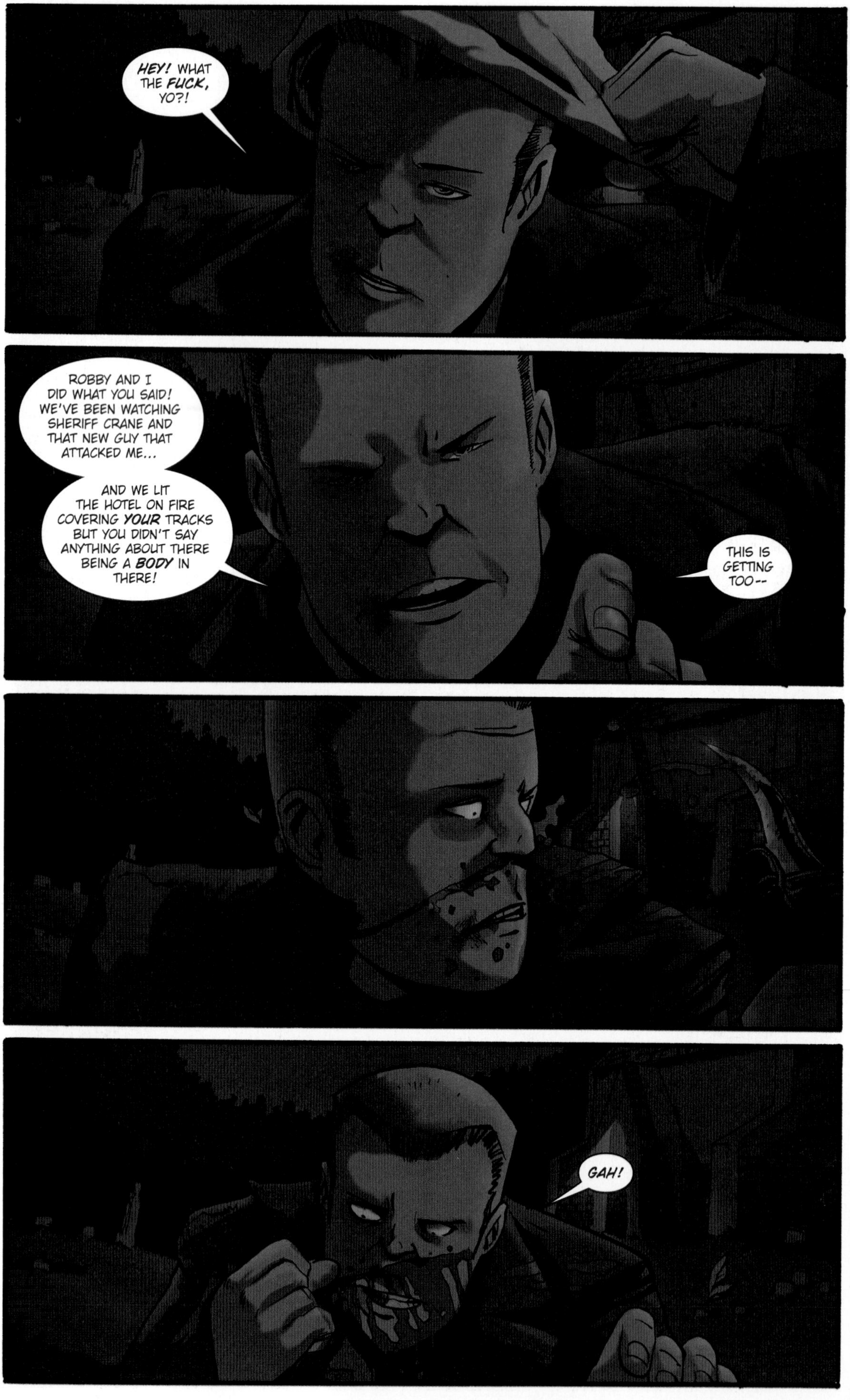
HEY! WHAT THE FUCK, YO?!
ROBBY AND I DID WHAT YOU SAID! WE'VE BEEN WATCHING SHERIFF CRANE AND THAT NEW GUY THAT ATTACKED ME...
AND WE LIT THE HOTEL ON FIRE COVERING YOUR TRACKS BUT YOU DIDN'T SAY ANYTHING ABOUT THERE BEING A BODY IN THERE!
THIS IS GETTING TOO--
GAH!

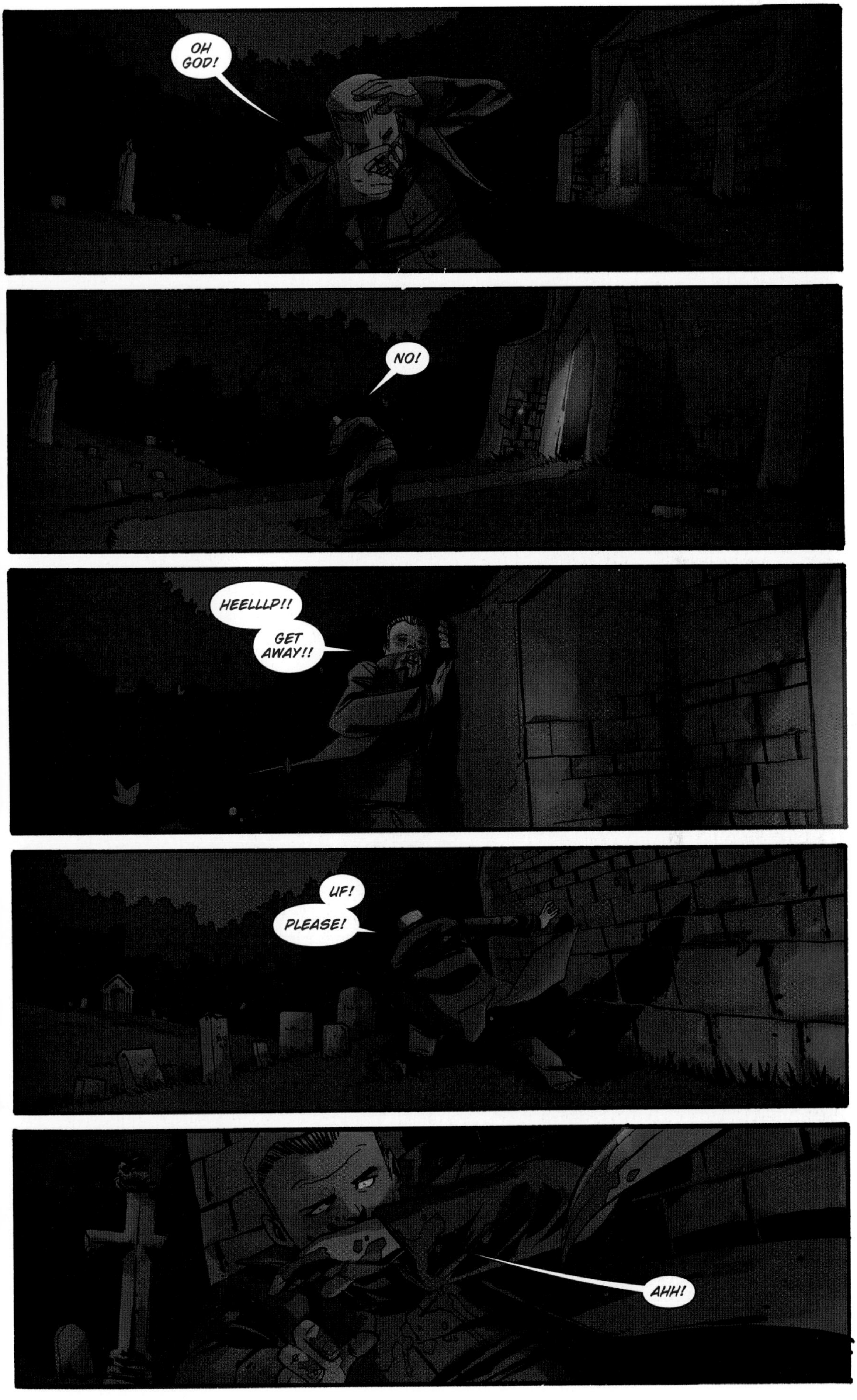
OH GOD!
NO!
HEELLLP!!
GET AWAY!!
UF!
PLEASE!
AHH!

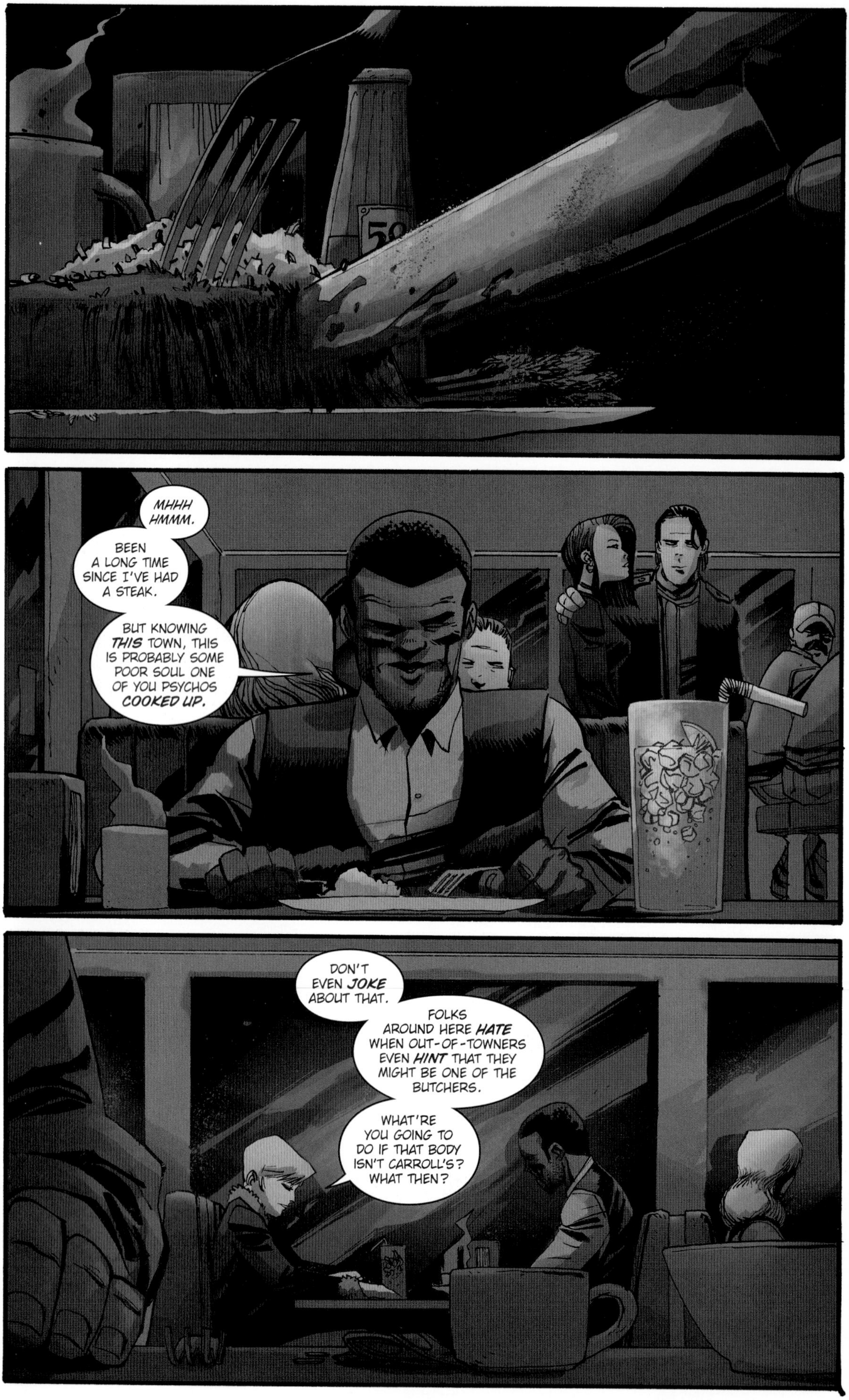
MHHH HMMM.
BEEN A LONG TIME SINCE I'VE HAD A STEAK.
BUT KNOWING THIS TOWN, THIS IS PROBABLY SOME POOR SOUL ONE OF YOU PSYCHOS COOKED UP.
DON'T EVEN JOKE ABOUT THAT.
FOLKS AROUND HERE HATE WHEN OUT-OF-TOWNERS EVEN HINT THAT THEY MIGHT BE ONE OF THE BUTCHERS.
WHAT'RE YOU GOING TO DO IF THAT BODY ISN'T CARROLL'S? WHAT THEN?

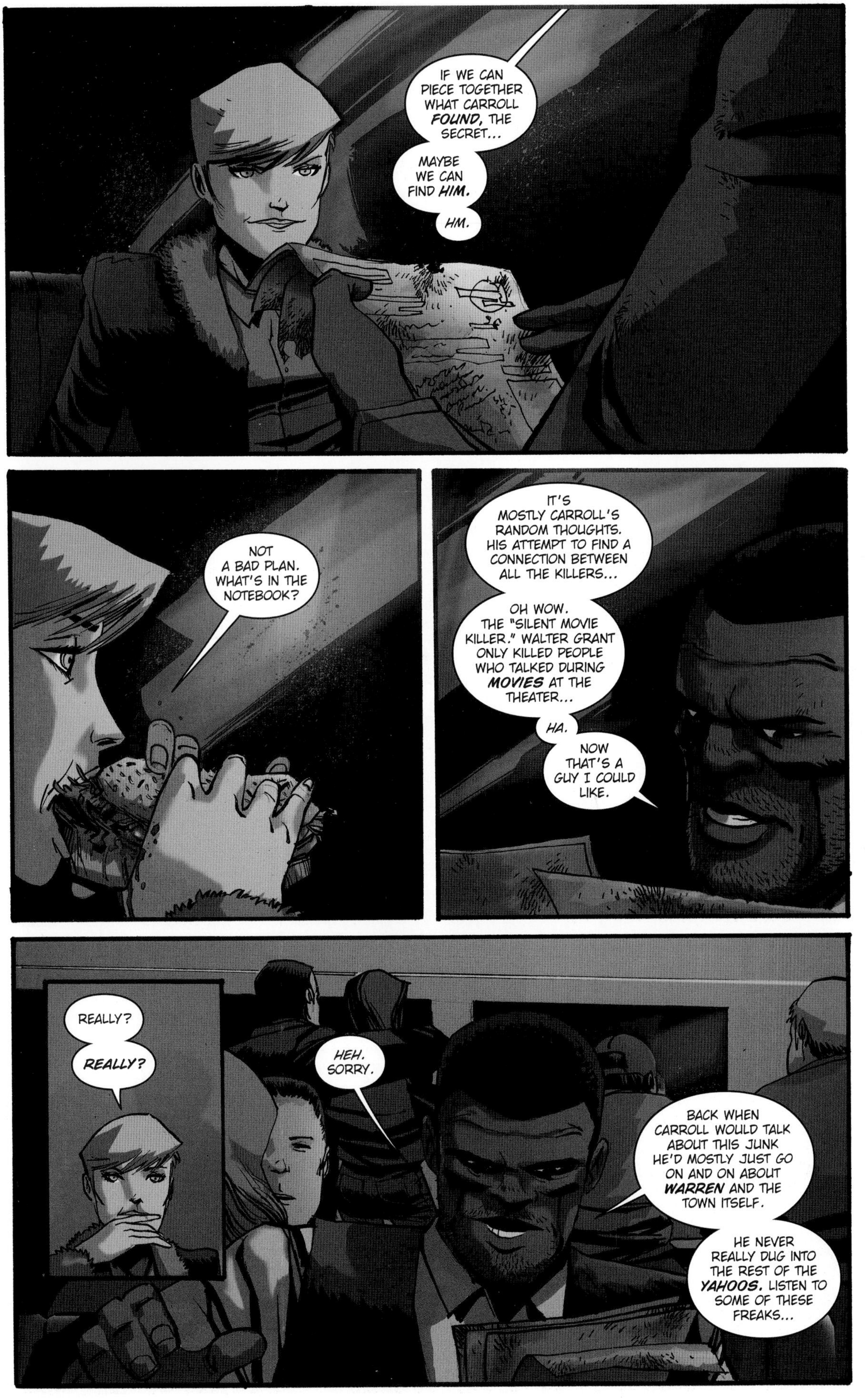
IF WE CAN PIECE TOGETHER WHAT CARROLL FOUND, THE SECRET...
MAYBE WE CAN FIND HIM.
HM.
NOT A BAD PLAN. WHAT'S IN THE NOTEBOOK?
IT'S MOSTLY CARROLL'S RANDOM THOUGHTS. HIS ATTEMPT TO FIND A CONNECTION BETWEEN ALL THE KILLERS...
OH WOW. THE "SILENT MOVIE KILLER." WALTER GRANT ONLY KILLED PEOPLE WHO TALKED DURING MOVIES AT THE THEATER...
HA.
NOW THAT'S A GUY I COULD LIKE.
REALLY?
REALLY?
HEH. SORRY.
BACK WHEN CARROLL WOULD TALK ABOUT THIS JUNK HE'D MOSTLY JUST GO ON AND ON ABOUT WARREN AND THE TOWN ITSELF.
HE NEVER REALLY DUG INTO THE REST OF THE YAHOOS. LISTEN TO SOME OF THESE FREAKS...

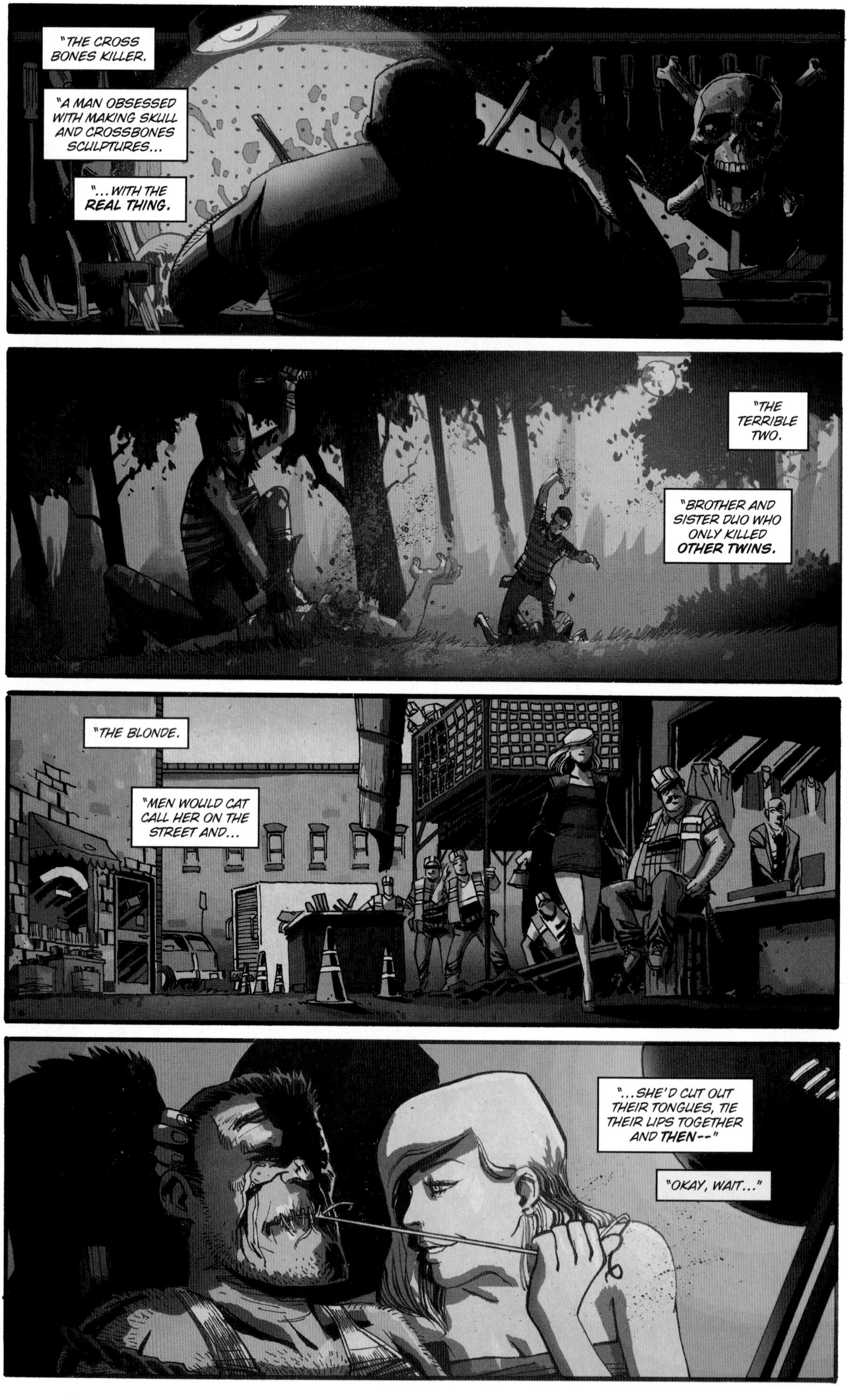
"THE CROSS BONES KILLER.
"A MAN OBSESSED WITH MAKING SKULL AND CROSSBONES SCULPTURES...
"...WITH THE REAL THING.
"THE TERRIBLE TWO.
"BROTHER AND SISTER DUO WHO ONLY KILLED OTHER TWINS.
"THE BLONDE.
"MEN WOULD CAT CALL HER ON THE STREET AND...
"...SHE'D CUT OUT THEIR TONGUES, TIE THEIR LIPS TOGETHER AND THEN--"
"OKAY, WAIT..."

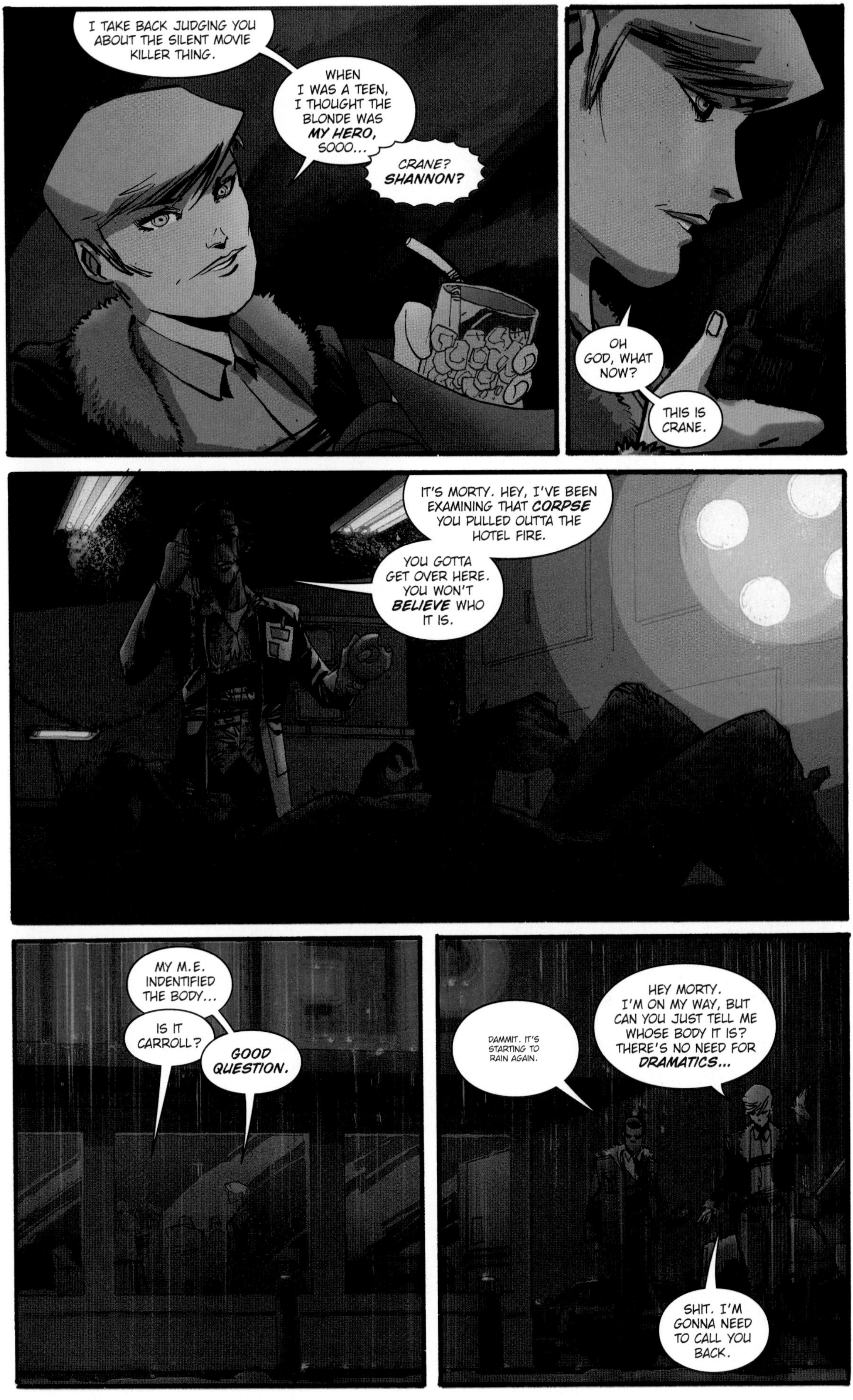

I TAKE BACK JUDGING YOU ABOUT THE SILENT MOVIE KILLER THING.
WHEN I WAS A TEEN, I THOUGHT THE BLONDE WAS **MY HERO,** SOOO...
CRANE? **SHANNON?**
OH GOD, WHAT NOW?
THIS IS CRANE.
IT'S MORTY. HEY, I'VE BEEN EXAMINING THAT **CORPSE** YOU PULLED OUTTA THE HOTEL FIRE.
YOU GOTTA GET OVER HERE. YOU WON'T **BELIEVE** WHO IT IS.
MY M.E. INDENTIFIED THE BODY...
IS IT CARROLL?
**GOOD QUESTION.**
DAMMIT. IT'S STARTING TO RAIN AGAIN.
HEY MORTY. I'M ON MY WAY, BUT CAN YOU JUST TELL ME WHOSE BODY IT IS? THERE'S NO NEED FOR **DRAMATICS...**
SHIT. I'M GONNA NEED TO CALL YOU BACK.

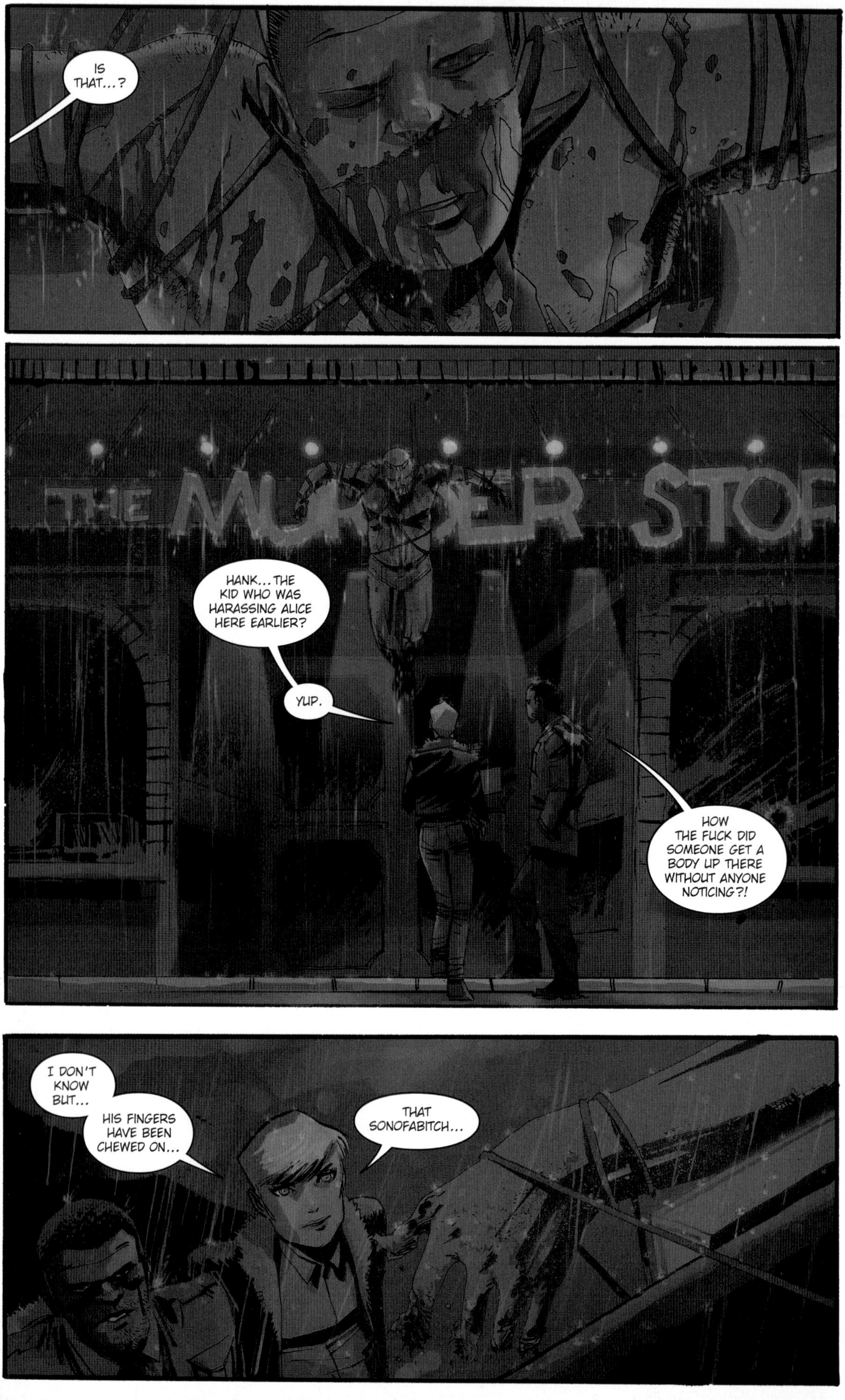
IS THAT...?
THE MURDER STOR
HANK...THE KID WHO WAS HARASSING ALICE HERE EARLIER?
YUP.
HOW THE FUCK DID SOMEONE GET A BODY UP THERE WITHOUT ANYONE NOTICING?!
I DON'T KNOW BUT...
HIS FINGERS HAVE BEEN CHEWED ON...
THAT SONOFABITCH...

# ISSUE THREE

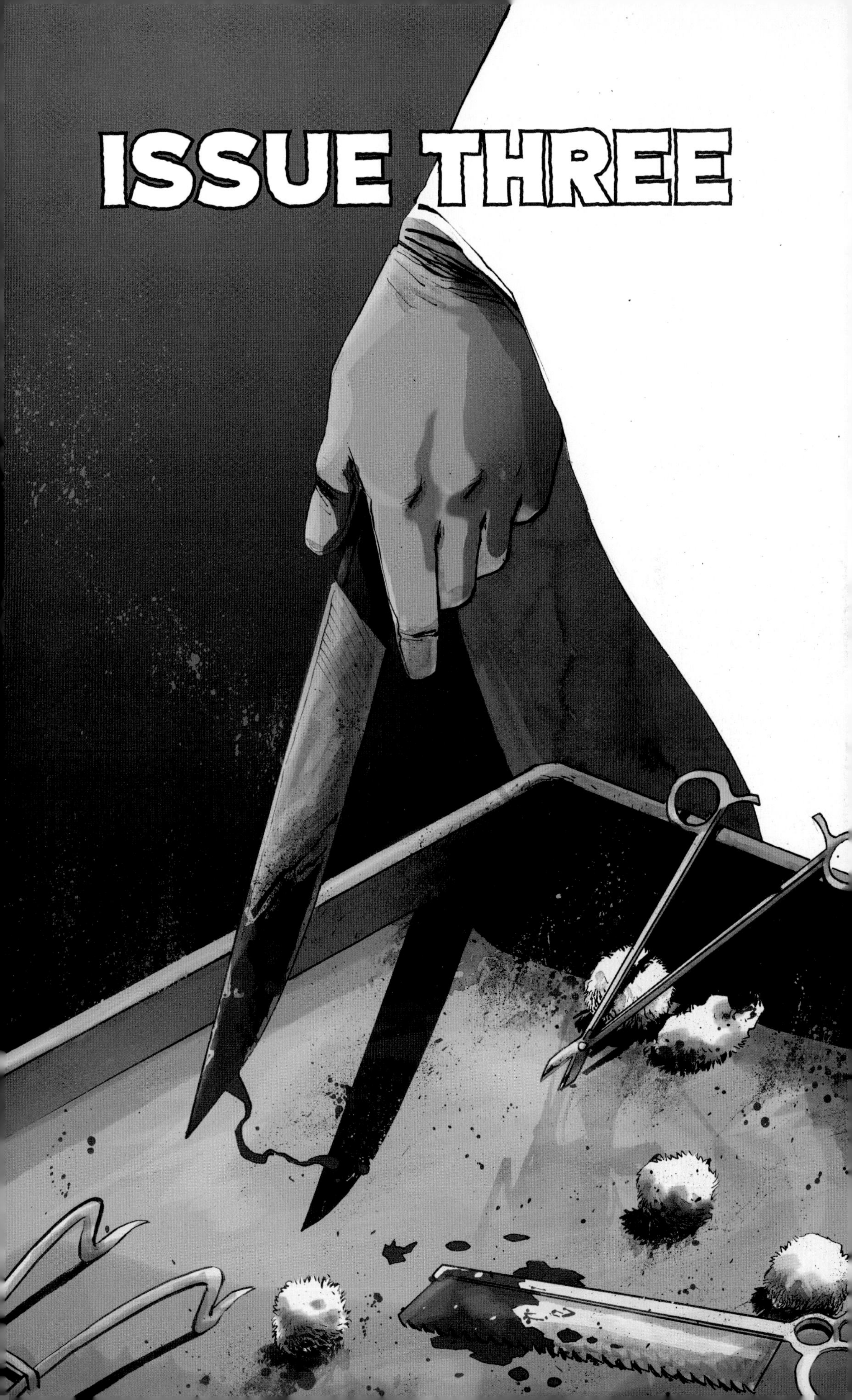

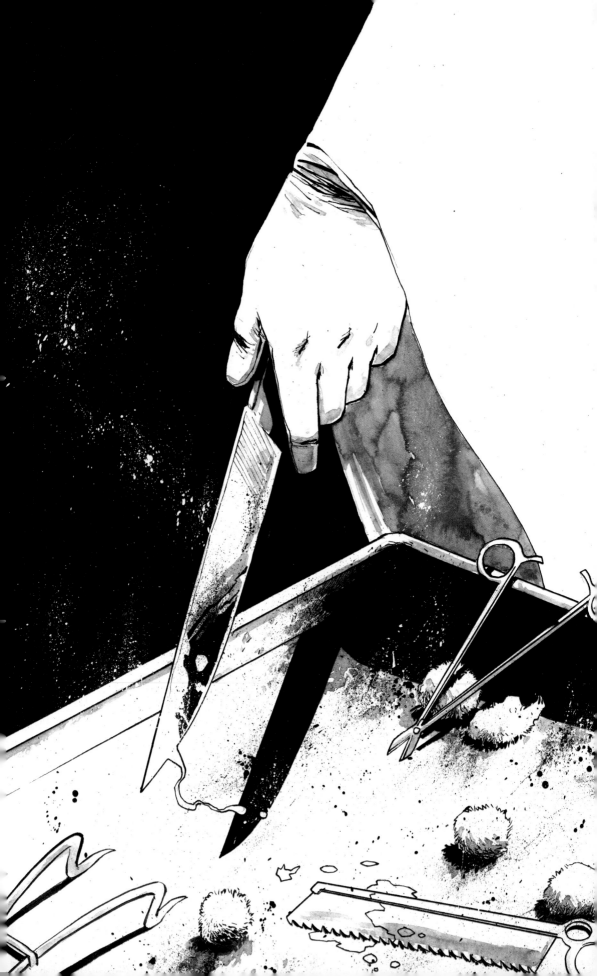

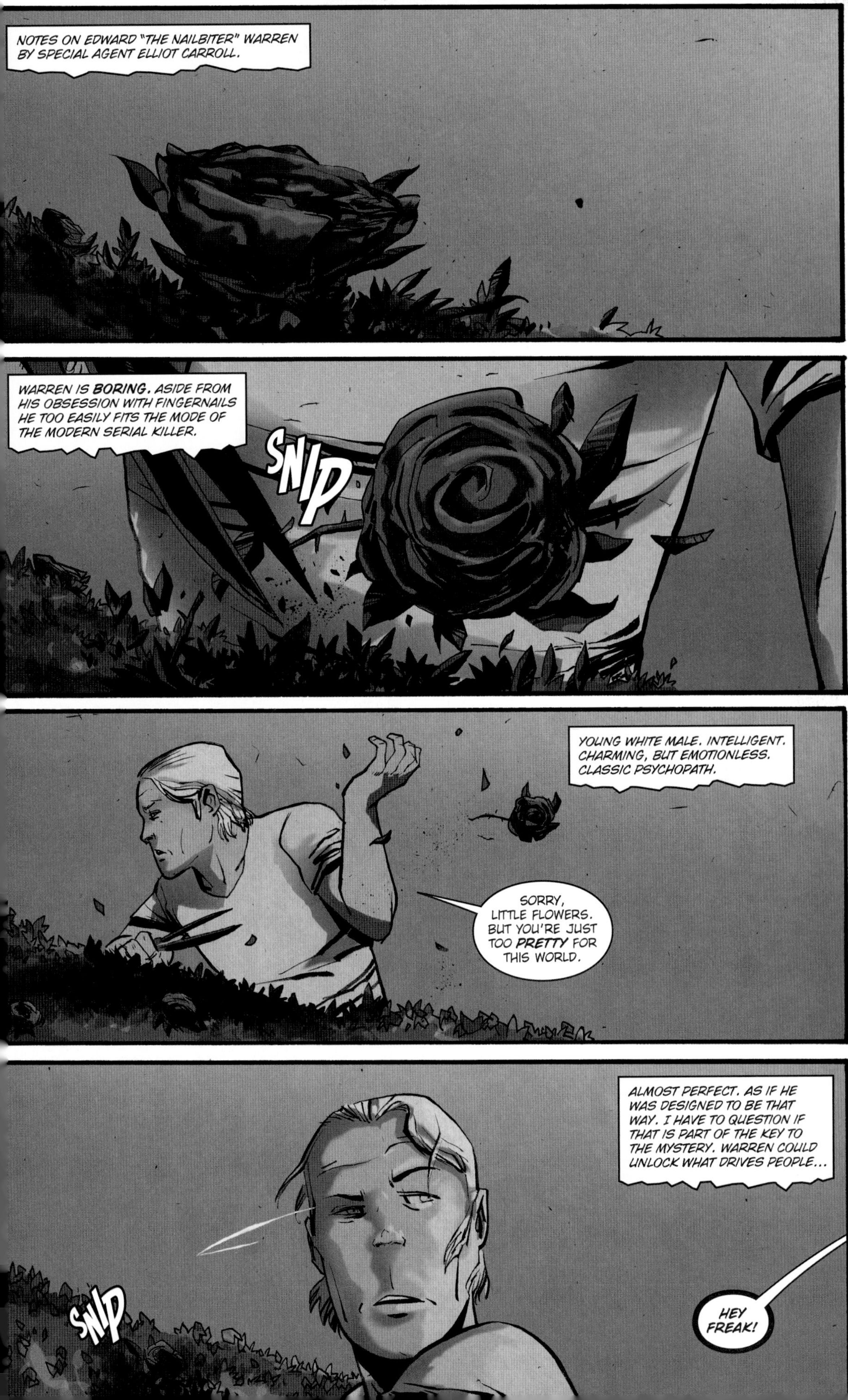
NOTES ON EDWARD "THE NAILBITER" WARREN BY SPECIAL AGENT ELLIOT CARROLL.
WARREN IS **BORING.** ASIDE FROM HIS OBSESSION WITH FINGERNAILS HE TOO EASILY FITS THE MODE OF THE MODERN SERIAL KILLER.
SNIP
YOUNG WHITE MALE. INTELLIGENT. CHARMING, BUT EMOTIONLESS. CLASSIC PSYCHOPATH.
SORRY, LITTLE FLOWERS. BUT YOU'RE JUST TOO ***PRETTY*** FOR THIS WORLD.
ALMOST PERFECT. AS IF HE WAS DESIGNED TO BE THAT WAY. I HAVE TO QUESTION IF THAT IS PART OF THE KEY TO THE MYSTERY. WARREN COULD UNLOCK WHAT DRIVES PEOPLE...
SNIP
HEY FREAK!

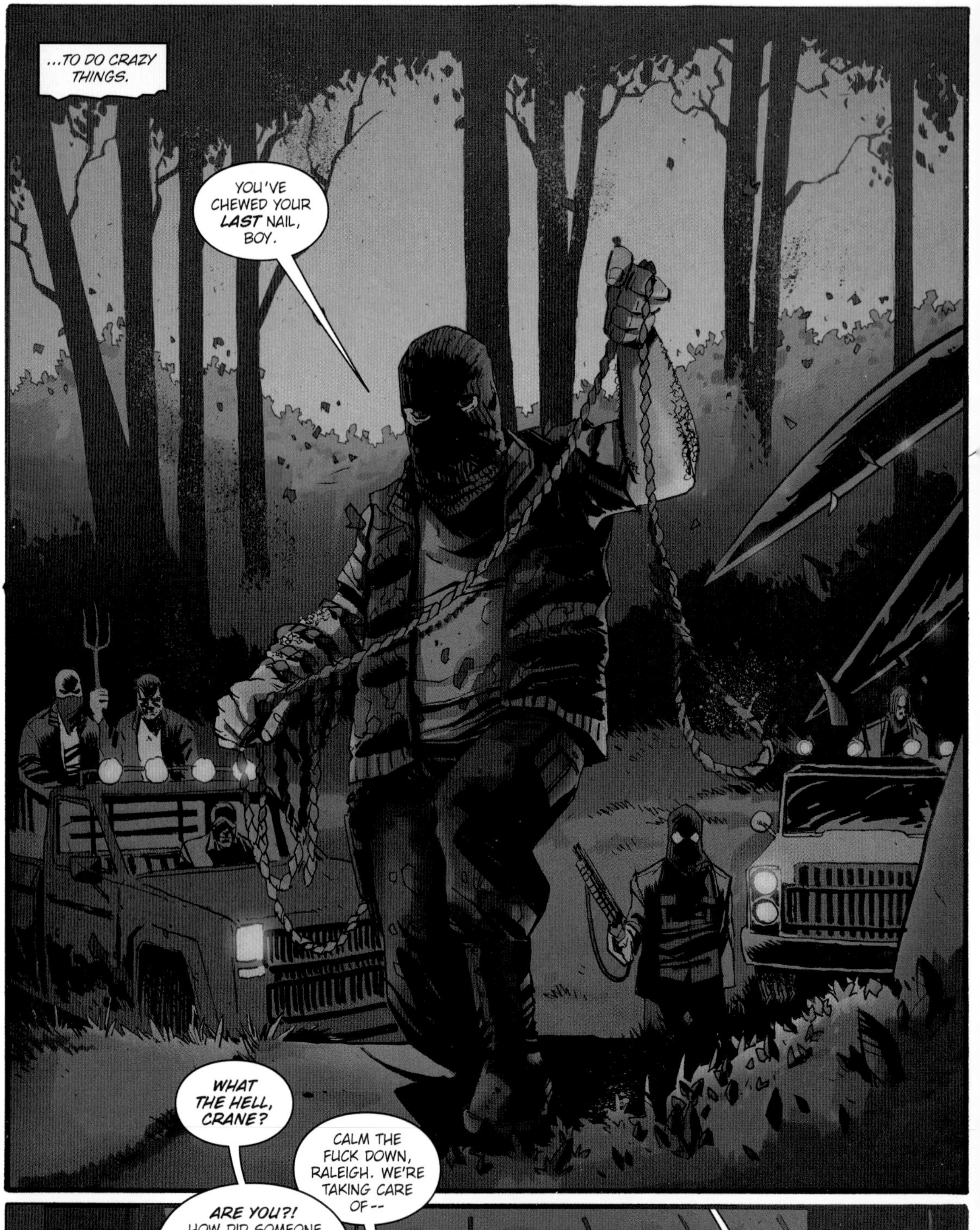
...TO DO CRAZY THINGS.
YOU'VE CHEWED YOUR LAST NAIL, BOY.
WHAT THE HELL, CRANE?
CALM THE FUCK DOWN, RALEIGH. WE'RE TAKING CARE OF --

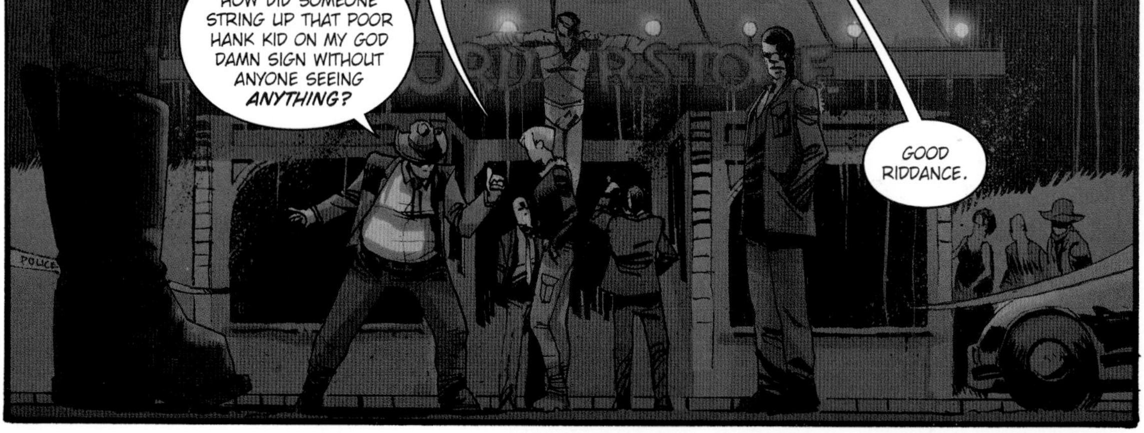
ARE YOU?! HOW DID SOMEONE STRING UP THAT POOR HANK KID ON MY GOD DAMN SIGN WITHOUT ANYONE SEEING ANYTHING?
GOOD RIDDANCE.
POLICE

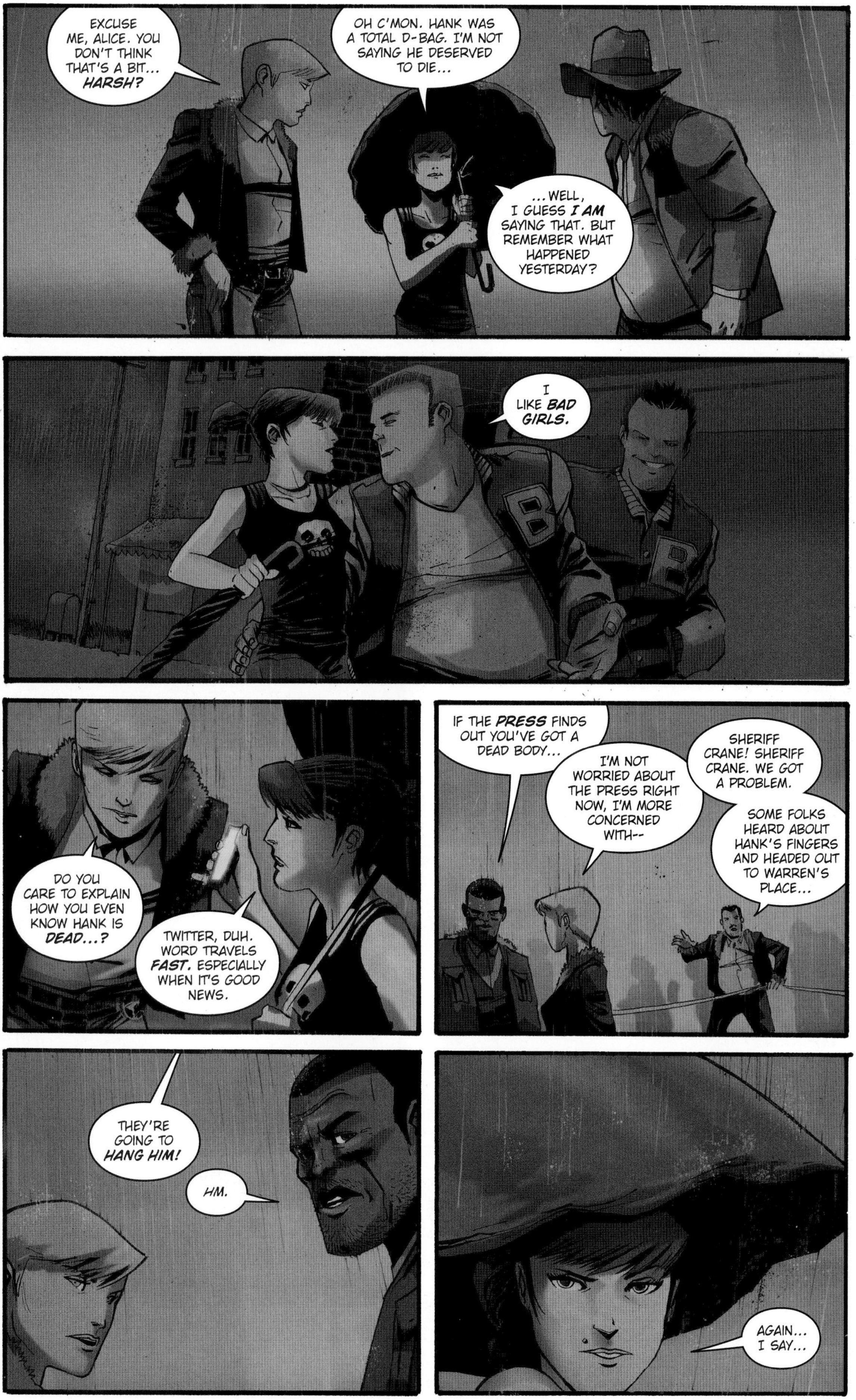
EXCUSE ME, ALICE. YOU DON'T THINK THAT'S A BIT... HARSH?
OH C'MON. HANK WAS A TOTAL D-BAG. I'M NOT SAYING HE DESERVED TO DIE...
...WELL, I GUESS I AM SAYING THAT. BUT REMEMBER WHAT HAPPENED YESTERDAY?
I LIKE BAD GIRLS.
DO YOU CARE TO EXPLAIN HOW YOU EVEN KNOW HANK IS DEAD...?
TWITTER, DUH. WORD TRAVELS FAST. ESPECIALLY WHEN IT'S GOOD NEWS.
IF THE PRESS FINDS OUT YOU'VE GOT A DEAD BODY...
I'M NOT WORRIED ABOUT THE PRESS RIGHT NOW, I'M MORE CONCERNED WITH--
SHERIFF CRANE! SHERIFF CRANE. WE GOT A PROBLEM.
SOME FOLKS HEARD ABOUT HANK'S FINGERS AND HEADED OUT TO WARREN'S PLACE...
THEY'RE GOING TO HANG HIM!
HM.
AGAIN... I SAY...

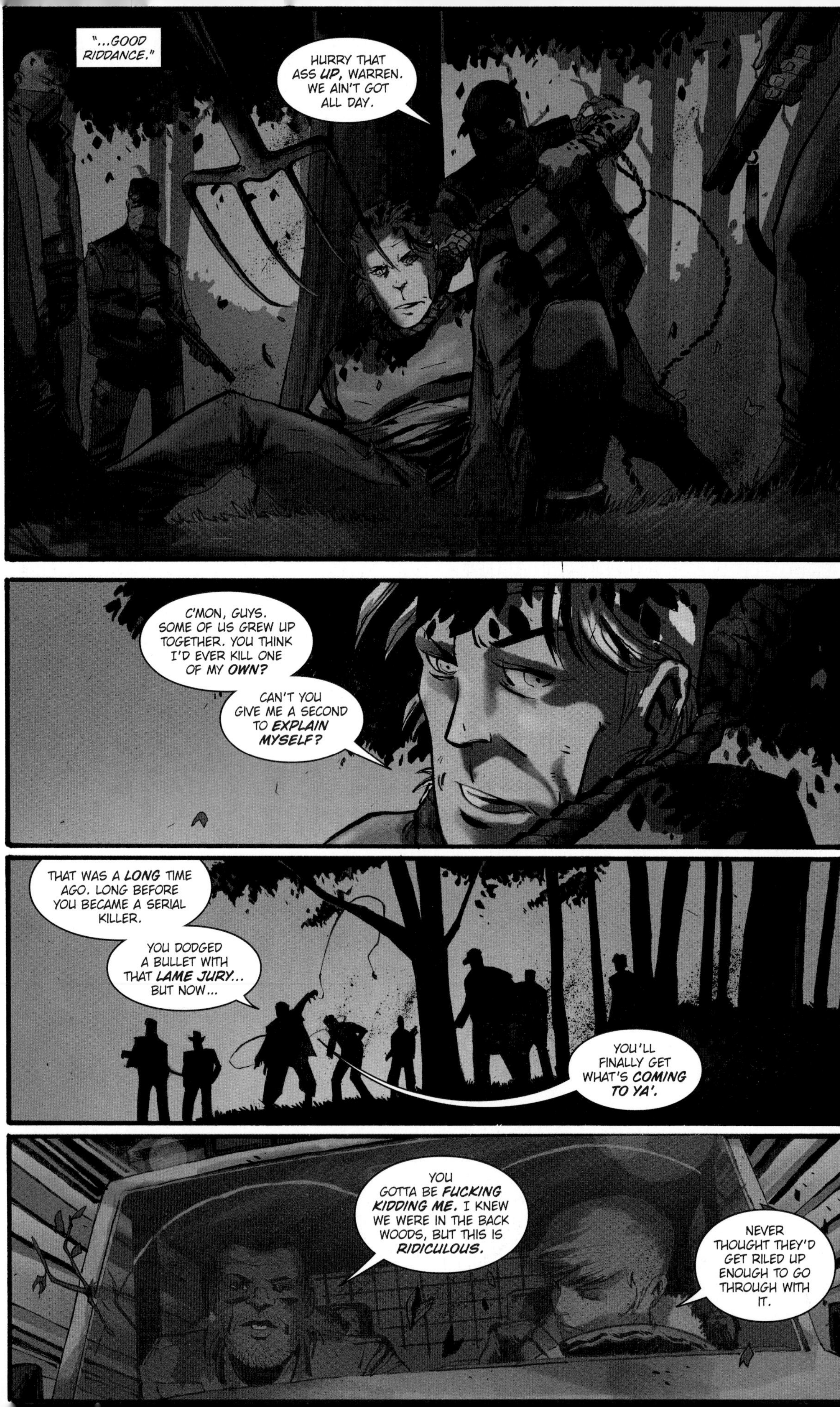
"...GOOD RIDDANCE."
HURRY THAT ASS UP, WARREN. WE AIN'T GOT ALL DAY.
C'MON, GUYS. SOME OF US GREW UP TOGETHER. YOU THINK I'D EVER KILL ONE OF MY OWN?
CAN'T YOU GIVE ME A SECOND TO EXPLAIN MYSELF?
THAT WAS A LONG TIME AGO. LONG BEFORE YOU BECAME A SERIAL KILLER.
YOU DODGED A BULLET WITH THAT LAME JURY... BUT NOW...
YOU'LL FINALLY GET WHAT'S COMING TO YA'.
YOU GOTTA BE FUCKING KIDDING ME. I KNEW WE WERE IN THE BACK WOODS, BUT THIS IS RIDICULOUS.
NEVER THOUGHT THEY'D GET RILED UP ENOUGH TO GO THROUGH WITH IT.

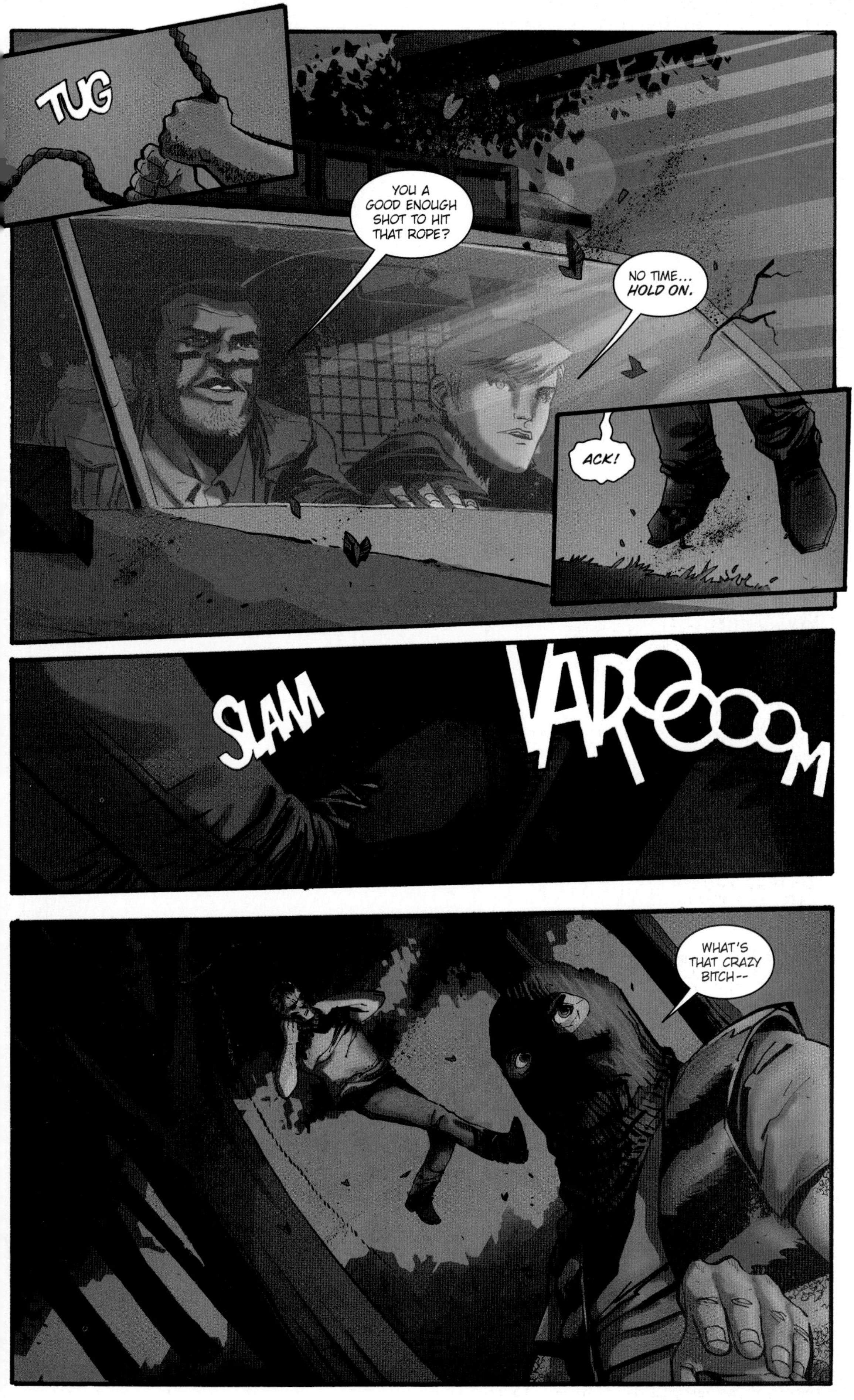
TUG
YOU A GOOD ENOUGH SHOT TO HIT THAT ROPE?
NO TIME... HOLD ON.
ACK!
SLAM
VAROoooOM
WHAT'S THAT CRAZY BITCH--

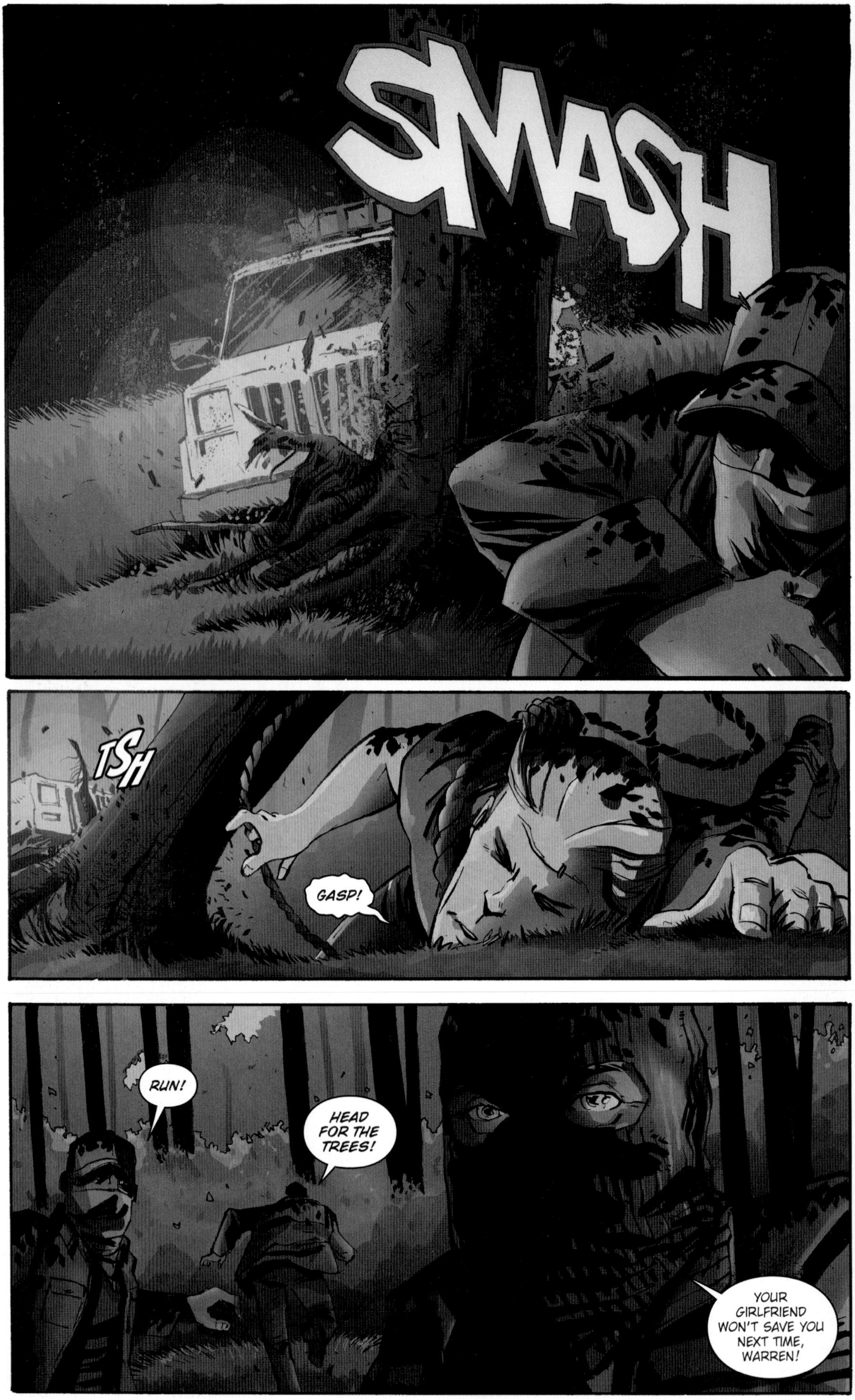
SMASH
TSH
GASP!
RUN!
HEAD FOR THE TREES!
YOUR GIRLFRIEND WON'T SAVE YOU NEXT TIME, WARREN!

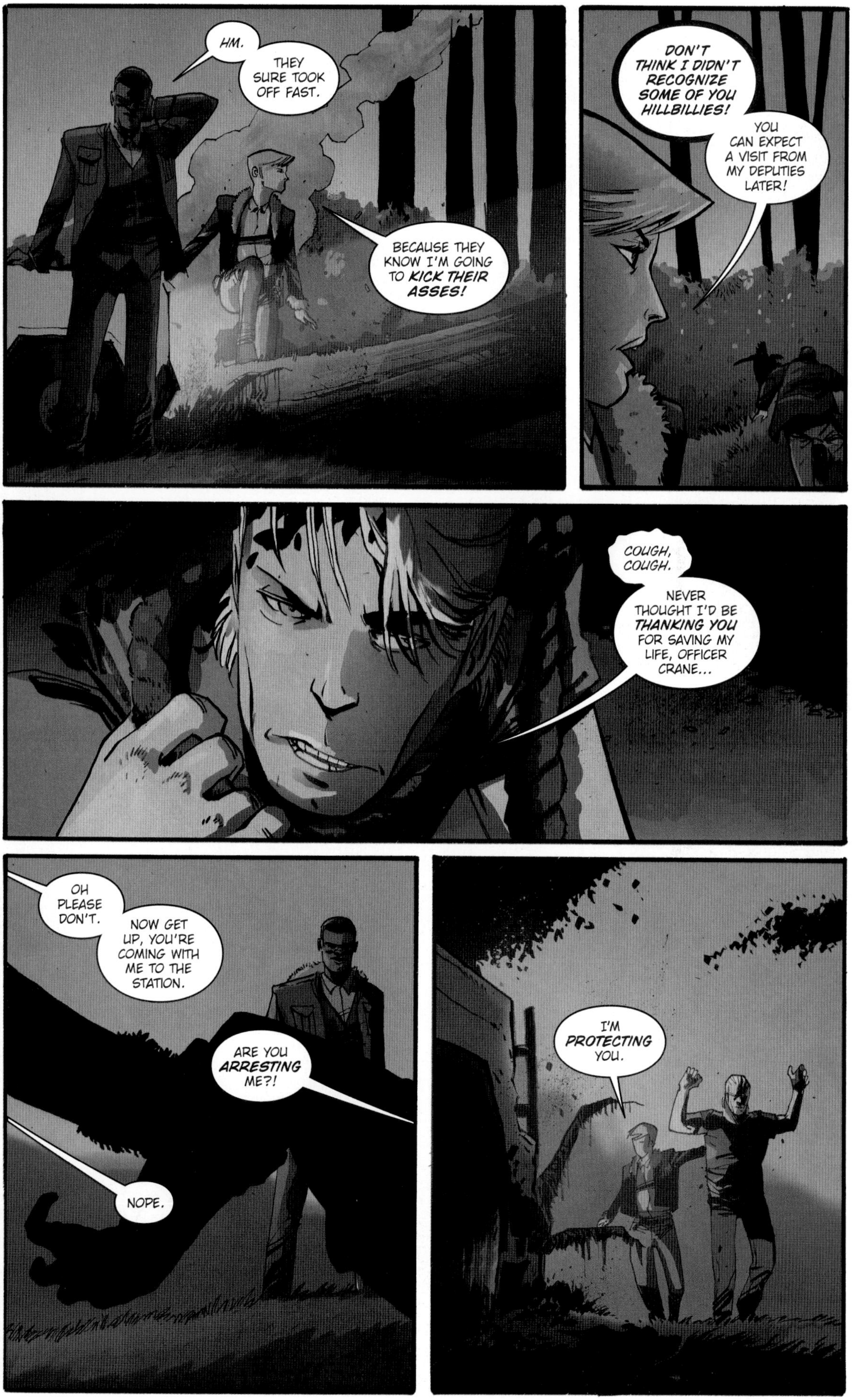
HM.
THEY SURE TOOK OFF FAST.
BECAUSE THEY KNOW I'M GOING TO KICK THEIR ASSES!
DON'T THINK I DIDN'T RECOGNIZE SOME OF YOU HILLBILLIES!
YOU CAN EXPECT A VISIT FROM MY DEPUTIES LATER!
COUGH, COUGH.
NEVER THOUGHT I'D BE THANKING YOU FOR SAVING MY LIFE, OFFICER CRANE...
OH PLEASE DON'T.
NOW GET UP, YOU'RE COMING WITH ME TO THE STATION.
ARE YOU ARRESTING ME?!
NOPE.
I'M PROTECTING YOU.

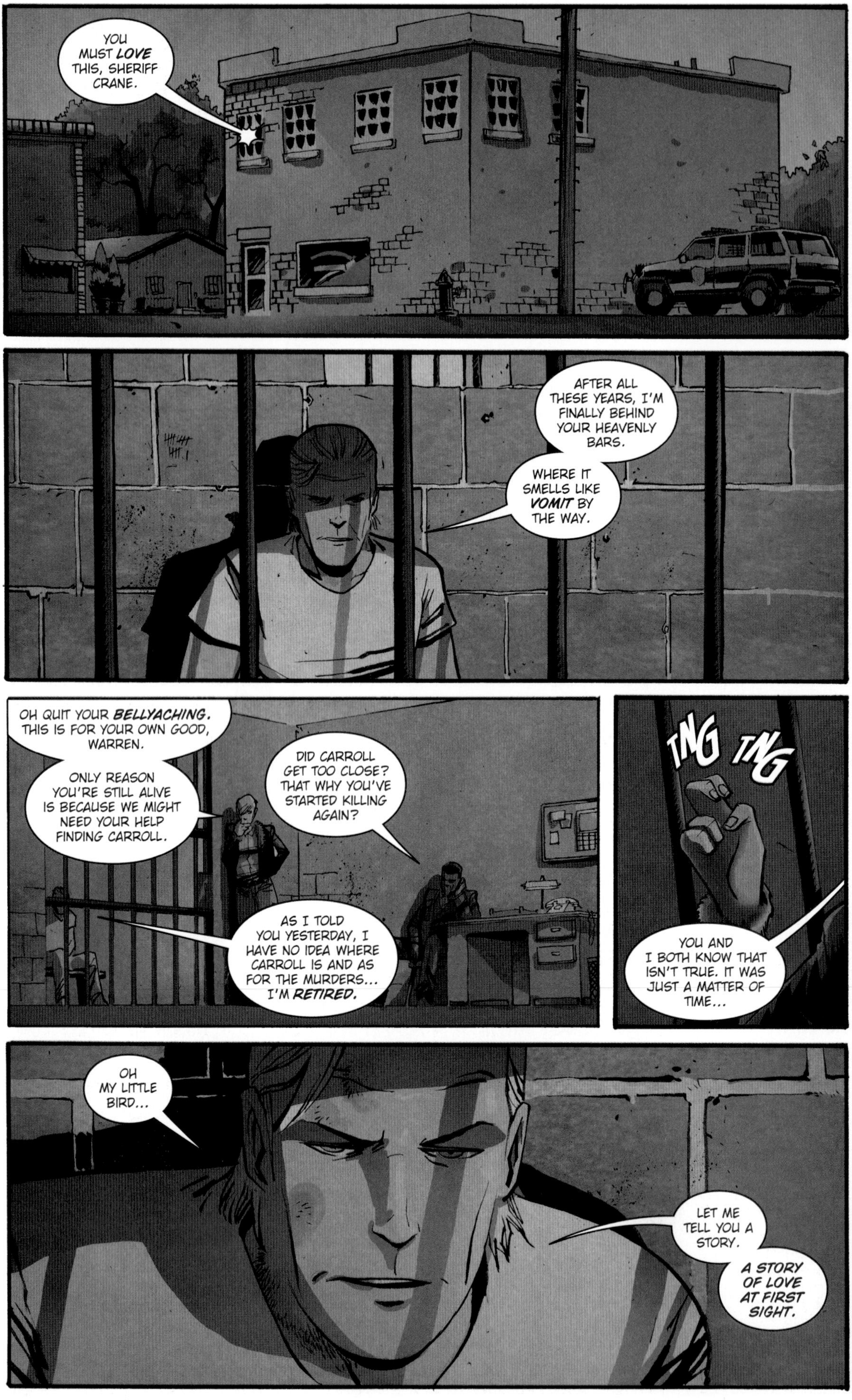
YOU MUST LOVE THIS, SHERIFF CRANE.
AFTER ALL THESE YEARS, I'M FINALLY BEHIND YOUR HEAVENLY BARS.
WHERE IT SMELLS LIKE VOMIT BY THE WAY.
OH QUIT YOUR BELLYACHING. THIS IS FOR YOUR OWN GOOD, WARREN.
ONLY REASON YOU'RE STILL ALIVE IS BECAUSE WE MIGHT NEED YOUR HELP FINDING CARROLL.
DID CARROLL GET TOO CLOSE? THAT WHY YOU'VE STARTED KILLING AGAIN?
AS I TOLD YOU YESTERDAY, I HAVE NO IDEA WHERE CARROLL IS AND AS FOR THE MURDERS... I'M RETIRED.
TNG TNG
YOU AND I BOTH KNOW THAT ISN'T TRUE. IT WAS JUST A MATTER OF TIME...
OH MY LITTLE BIRD...
LET ME TELL YOU A STORY.
A STORY OF LOVE AT FIRST SIGHT.

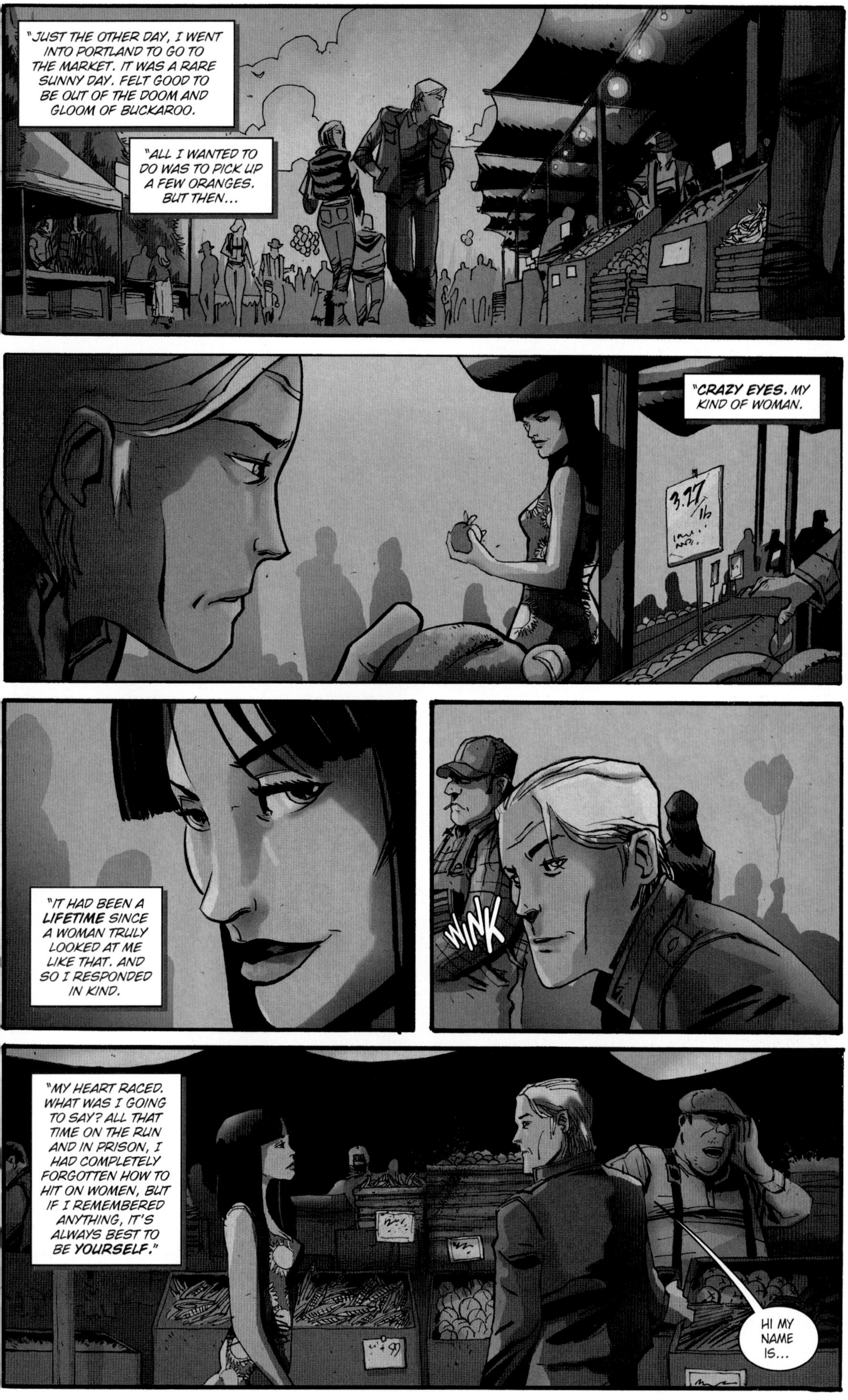
"JUST THE OTHER DAY, I WENT INTO PORTLAND TO GO TO THE MARKET. IT WAS A RARE SUNNY DAY. FELT GOOD TO BE OUT OF THE DOOM AND GLOOM OF BUCKAROO.
"ALL I WANTED TO DO WAS TO PICK UP A FEW ORANGES. BUT THEN...
"CRAZY EYES. MY KIND OF WOMAN.
3.27 /lb
"IT HAD BEEN A LIFETIME SINCE A WOMAN TRULY LOOKED AT ME LIKE THAT. AND SO I RESPONDED IN KIND.
WINK
"MY HEART RACED. WHAT WAS I GOING TO SAY? ALL THAT TIME ON THE RUN AND IN PRISON, I HAD COMPLETELY FORGOTTEN HOW TO HIT ON WOMEN, BUT IF I REMEMBERED ANYTHING, IT'S ALWAYS BEST TO BE YOURSELF."
HI MY NAME IS...

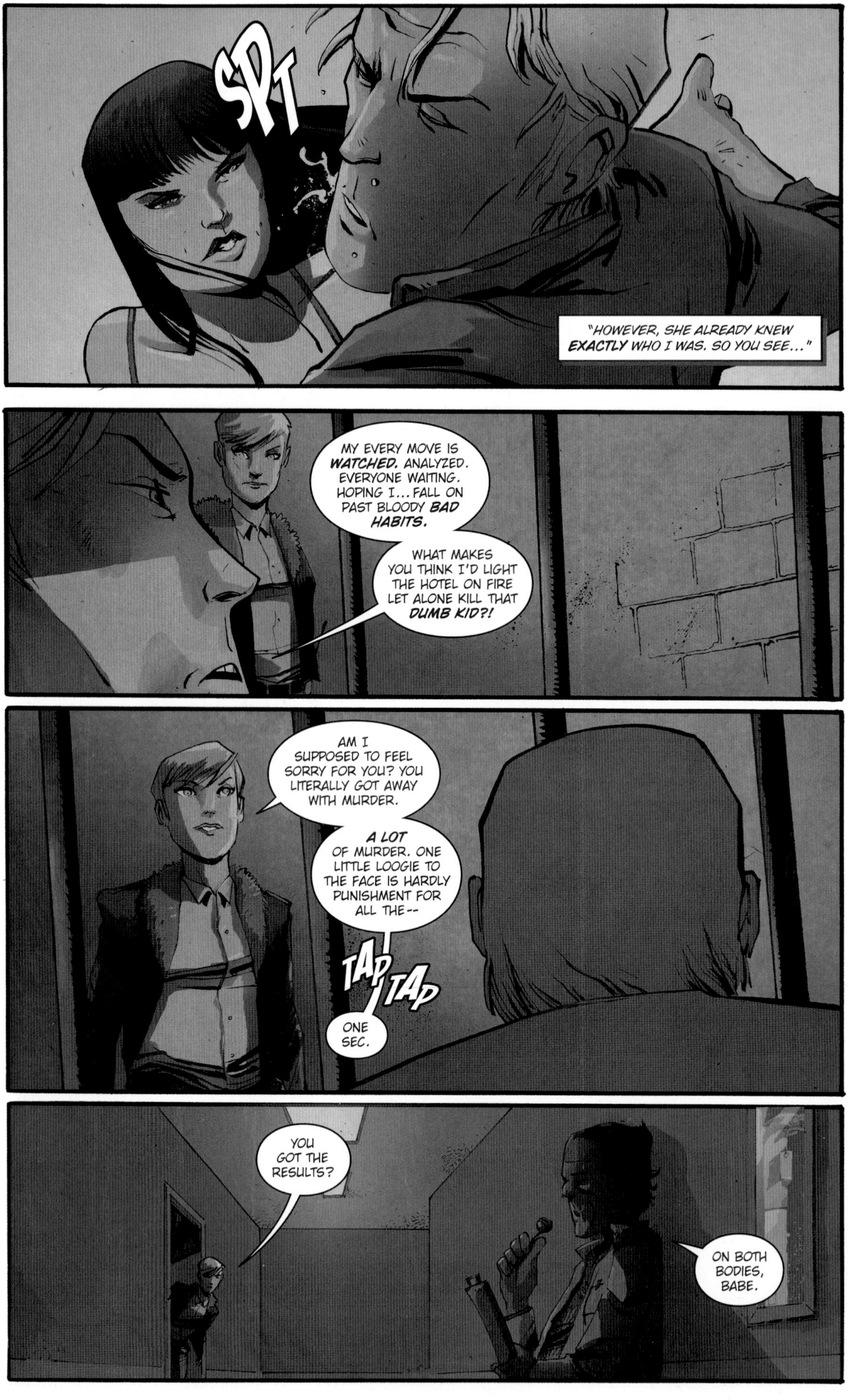
SPT
"HOWEVER, SHE ALREADY KNEW **EXACTLY** WHO I WAS. SO YOU SEE..."
MY EVERY MOVE IS **WATCHED.** ANALYZED. EVERYONE WAITING. HOPING I... FALL ON PAST BLOODY **BAD HABITS.**
WHAT MAKES YOU THINK I'D LIGHT THE HOTEL ON FIRE LET ALONE KILL THAT **DUMB KID?!**
AM I SUPPOSED TO FEEL SORRY FOR YOU? YOU LITERALLY GOT AWAY WITH MURDER.
**A LOT** OF MURDER. ONE LITTLE LOOGIE TO THE FACE IS HARDLY PUNISHMENT FOR ALL THE--
TAP TAP
ONE SEC.
YOU GOT THE RESULTS?
ON BOTH BODIES, BABE.

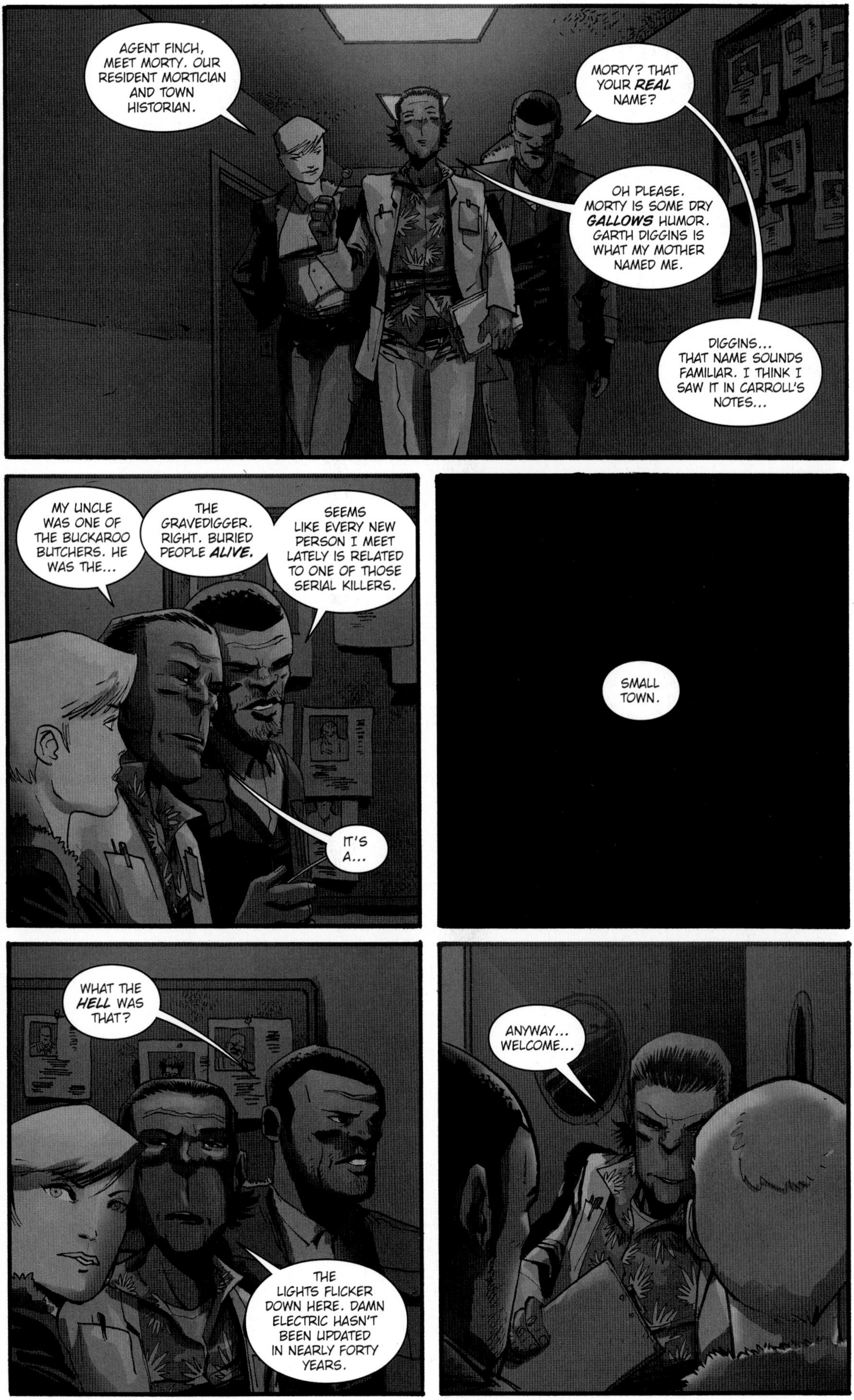
AGENT FINCH, MEET MORTY. OUR RESIDENT MORTICIAN AND TOWN HISTORIAN.
MORTY? THAT YOUR **REAL** NAME?
OH PLEASE. MORTY IS SOME DRY **GALLOWS** HUMOR. GARTH DIGGINS IS WHAT MY MOTHER NAMED ME.
DIGGINS... THAT NAME SOUNDS FAMILIAR. I THINK I SAW IT IN CARROLL'S NOTES...
MY UNCLE WAS ONE OF THE BUCKAROO BUTCHERS. HE WAS THE...
THE GRAVEDIGGER. RIGHT. BURIED PEOPLE **ALIVE.**
SEEMS LIKE EVERY NEW PERSON I MEET LATELY IS RELATED TO ONE OF THOSE SERIAL KILLERS.
IT'S A...
SMALL TOWN.
WHAT THE **HELL** WAS THAT?
THE LIGHTS FLICKER DOWN HERE. DAMN ELECTRIC HASN'T BEEN UPDATED IN NEARLY FORTY YEARS.
ANYWAY... WELCOME...

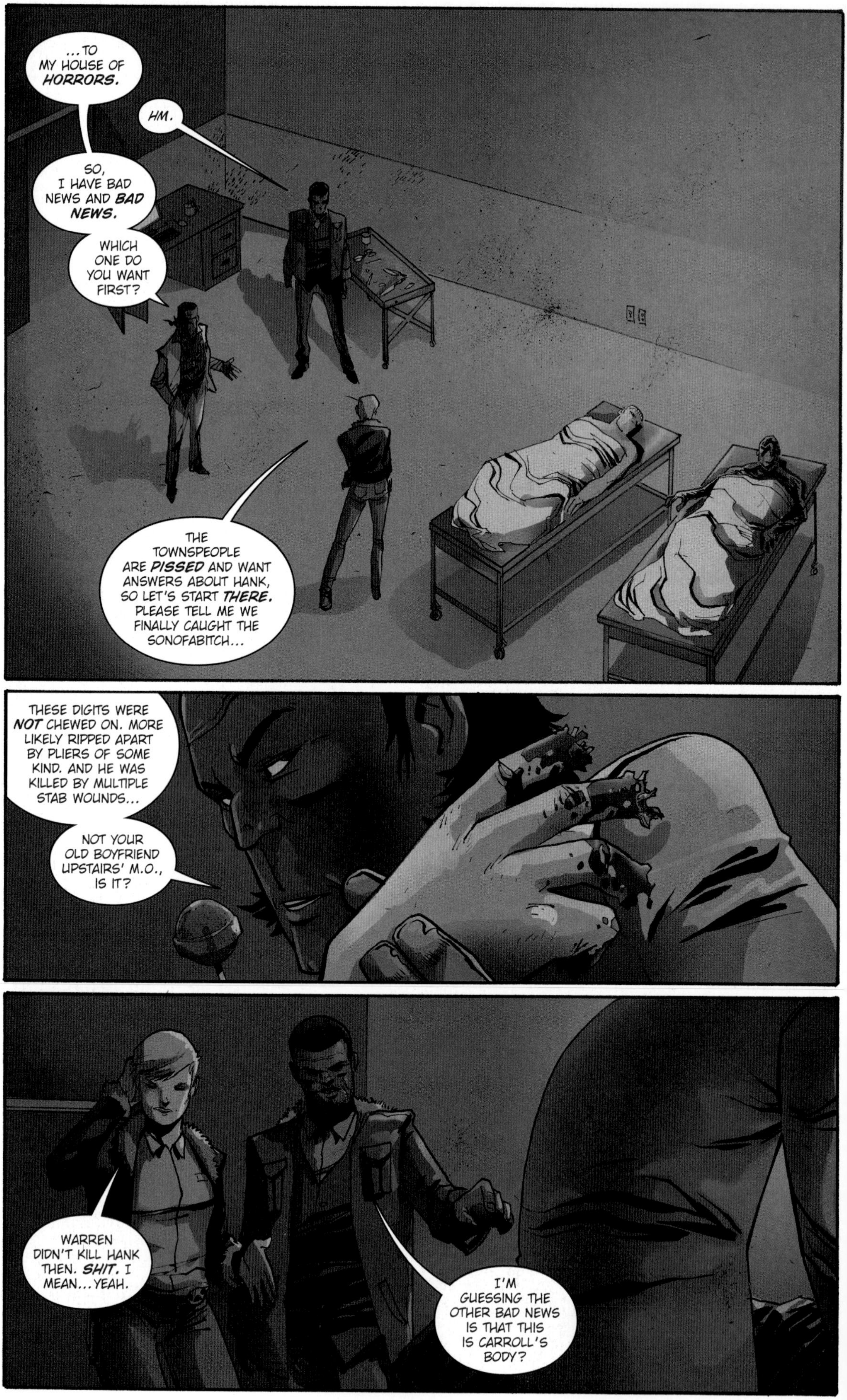
...TO MY HOUSE OF **HORRORS.**
HM.
SO, I HAVE BAD NEWS AND **BAD NEWS.**
WHICH ONE DO YOU WANT FIRST?
THE TOWNSPEOPLE ARE **PISSED** AND WANT ANSWERS ABOUT HANK, SO LET'S START **THERE.** PLEASE TELL ME WE FINALLY CAUGHT THE SONOFABITCH...
THESE DIGITS WERE **NOT** CHEWED ON. MORE LIKELY RIPPED APART BY PLIERS OF SOME KIND. AND HE WAS KILLED BY MULTIPLE STAB WOUNDS...
NOT YOUR OLD BOYFRIEND UPSTAIRS' M.O., IS IT?
WARREN DIDN'T KILL HANK THEN. **SHIT.** I MEAN...YEAH.
I'M GUESSING THE OTHER BAD NEWS IS THAT THIS IS CARROLL'S BODY?

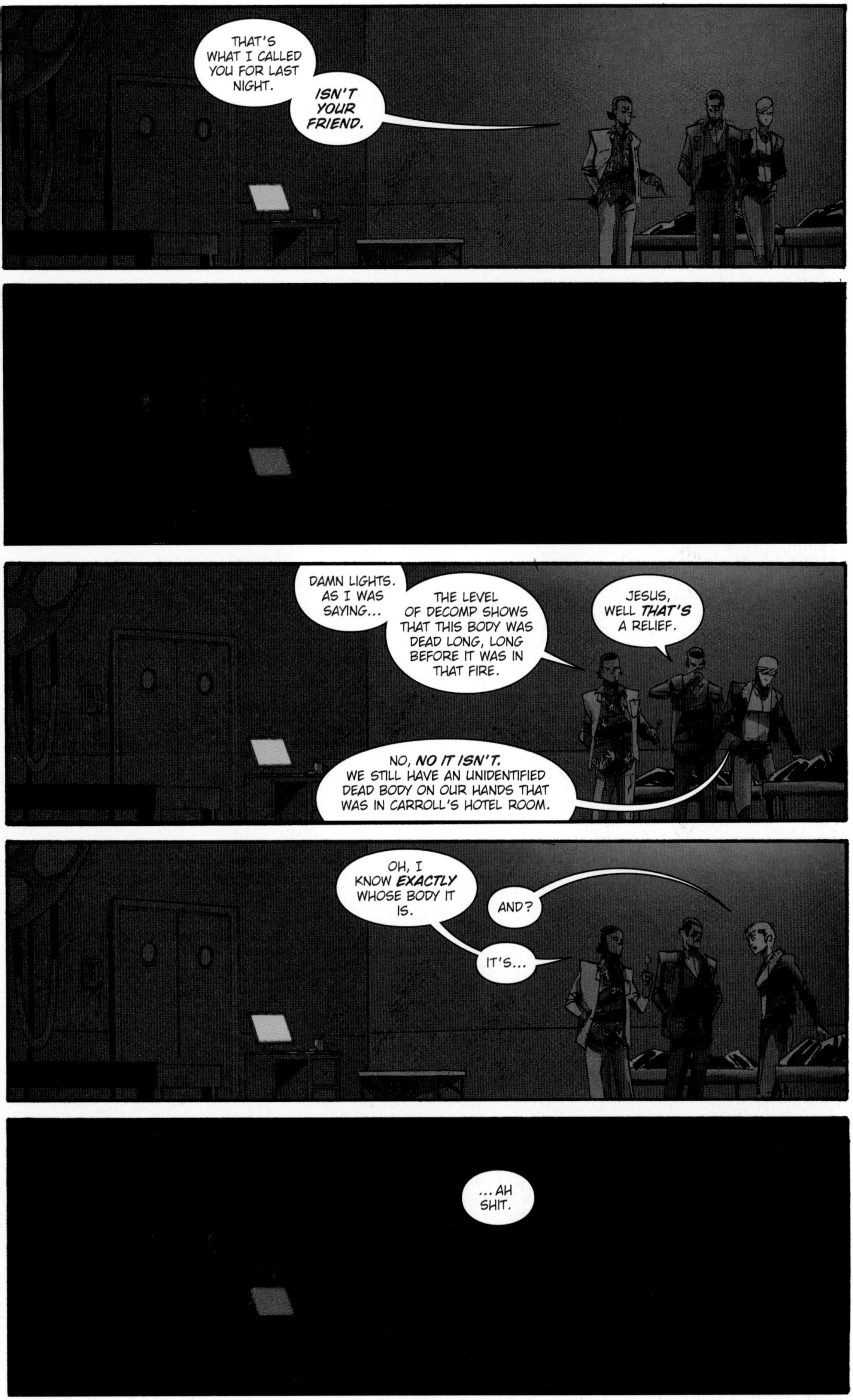
THAT'S WHAT I CALLED YOU FOR LAST NIGHT.
ISN'T YOUR FRIEND.
DAMN LIGHTS. AS I WAS SAYING...
THE LEVEL OF DECOMP SHOWS THAT THIS BODY WAS DEAD LONG, LONG BEFORE IT WAS IN THAT FIRE.
JESUS, WELL THAT'S A RELIEF.
NO, NO IT ISN'T. WE STILL HAVE AN UNIDENTIFIED DEAD BODY ON OUR HANDS THAT WAS IN CARROLL'S HOTEL ROOM.
OH, I KNOW EXACTLY WHOSE BODY IT IS.
AND?
IT'S...
...AH SHIT.

SORRY, ANYWAY... THE BODY IS THE BOOK BURNER'S.
WHAT? THAT'S IMPOSSIBLE.
YOU REALLY NEED TO GET THE LIGHTS FIXED.
YOU WANT TO PAY THE BUDGET? ANYWAY.
YEAH, HE'S THE BOOK BURNER.
THE TESTS ARE POINTING ME IN THAT DIRECTION. THIS IS THE ORIGINAL BUCKAROO BUTCHER'S DEAD BODY. THAT SHOULD BE BURIED OUT IN...
I FEEL LIKE THAT'S MY SIGN TO LEAVE. NICE KNOWING YA'.
WAIT, WHAT?

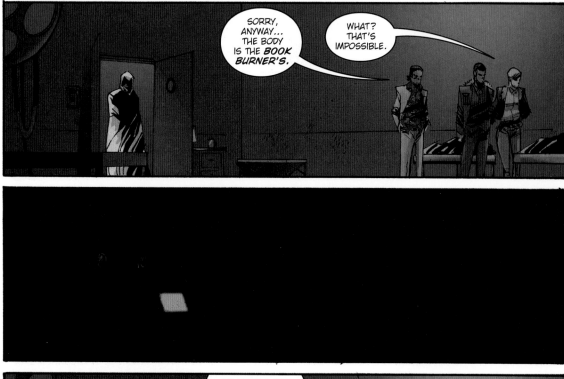

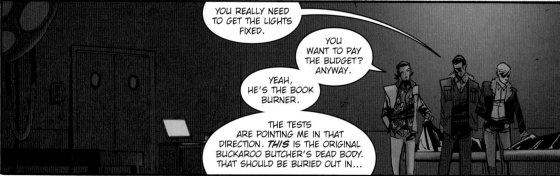

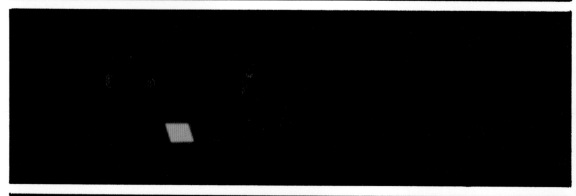

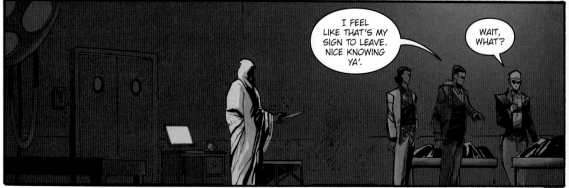

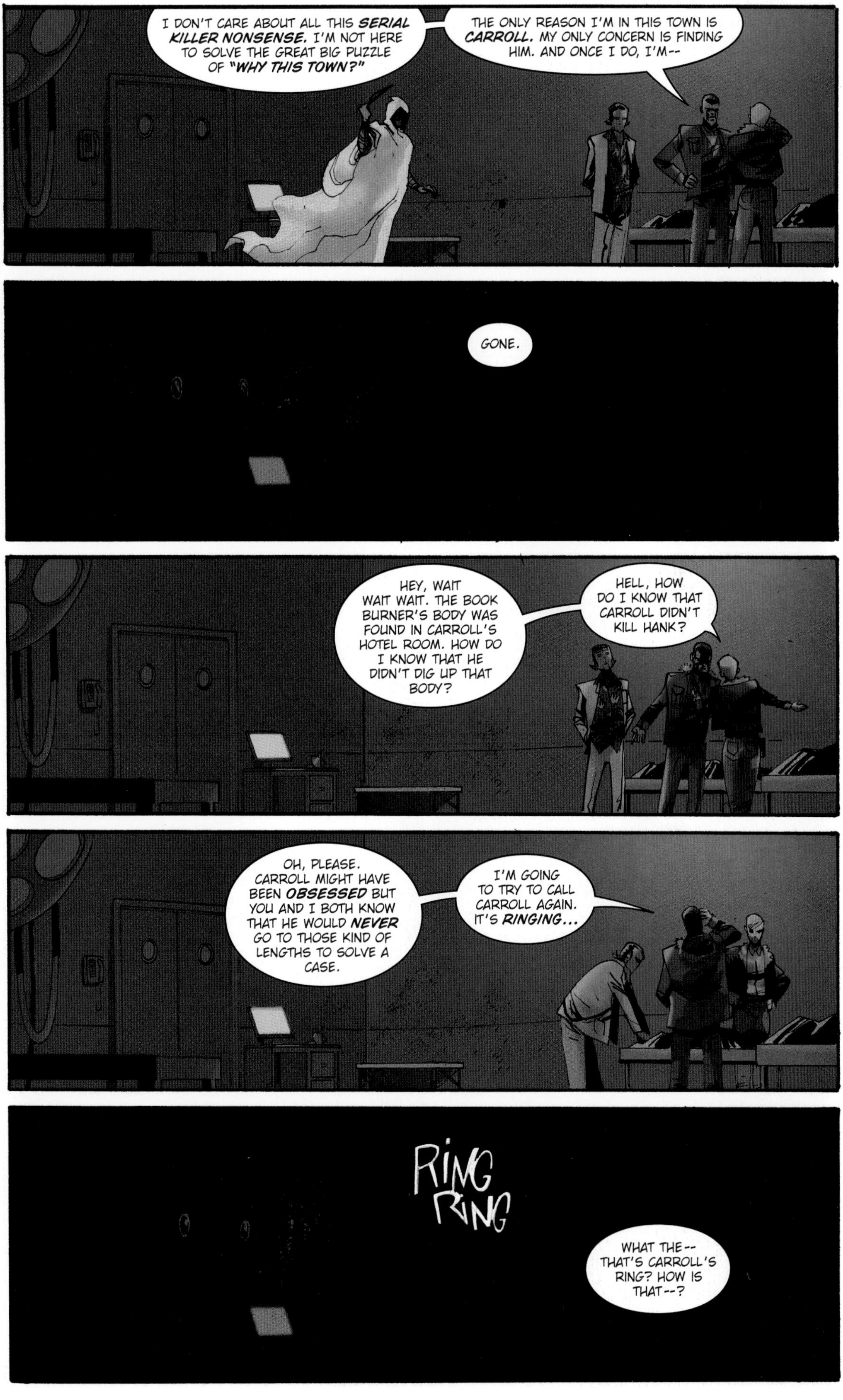
I DON'T CARE ABOUT ALL THIS SERIAL KILLER NONSENSE. I'M NOT HERE TO SOLVE THE GREAT BIG PUZZLE OF "WHY THIS TOWN?"
THE ONLY REASON I'M IN THIS TOWN IS CARROLL. MY ONLY CONCERN IS FINDING HIM. AND ONCE I DO, I'M--
GONE.
HEY, WAIT WAIT WAIT. THE BOOK BURNER'S BODY WAS FOUND IN CARROLL'S HOTEL ROOM. HOW DO I KNOW THAT HE DIDN'T DIG UP THAT BODY?
HELL, HOW DO I KNOW THAT CARROLL DIDN'T KILL HANK?
OH, PLEASE. CARROLL MIGHT HAVE BEEN OBSESSED BUT YOU AND I BOTH KNOW THAT HE WOULD NEVER GO TO THOSE KIND OF LENGTHS TO SOLVE A CASE.
I'M GOING TO TRY TO CALL CARROLL AGAIN. IT'S RINGING...
RING RING
WHAT THE-- THAT'S CARROLL'S RING? HOW IS THAT--?

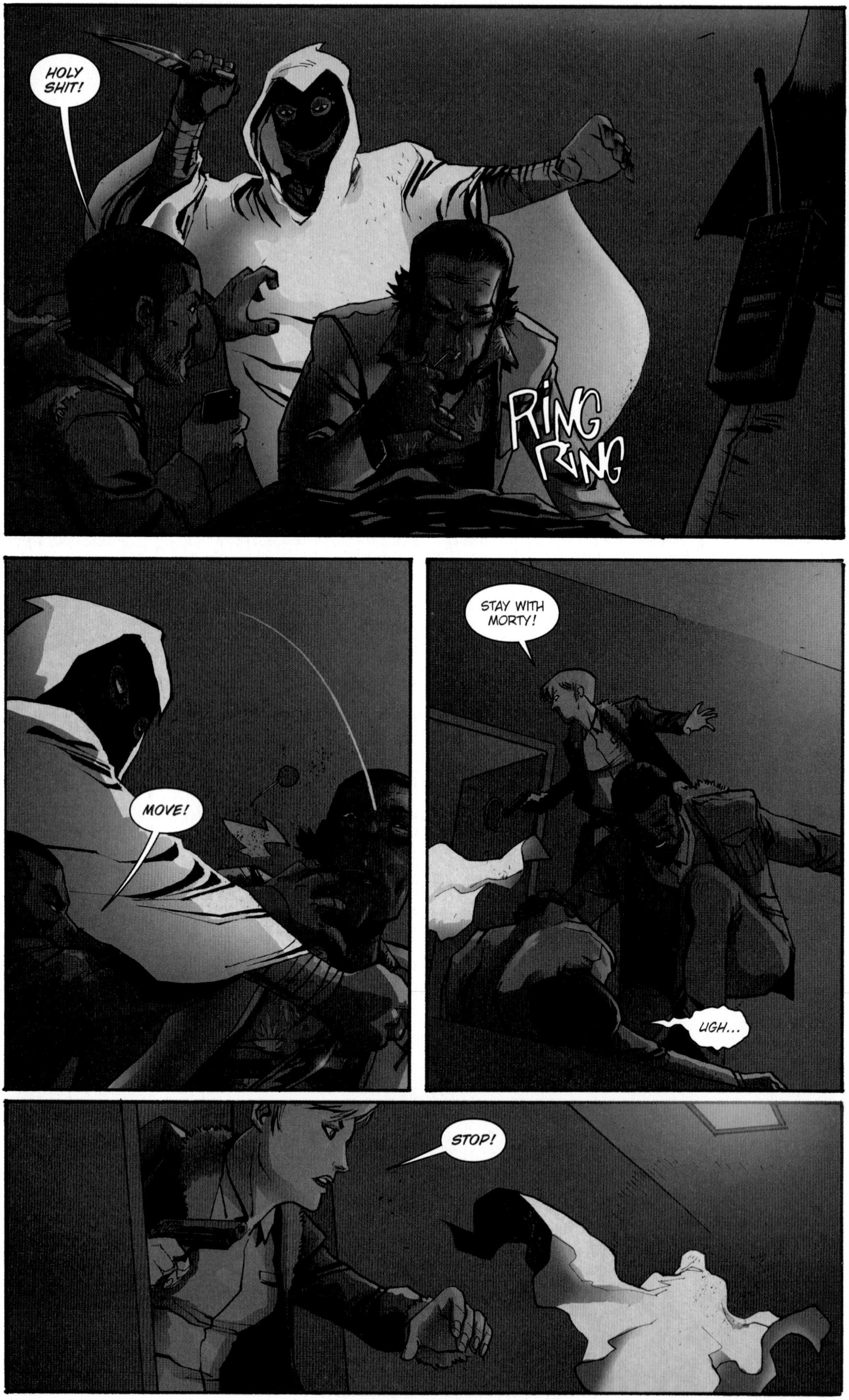
HOLY SHIT!
RING RING
MOVE!
STAY WITH MORTY!
UGH...
STOP!

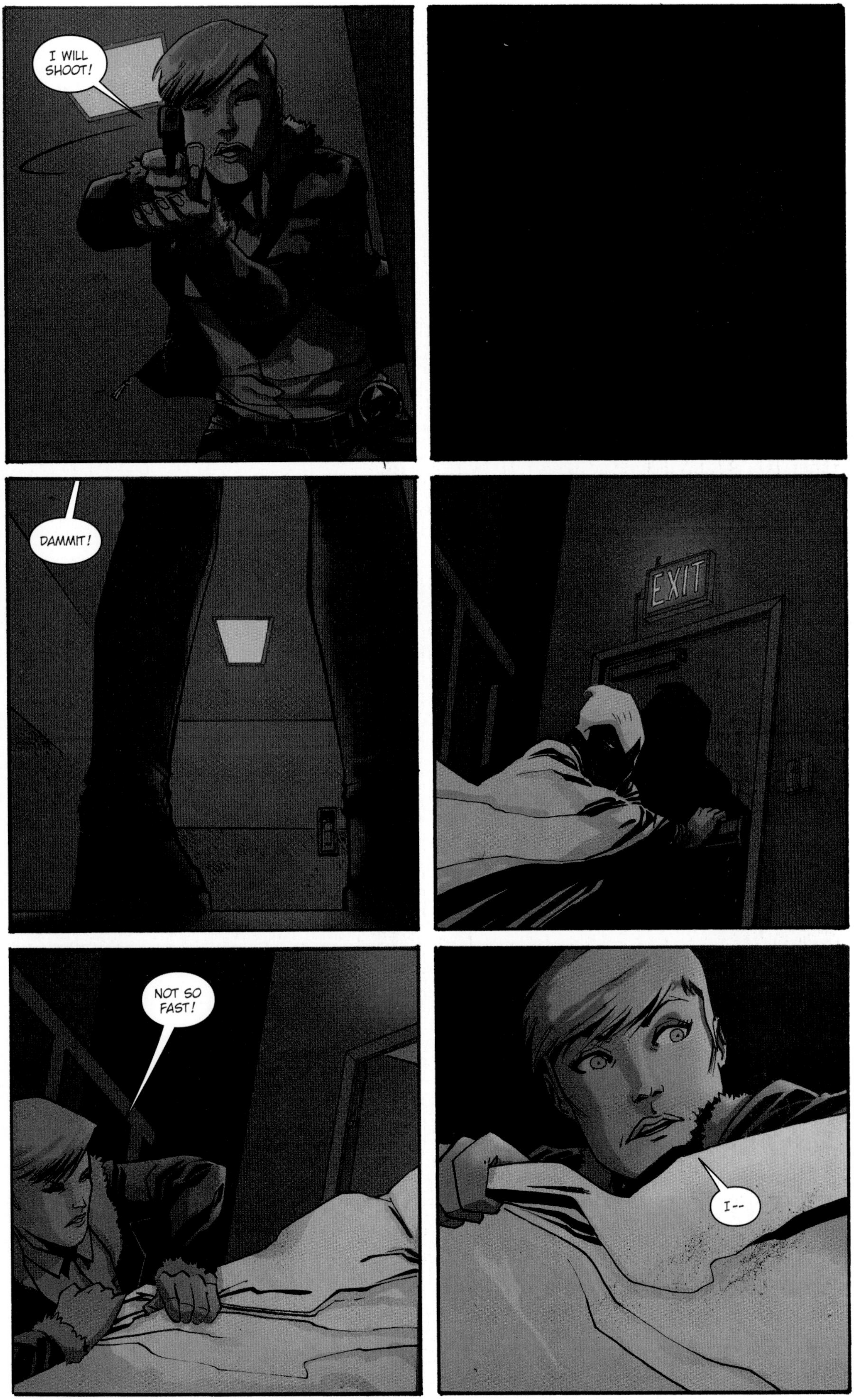
I WILL SHOOT!
DAMMIT!
NOT SO FAST!
I--

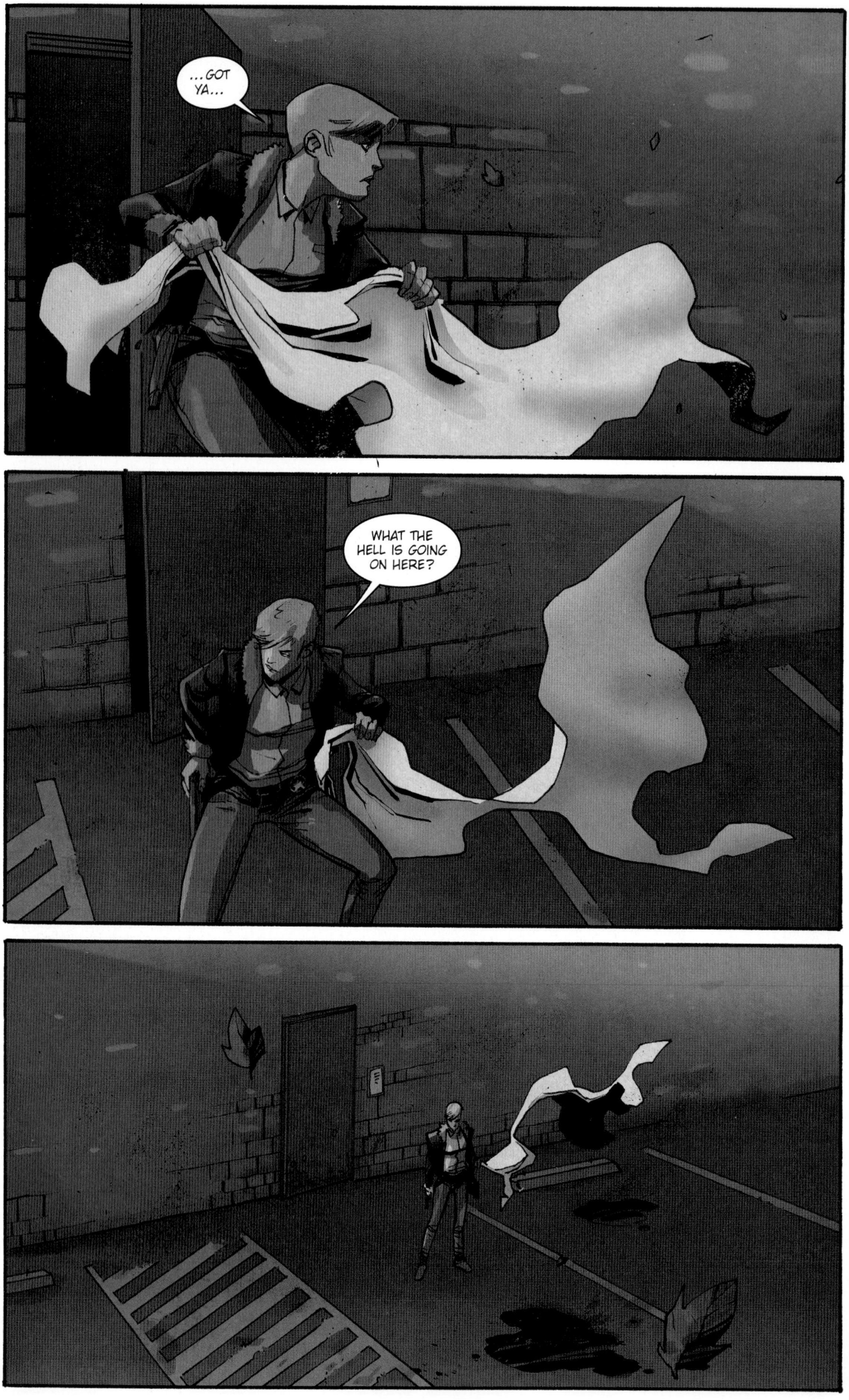
...GOT YA...
WHAT THE HELL IS GOING ON HERE?

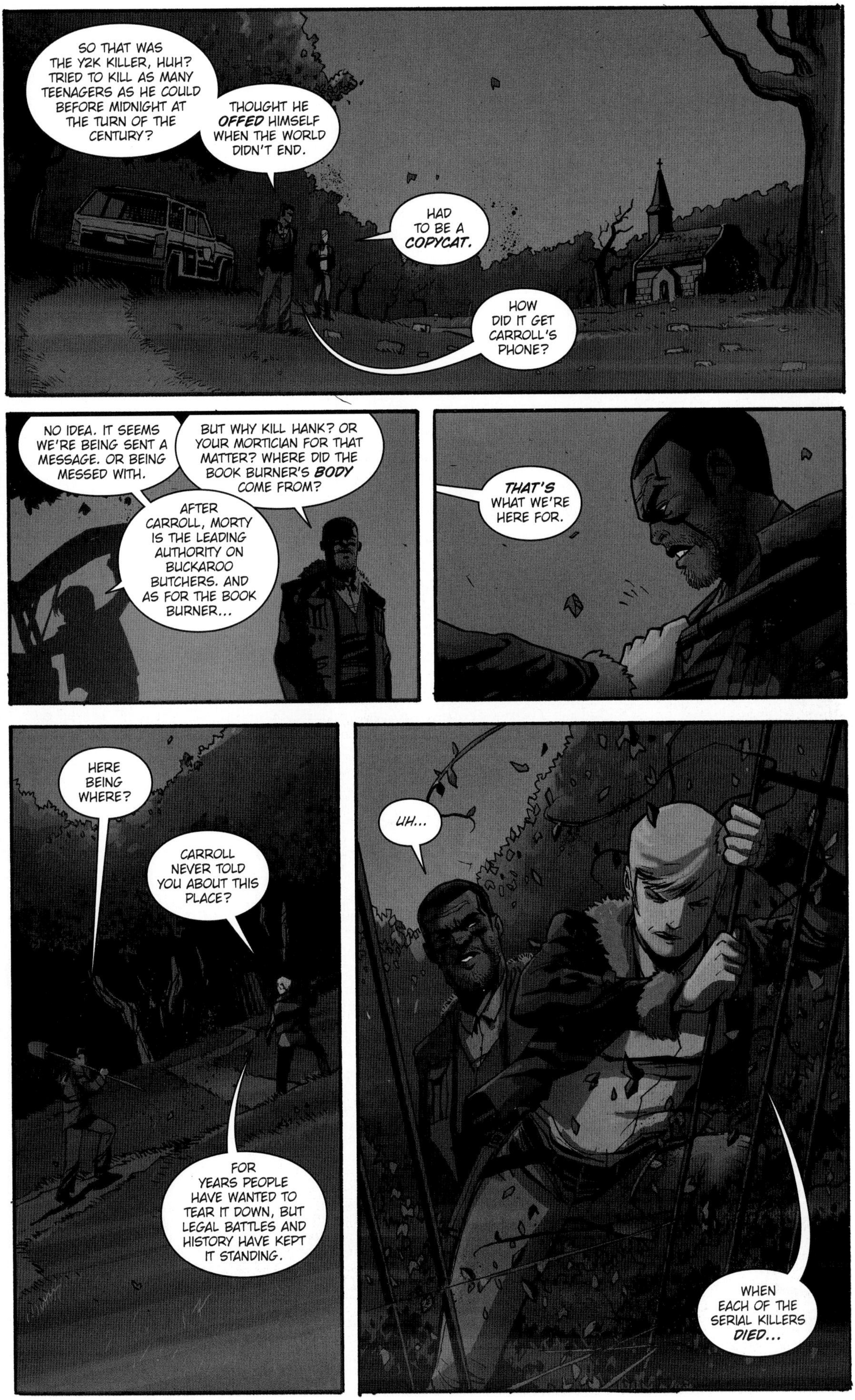

SO THAT WAS THE Y2K KILLER, HUH? TRIED TO KILL AS MANY TEENAGERS AS HE COULD BEFORE MIDNIGHT AT THE TURN OF THE CENTURY?
THOUGHT HE *OFFED* HIMSELF WHEN THE WORLD DIDN'T END.
HAD TO BE A *COPYCAT.*
HOW DID IT GET CARROLL'S PHONE?
NO IDEA. IT SEEMS WE'RE BEING SENT A MESSAGE. OR BEING MESSED WITH.
BUT WHY KILL HANK? OR YOUR MORTICIAN FOR THAT MATTER? WHERE DID THE BOOK BURNER'S *BODY* COME FROM?
AFTER CARROLL, MORTY IS THE LEADING AUTHORITY ON BUCKAROO BUTCHERS. AND AS FOR THE BOOK BURNER...
*THAT'S* WHAT WE'RE HERE FOR.
HERE BEING WHERE?
CARROLL NEVER TOLD YOU ABOUT THIS PLACE?
FOR YEARS PEOPLE HAVE WANTED TO TEAR IT DOWN, BUT LEGAL BATTLES AND HISTORY HAVE KEPT IT STANDING.
UH...
WHEN EACH OF THE SERIAL KILLERS *DIED...*

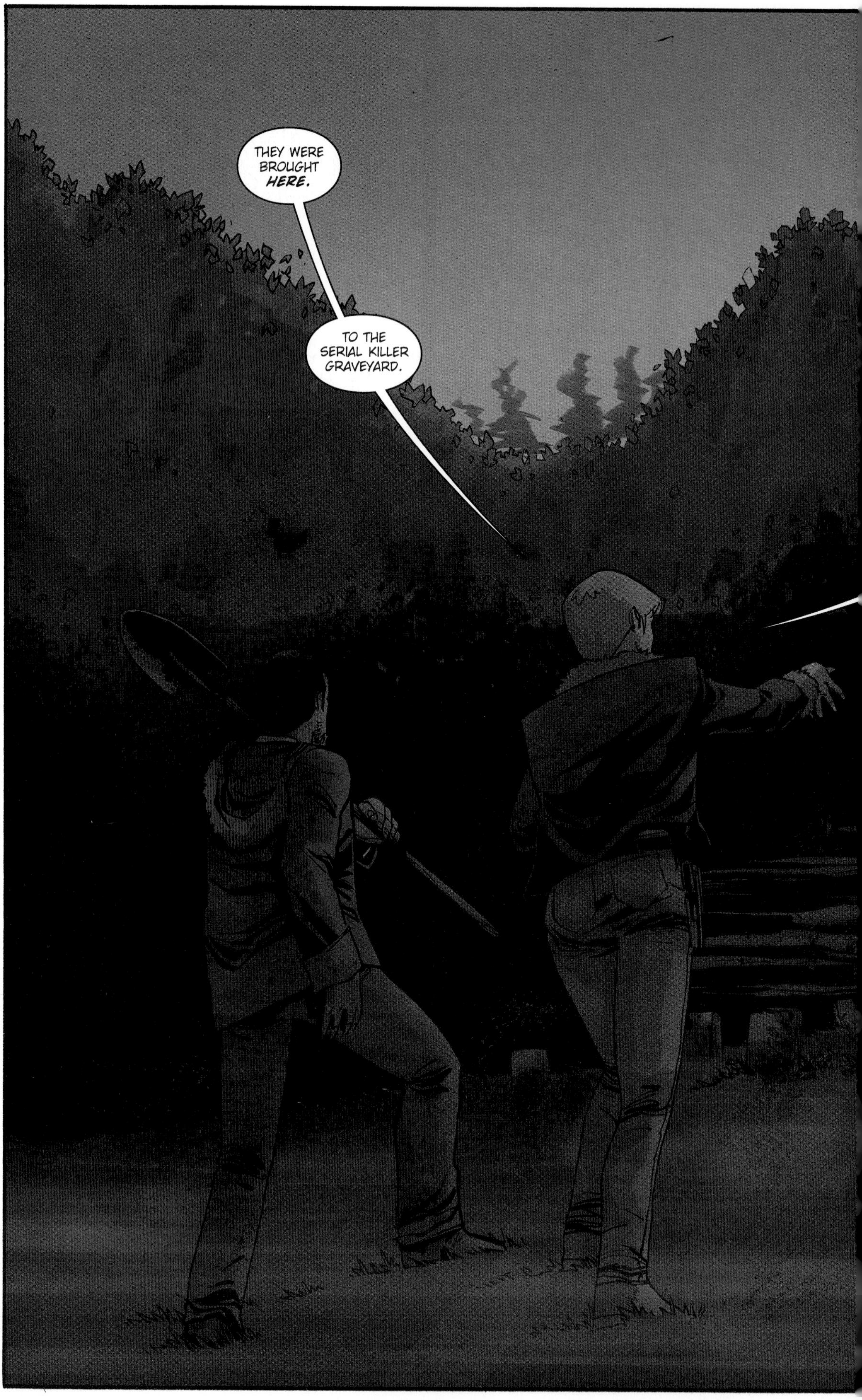
THEY WERE BROUGHT *HERE.*
TO THE SERIAL KILLER GRAVEYARD.

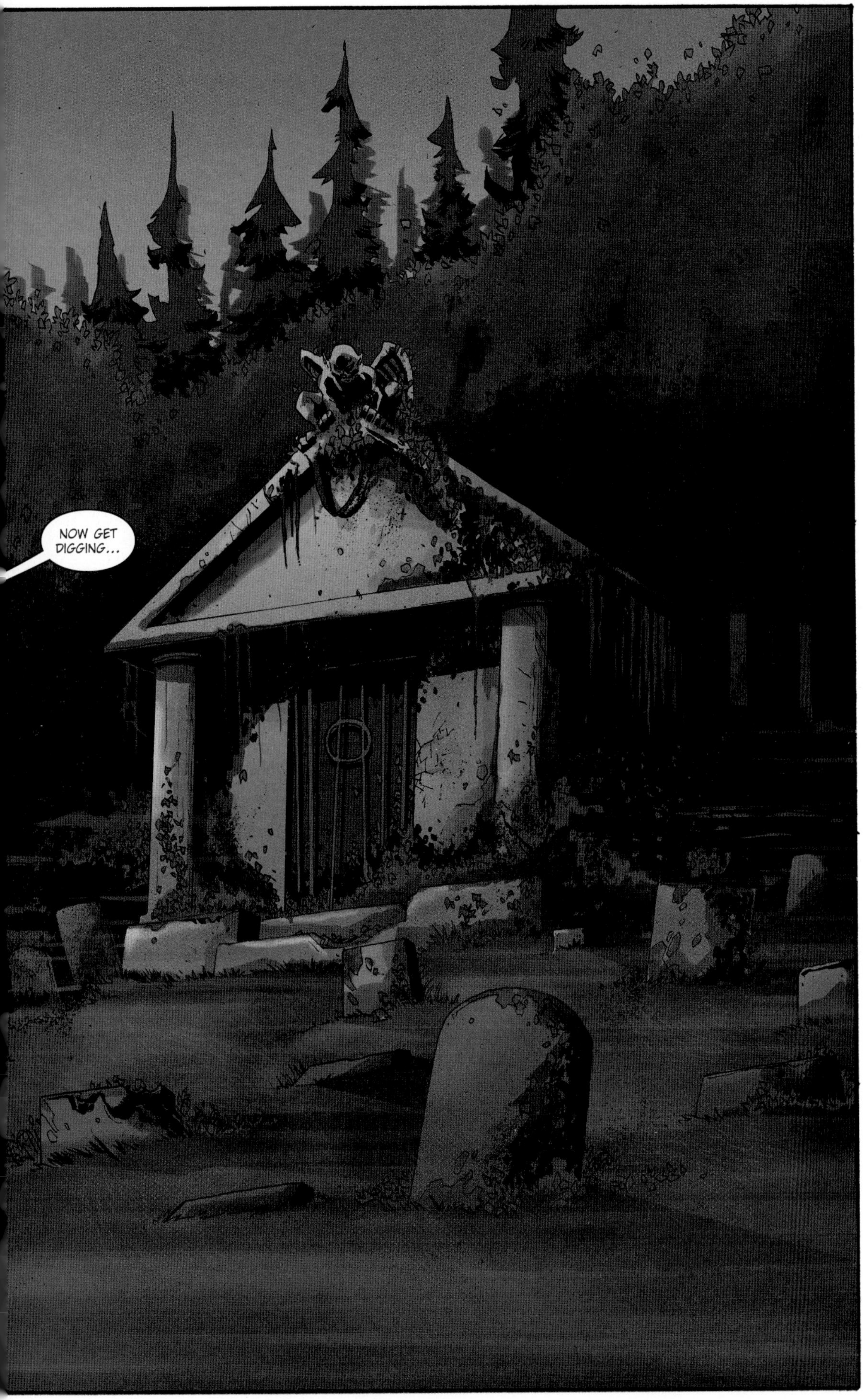
NOW GET DIGGING...

# ISSUE FOUR

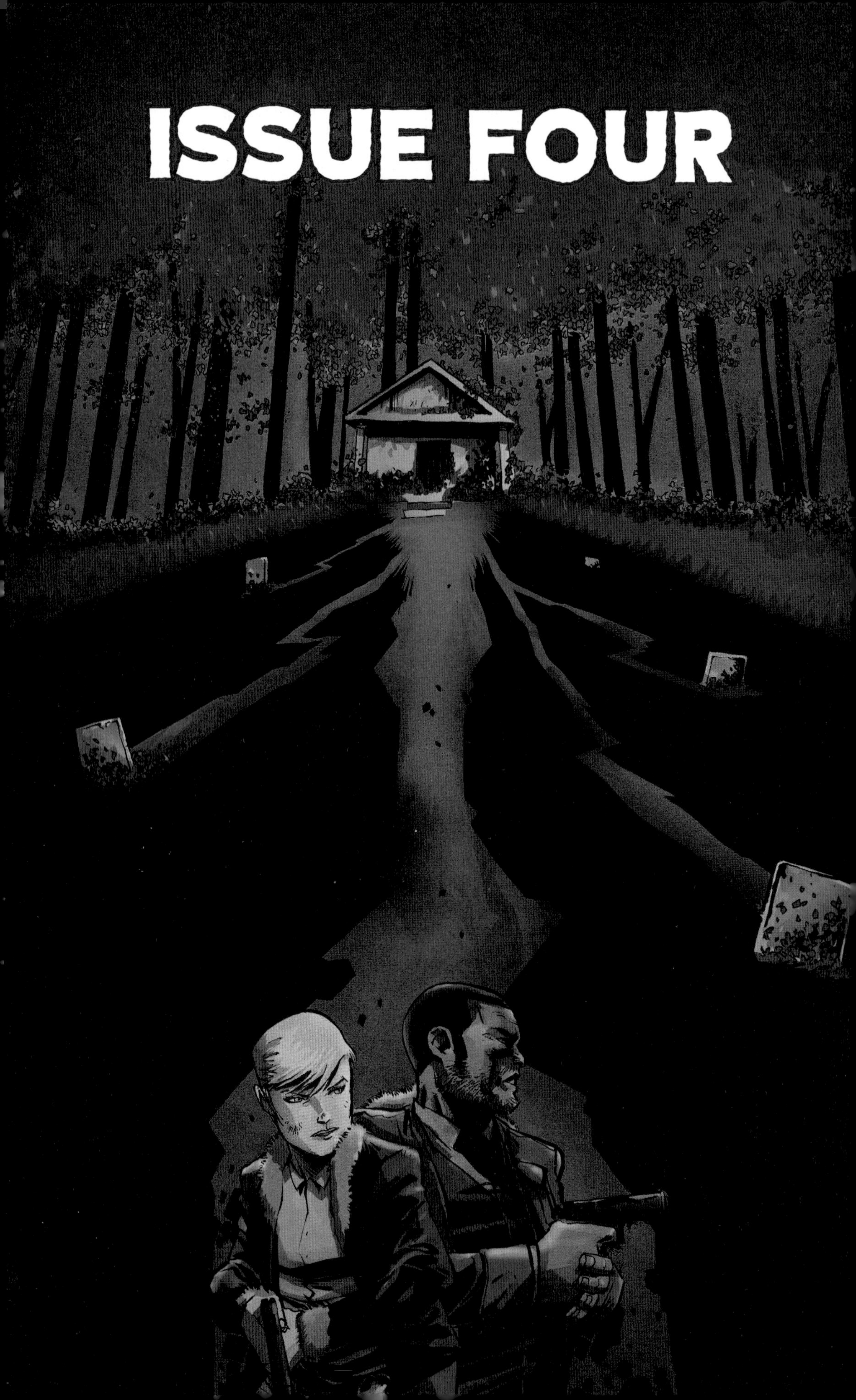

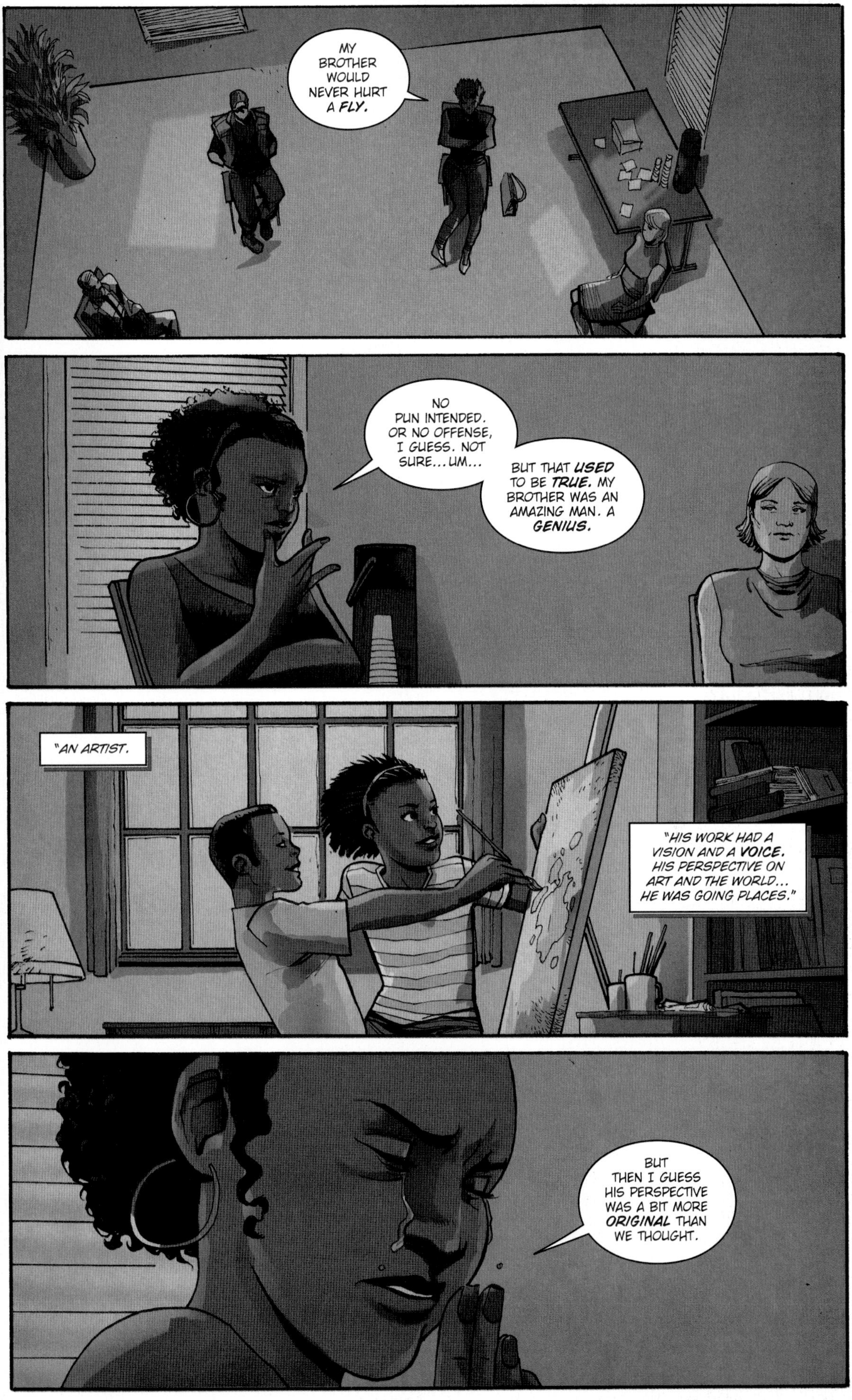
MY BROTHER WOULD NEVER HURT A FLY.
NO PUN INTENDED. OR NO OFFENSE, I GUESS. NOT SURE... UM...
BUT THAT USED TO BE TRUE. MY BROTHER WAS AN AMAZING MAN. A GENIUS.
"AN ARTIST.
"HIS WORK HAD A VISION AND A VOICE. HIS PERSPECTIVE ON ART AND THE WORLD... HE WAS GOING PLACES."
BUT THEN I GUESS HIS PERSPECTIVE WAS A BIT MORE ORIGINAL THAN WE THOUGHT.

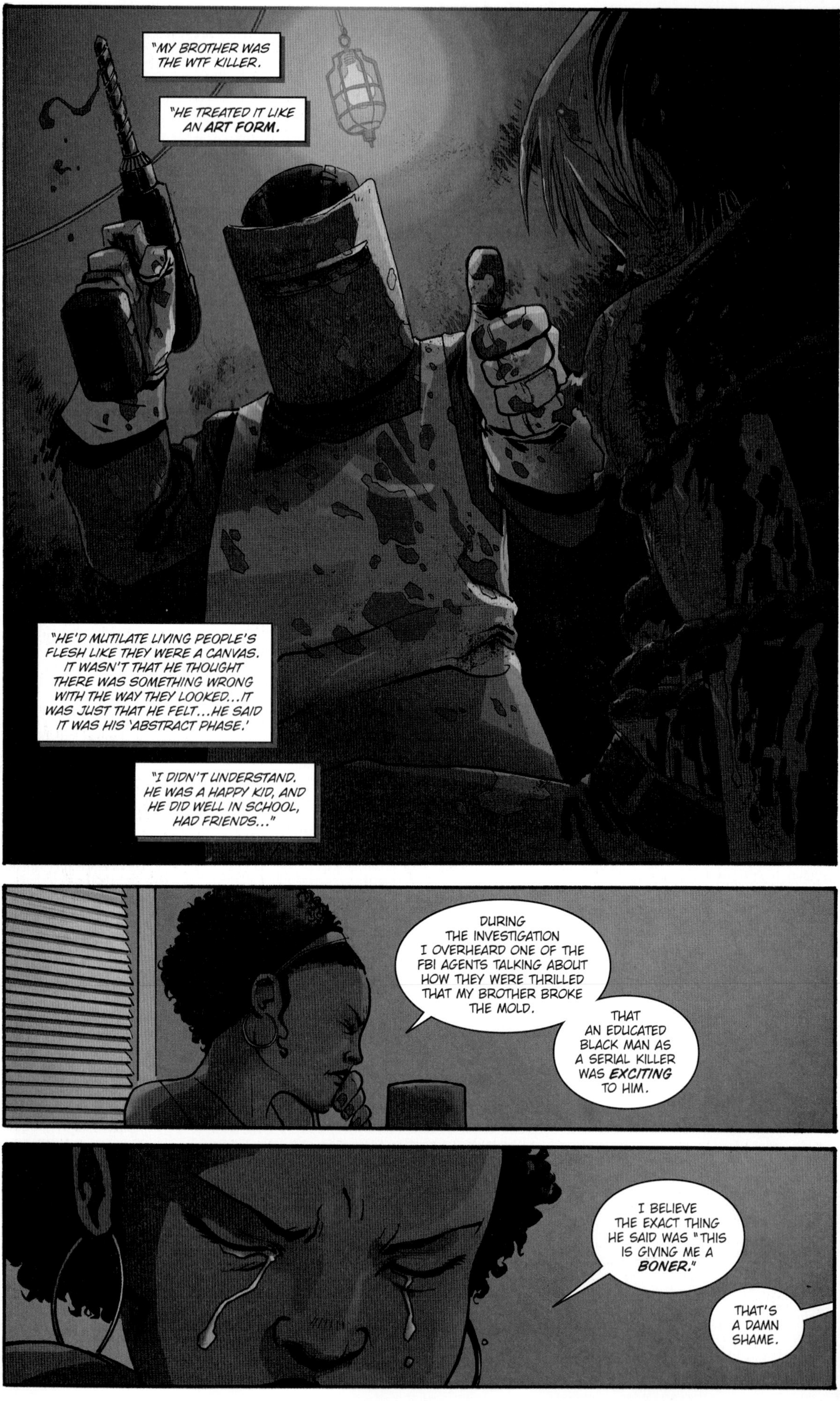
"MY BROTHER WAS THE WTF KILLER.
"HE TREATED IT LIKE AN **ART FORM.**
"HE'D MUTILATE LIVING PEOPLE'S FLESH LIKE THEY WERE A CANVAS. IT WASN'T THAT HE THOUGHT THERE WAS SOMETHING WRONG WITH THE WAY THEY LOOKED...IT WAS JUST THAT HE FELT...HE SAID IT WAS HIS 'ABSTRACT PHASE.'
"I DIDN'T UNDERSTAND. HE WAS A HAPPY KID, AND HE DID WELL IN SCHOOL, HAD FRIENDS..."
DURING THE INVESTIGATION I OVERHEARD ONE OF THE FBI AGENTS TALKING ABOUT HOW THEY WERE THRILLED THAT MY BROTHER BROKE THE MOLD.
THAT AN EDUCATED BLACK MAN AS A SERIAL KILLER WAS **EXCITING** TO HIM.
I BELIEVE THE EXACT THING HE SAID WAS "THIS IS GIVING ME A **BONER.**"
THAT'S A DAMN SHAME.

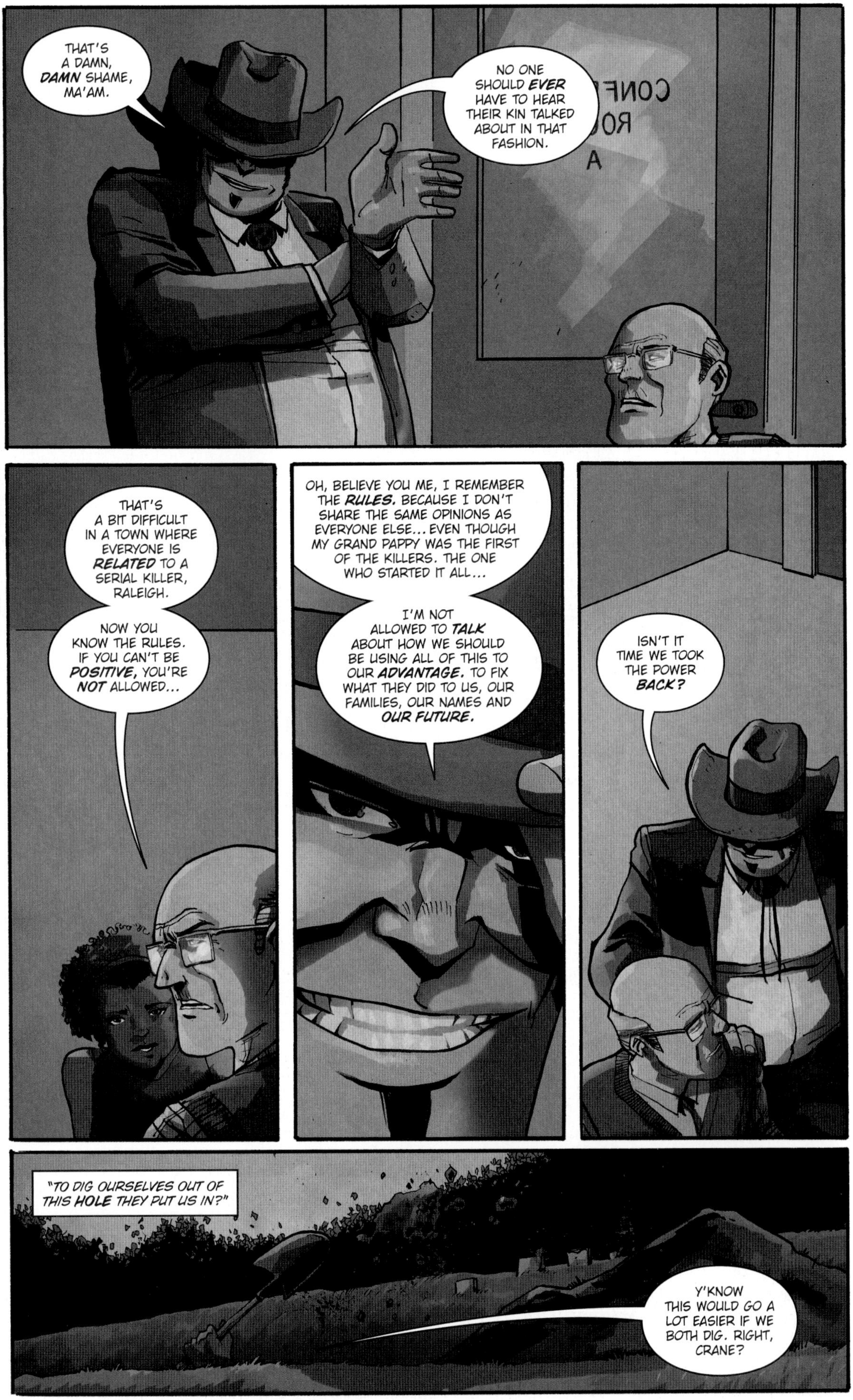
THAT'S A DAMN, DAMN SHAME, MA'AM.
NO ONE SHOULD EVER HAVE TO HEAR THEIR KIN TALKED ABOUT IN THAT FASHION.
CONF RO A
THAT'S A BIT DIFFICULT IN A TOWN WHERE EVERYONE IS RELATED TO A SERIAL KILLER, RALEIGH.
NOW YOU KNOW THE RULES. IF YOU CAN'T BE POSITIVE, YOU'RE NOT ALLOWED...
OH, BELIEVE YOU ME, I REMEMBER THE RULES. BECAUSE I DON'T SHARE THE SAME OPINIONS AS EVERYONE ELSE... EVEN THOUGH MY GRAND PAPPY WAS THE FIRST OF THE KILLERS. THE ONE WHO STARTED IT ALL...
I'M NOT ALLOWED TO TALK ABOUT HOW WE SHOULD BE USING ALL OF THIS TO OUR ADVANTAGE. TO FIX WHAT THEY DID TO US, OUR FAMILIES, OUR NAMES AND OUR FUTURE.
ISN'T IT TIME WE TOOK THE POWER BACK?
"TO DIG OURSELVES OUT OF THIS HOLE THEY PUT US IN?"
Y'KNOW THIS WOULD GO A LOT EASIER IF WE BOTH DIG. RIGHT, CRANE?

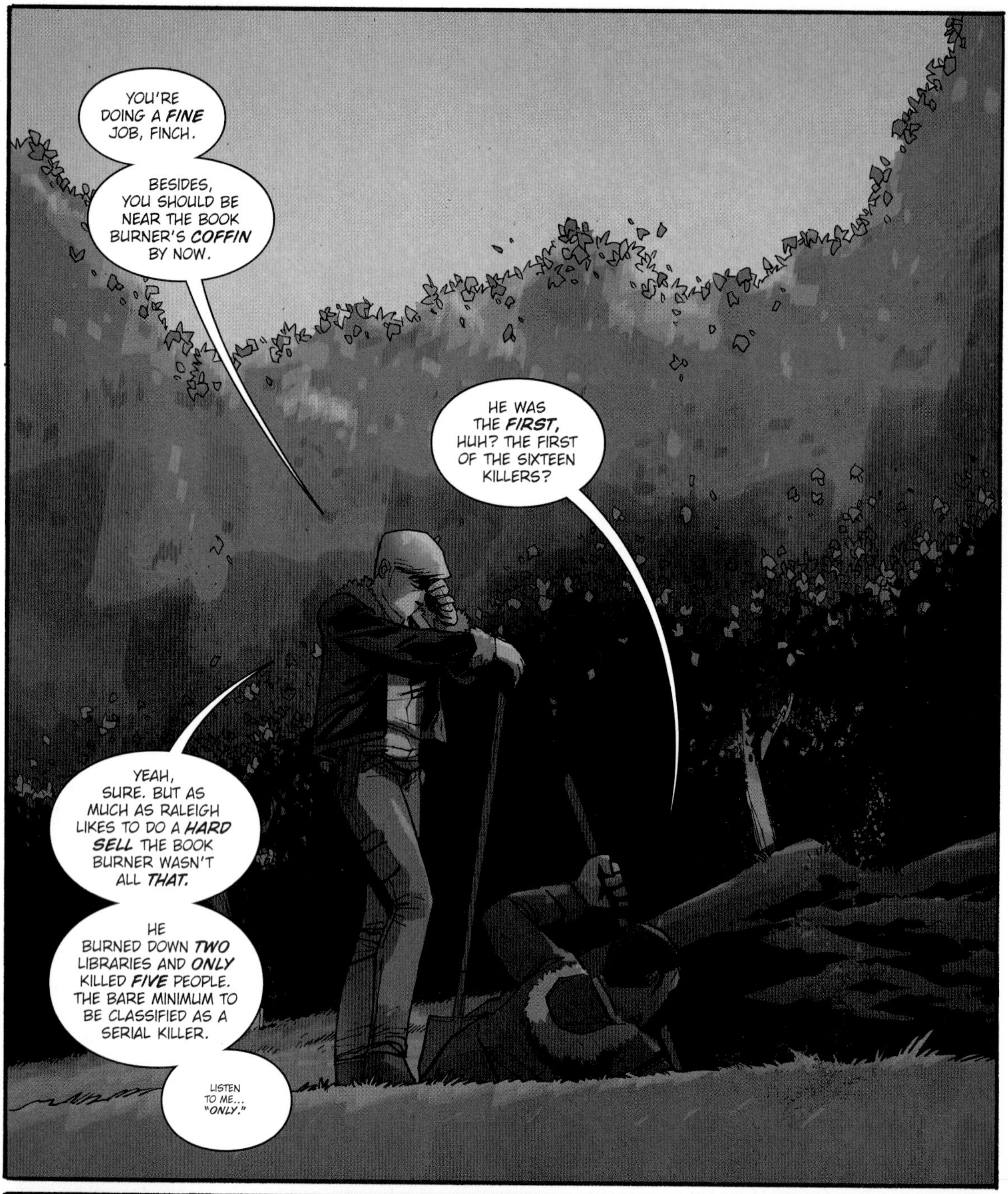
YOU'RE DOING A *FINE* JOB, FINCH.
BESIDES, YOU SHOULD BE NEAR THE BOOK BURNER'S *COFFIN* BY NOW.
HE WAS THE *FIRST,* HUH? THE FIRST OF THE SIXTEEN KILLERS?
YEAH, SURE. BUT AS MUCH AS RALEIGH LIKES TO DO A *HARD SELL* THE BOOK BURNER WASN'T ALL *THAT.*
HE BURNED DOWN *TWO* LIBRARIES AND *ONLY* KILLED *FIVE* PEOPLE. THE BARE MINIMUM TO BE CLASSIFIED AS A SERIAL KILLER.
LISTEN TO ME... *"ONLY."*

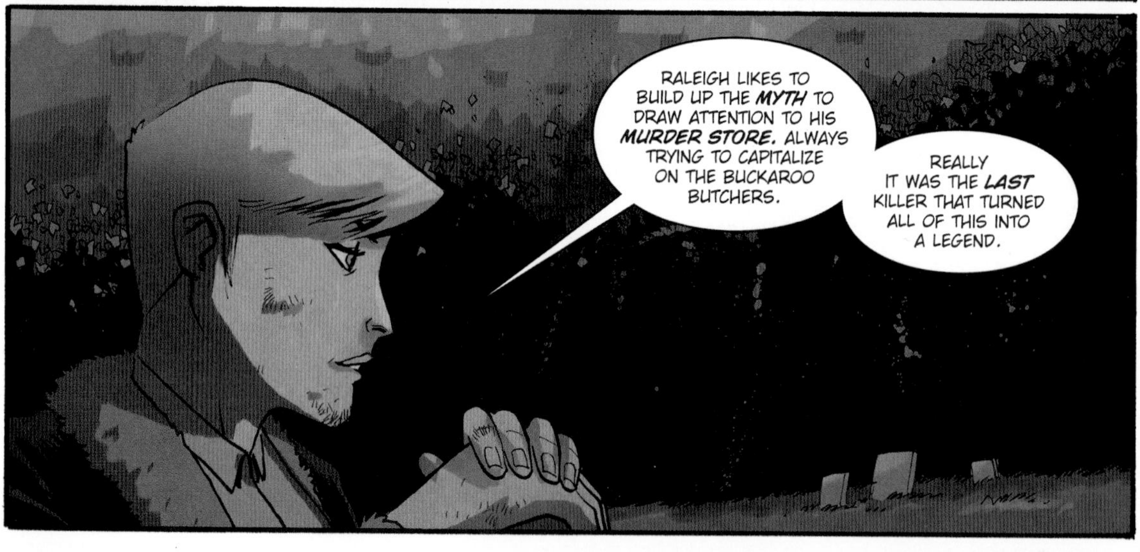
RALEIGH LIKES TO BUILD UP THE *MYTH* TO DRAW ATTENTION TO HIS *MURDER STORE.* ALWAYS TRYING TO CAPITALIZE ON THE BUCKAROO BUTCHERS.
REALLY IT WAS THE *LAST* KILLER THAT TURNED ALL OF THIS INTO A LEGEND.

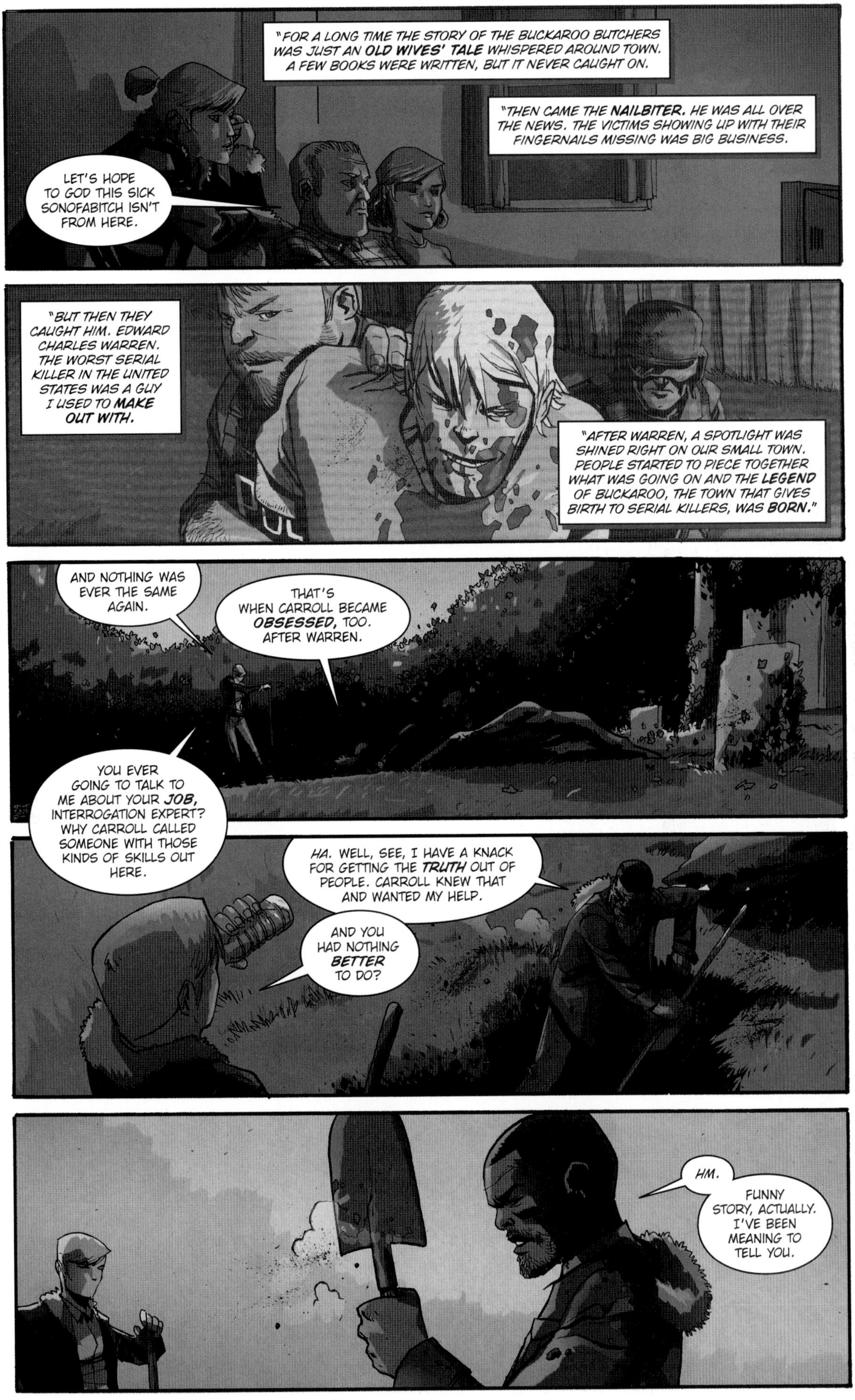
"FOR A LONG TIME THE STORY OF THE BUCKAROO BUTCHERS WAS JUST AN OLD WIVES' TALE WHISPERED AROUND TOWN. A FEW BOOKS WERE WRITTEN, BUT IT NEVER CAUGHT ON.
"THEN CAME THE NAILBITER. HE WAS ALL OVER THE NEWS. THE VICTIMS SHOWING UP WITH THEIR FINGERNAILS MISSING WAS BIG BUSINESS.
LET'S HOPE TO GOD THIS SICK SONOFABITCH ISN'T FROM HERE.
"BUT THEN THEY CAUGHT HIM. EDWARD CHARLES WARREN. THE WORST SERIAL KILLER IN THE UNITED STATES WAS A GUY I USED TO MAKE OUT WITH.
"AFTER WARREN, A SPOTLIGHT WAS SHINED RIGHT ON OUR SMALL TOWN. PEOPLE STARTED TO PIECE TOGETHER WHAT WAS GOING ON AND THE LEGEND OF BUCKAROO, THE TOWN THAT GIVES BIRTH TO SERIAL KILLERS, WAS BORN."
AND NOTHING WAS EVER THE SAME AGAIN.
THAT'S WHEN CARROLL BECAME OBSESSED, TOO. AFTER WARREN.
YOU EVER GOING TO TALK TO ME ABOUT YOUR JOB, INTERROGATION EXPERT? WHY CARROLL CALLED SOMEONE WITH THOSE KINDS OF SKILLS OUT HERE.
HA. WELL, SEE, I HAVE A KNACK FOR GETTING THE TRUTH OUT OF PEOPLE. CARROLL KNEW THAT AND WANTED MY HELP.
AND YOU HAD NOTHING BETTER TO DO?
HM.
FUNNY STORY, ACTUALLY. I'VE BEEN MEANING TO TELL YOU.

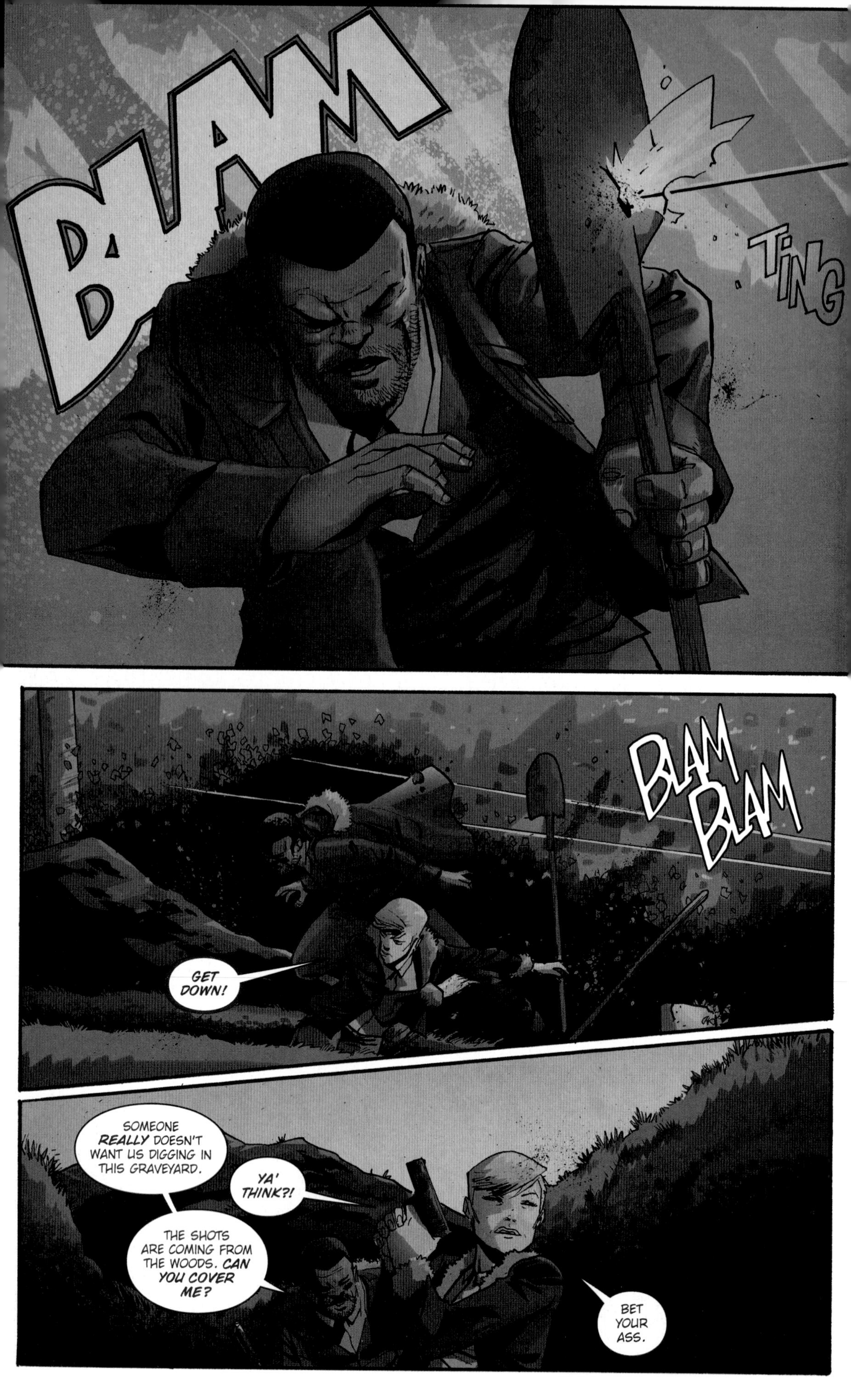
BLAM
TING
BLAM BLAM
GET DOWN!
SOMEONE REALLY DOESN'T WANT US DIGGING IN THIS GRAVEYARD.
YA' THINK?!
THE SHOTS ARE COMING FROM THE WOODS. CAN YOU COVER ME?
BET YOUR ASS.

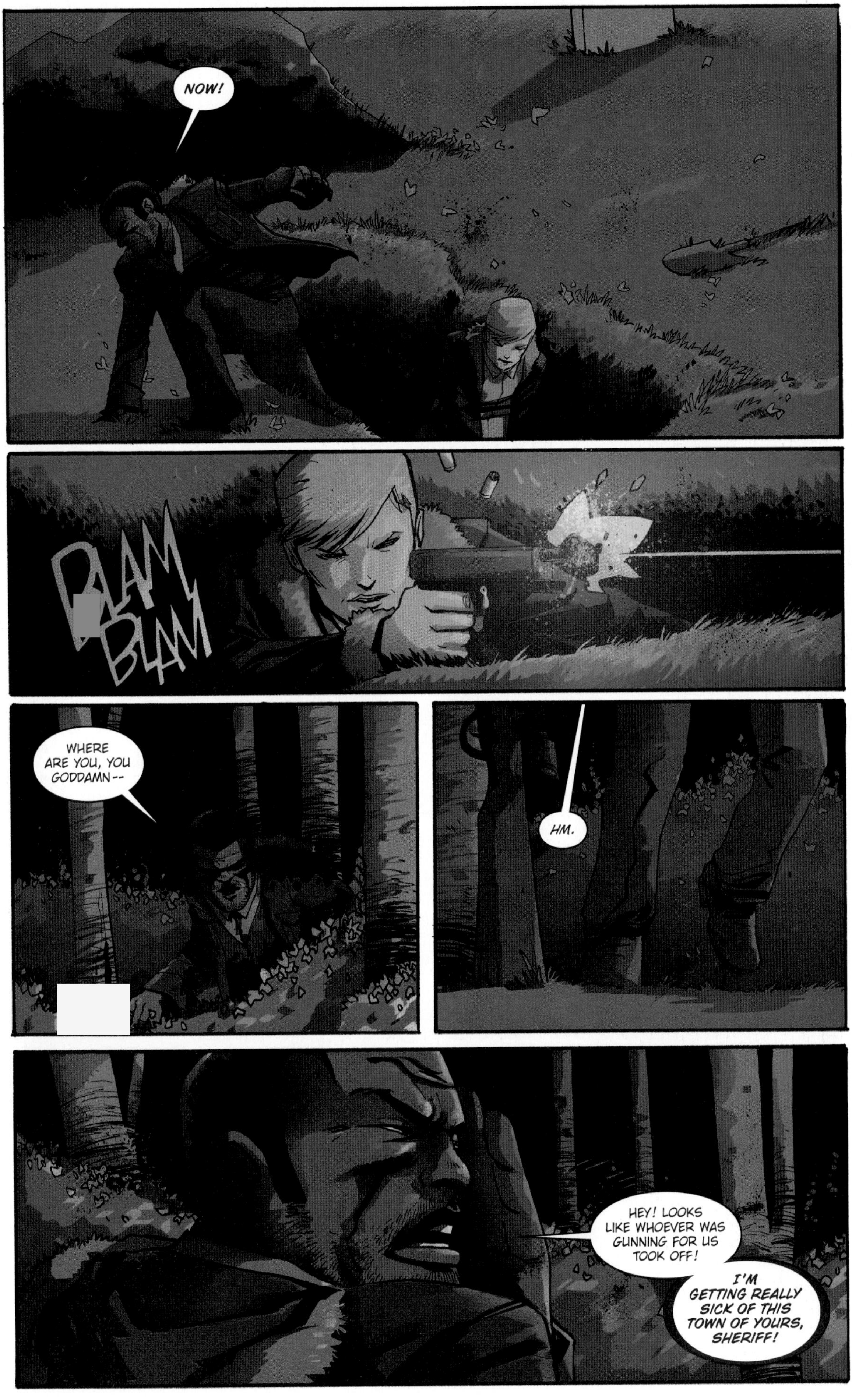
NOW!
BLAM BLAM
WHERE ARE YOU, YOU GODDAMN--
HM.
HEY! LOOKS LIKE WHOEVER WAS GUNNING FOR US TOOK OFF!
I'M GETTING REALLY SICK OF THIS TOWN OF YOURS, SHERIFF!

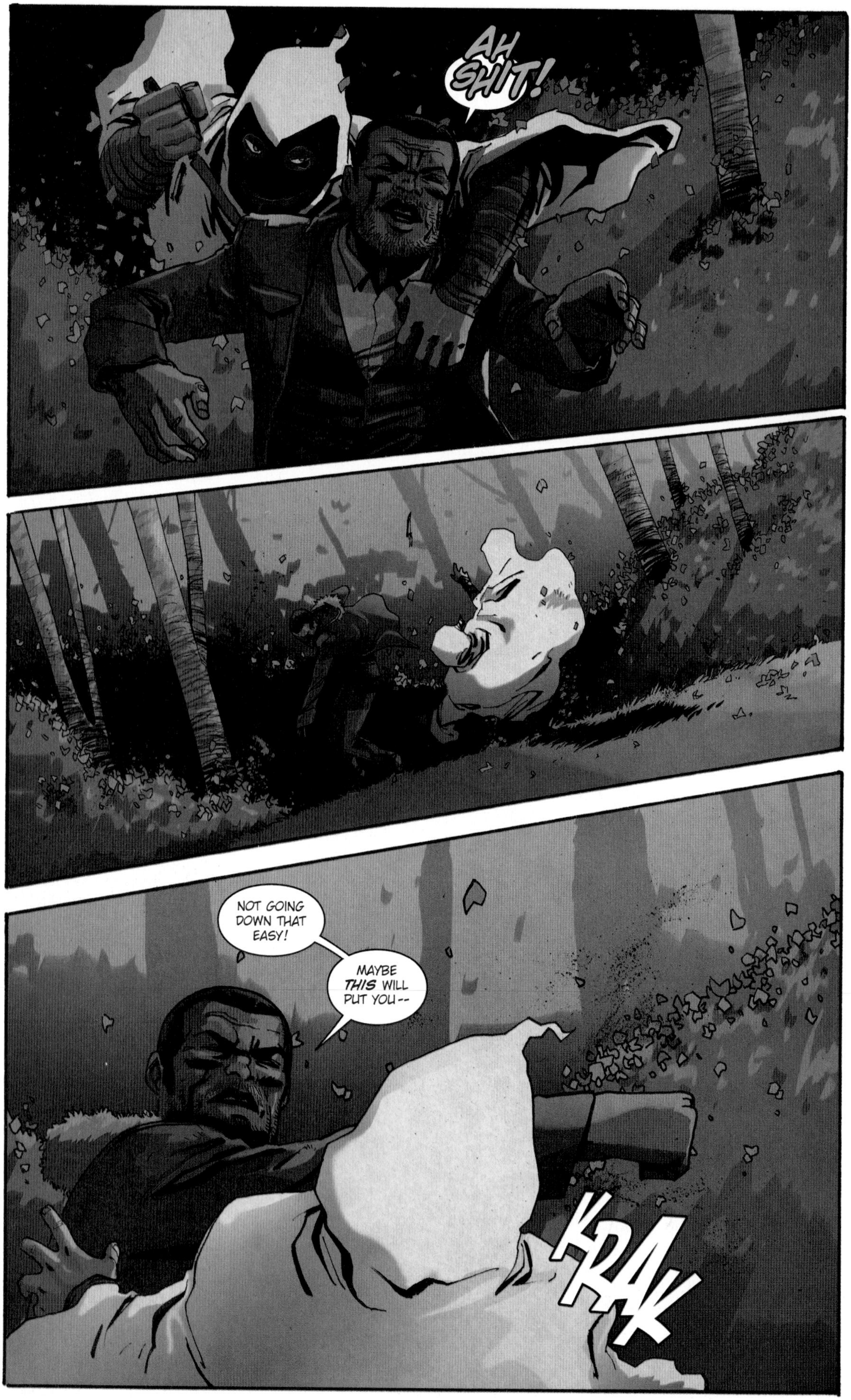
AH SHIT!
NOT GOING DOWN THAT EASY!
MAYBE THIS WILL PUT YOU--
KRAK

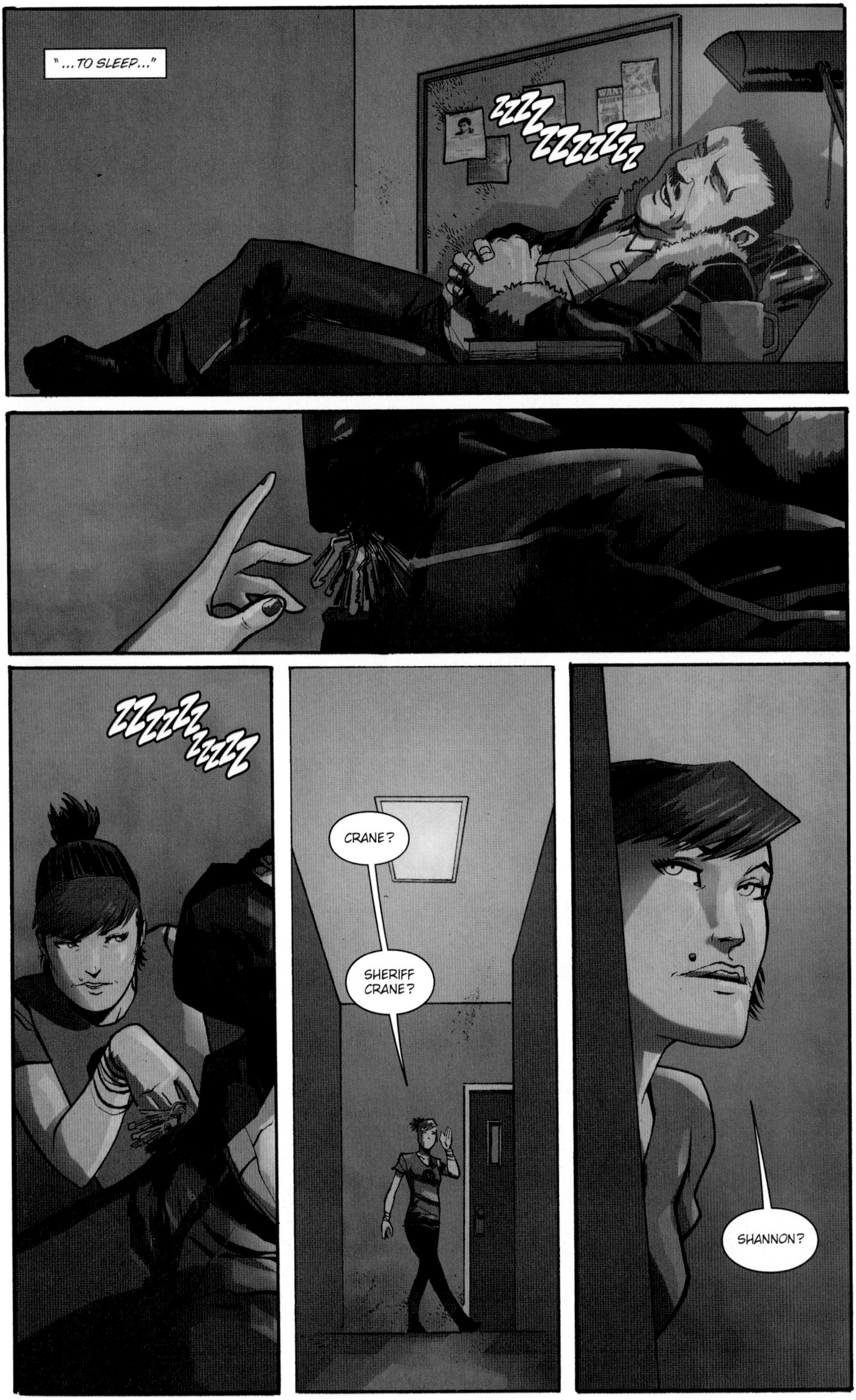
"...TO SLEEP..."
ZZZZZZZZZZ
ZZZZZZZZZZ
CRANE?
SHERIFF CRANE?
SHANNON?

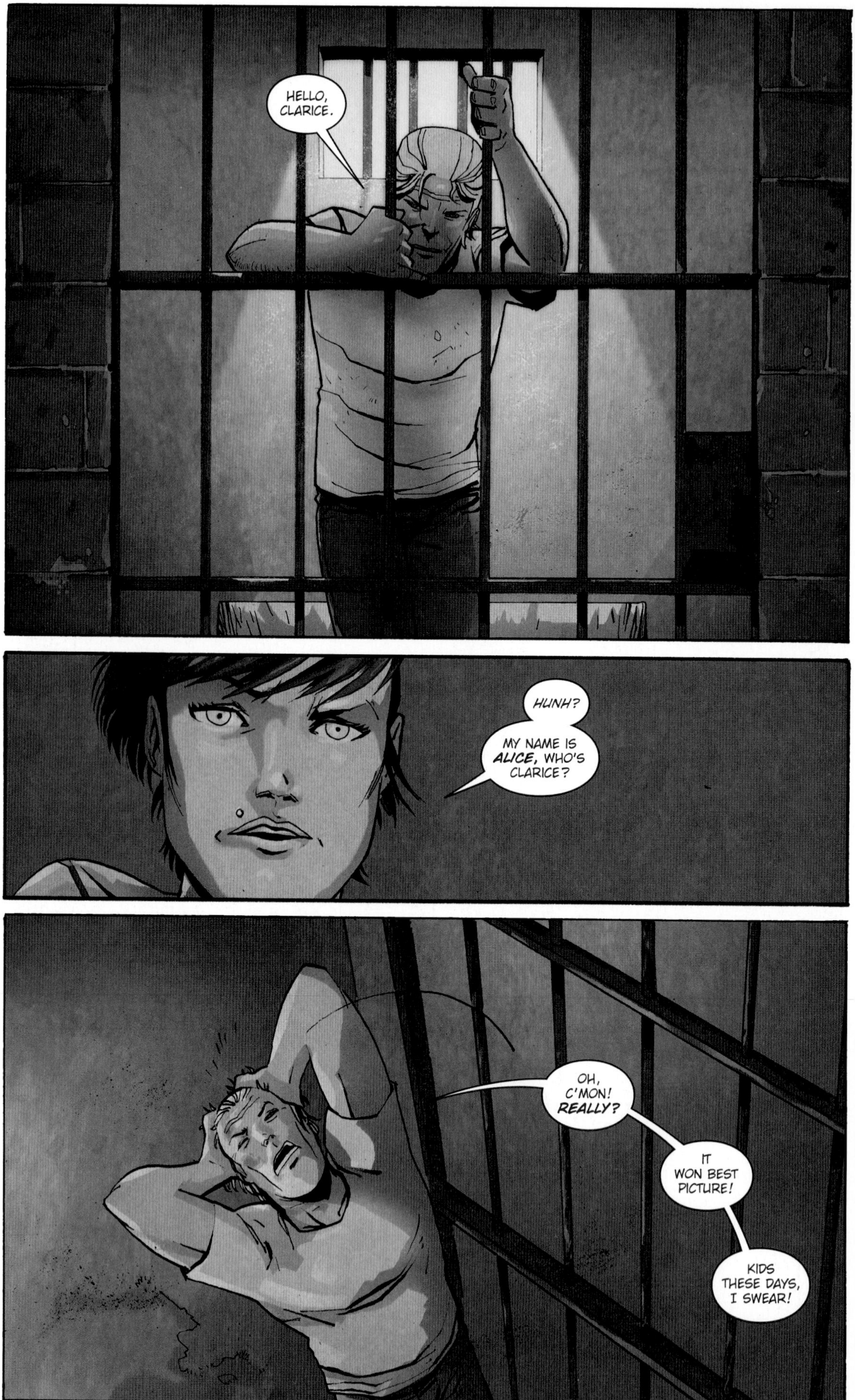
HELLO, CLARICE.
HUNH?
MY NAME IS ALICE, WHO'S CLARICE?
OH, C'MON! REALLY?
IT WON BEST PICTURE!
KIDS THESE DAYS, I SWEAR!

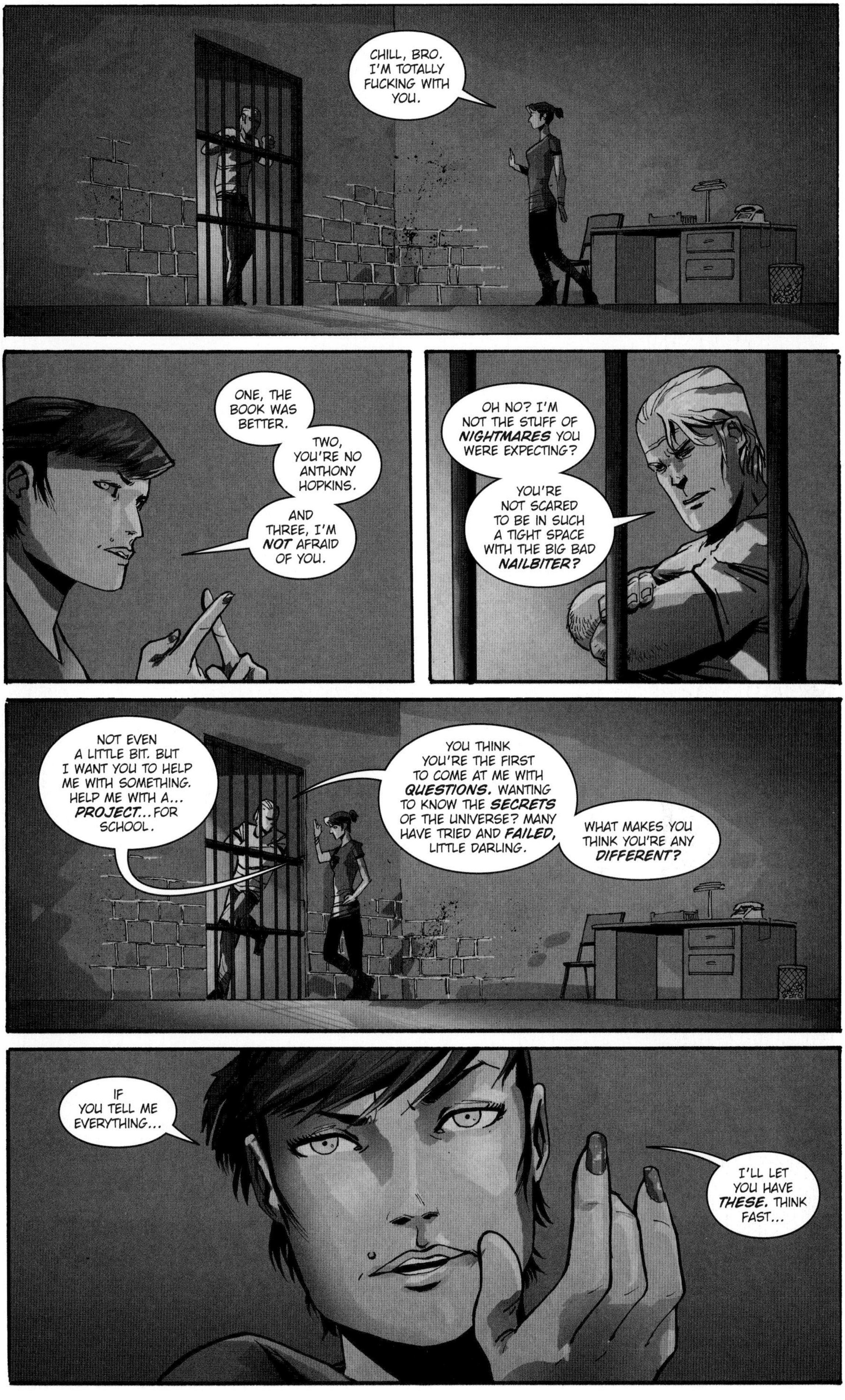
CHILL, BRO. I'M TOTALLY FUCKING WITH YOU.
ONE, THE BOOK WAS BETTER.
TWO, YOU'RE NO ANTHONY HOPKINS.
AND THREE, I'M NOT AFRAID OF YOU.
OH NO? I'M NOT THE STUFF OF NIGHTMARES YOU WERE EXPECTING?
YOU'RE NOT SCARED TO BE IN SUCH A TIGHT SPACE WITH THE BIG BAD NAILBITER?
NOT EVEN A LITTLE BIT. BUT I WANT YOU TO HELP ME WITH SOMETHING. HELP ME WITH A... PROJECT...FOR SCHOOL.
YOU THINK YOU'RE THE FIRST TO COME AT ME WITH QUESTIONS. WANTING TO KNOW THE SECRETS OF THE UNIVERSE? MANY HAVE TRIED AND FAILED, LITTLE DARLING.
WHAT MAKES YOU THINK YOU'RE ANY DIFFERENT?
IF YOU TELL ME EVERYTHING...
I'LL LET YOU HAVE THESE. THINK FAST...

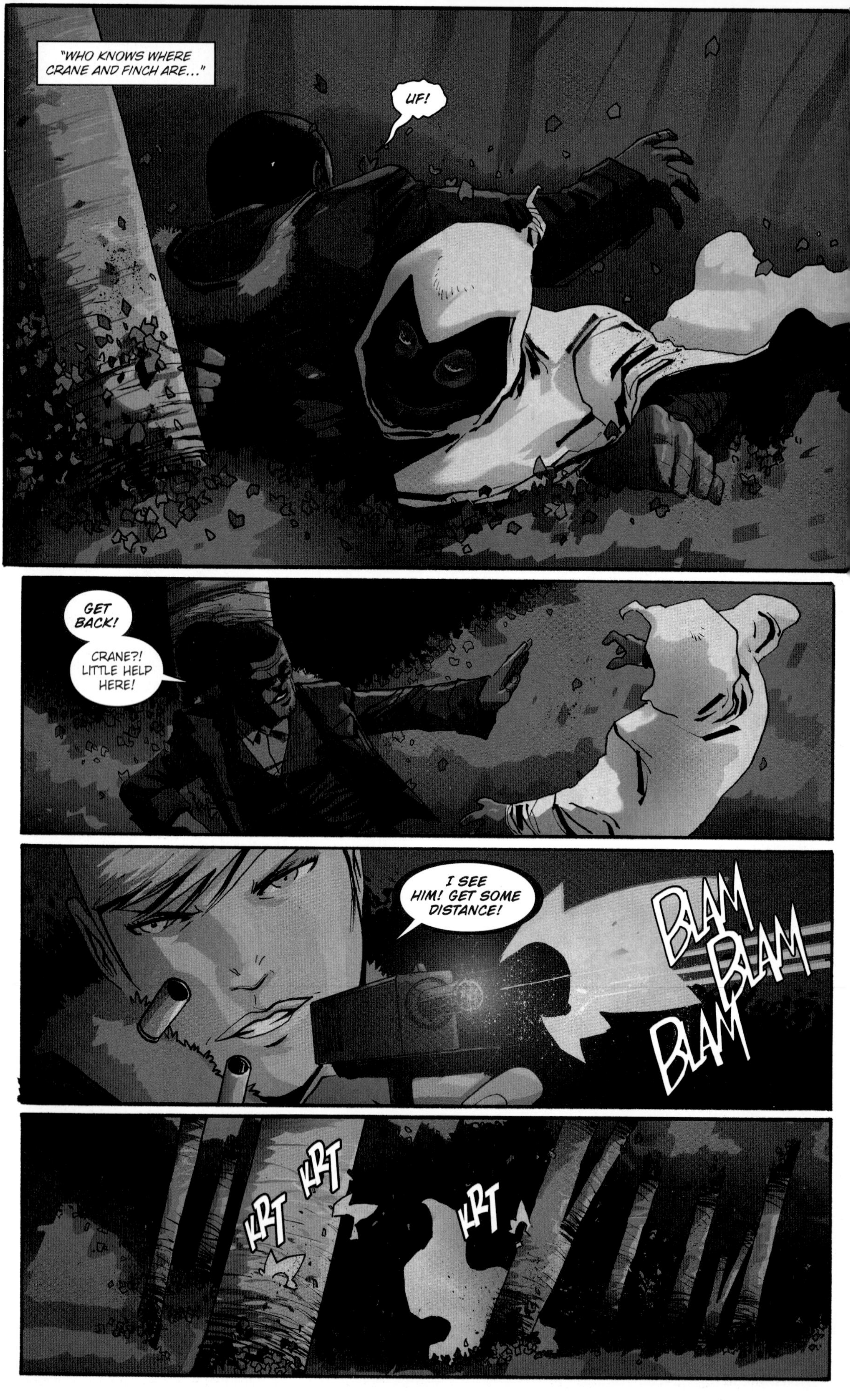
"WHO KNOWS WHERE CRANE AND FINCH ARE..."
UF!
GET BACK!
CRANE?! LITTLE HELP HERE!
I SEE HIM! GET SOME DISTANCE!
BLAM BLAM BLAM
KRT KRT KRT

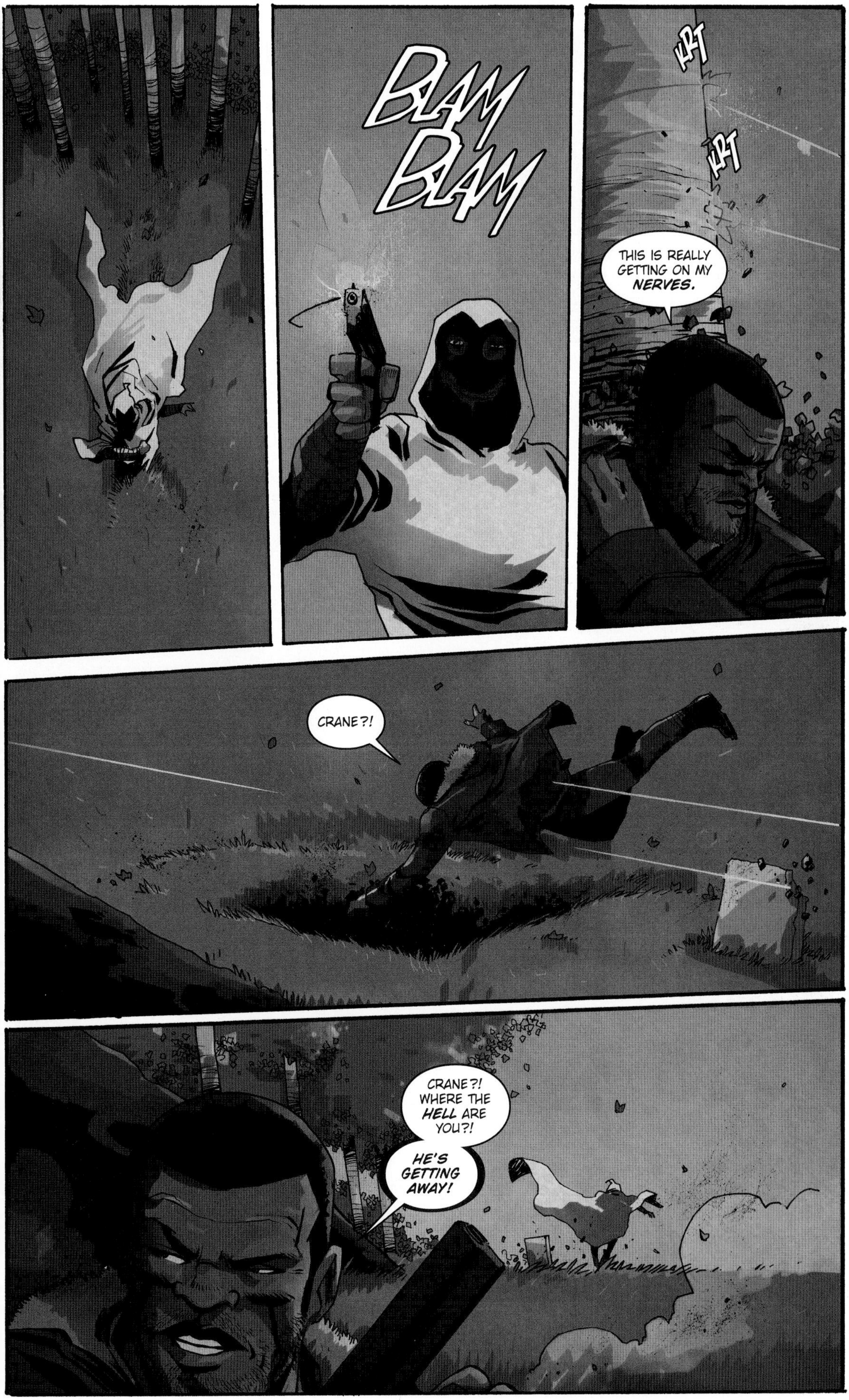

BLAM BLAM
KRT
KRT
THIS IS REALLY GETTING ON MY **NERVES.**
CRANE?!
CRANE?! WHERE THE **HELL** ARE YOU?!
**HE'S GETTING AWAY!**

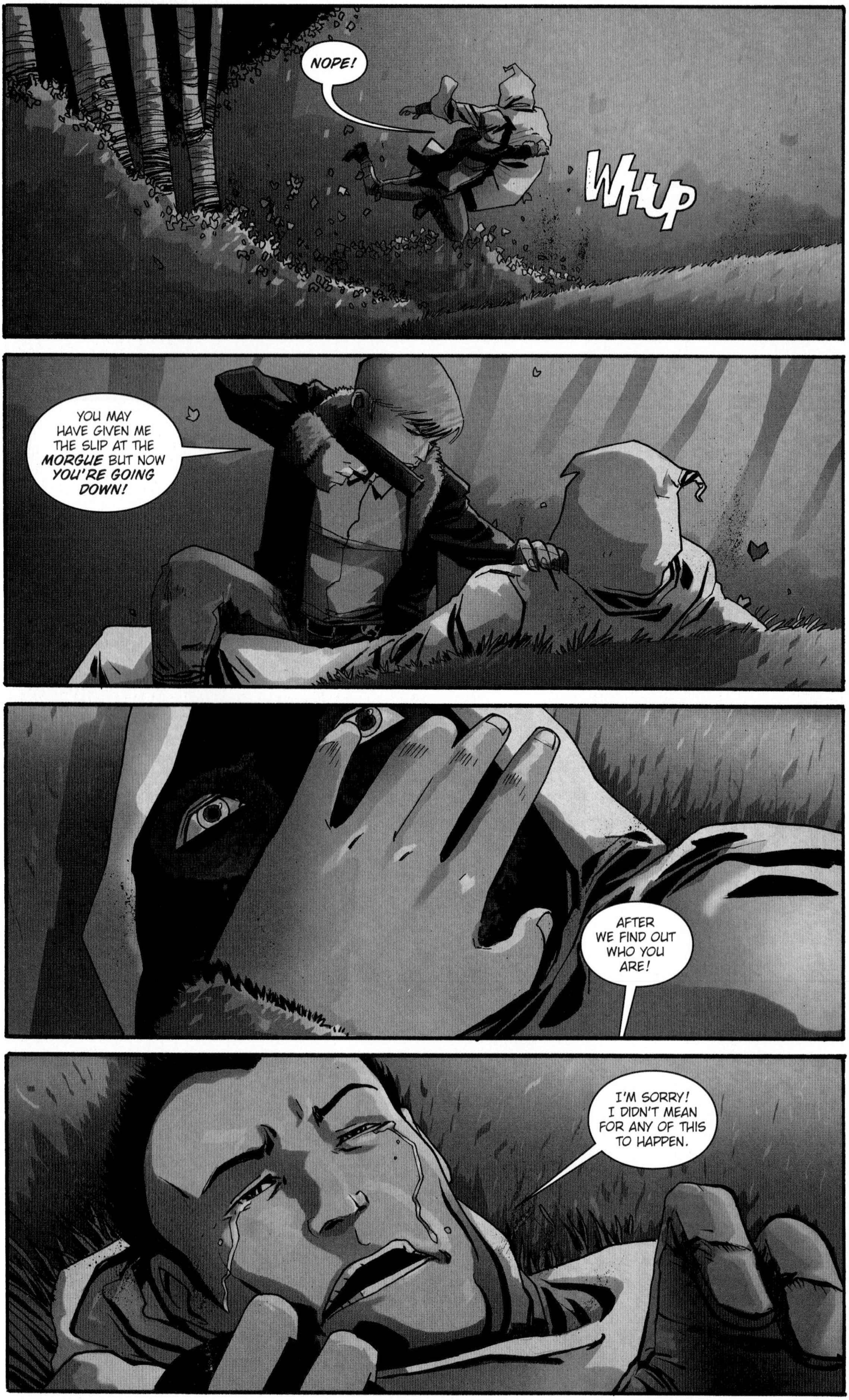
NOPE!
WHUP
YOU MAY HAVE GIVEN ME THE SLIP AT THE MORGUE BUT NOW YOU'RE GOING DOWN!
AFTER WE FIND OUT WHO YOU ARE!
I'M SORRY! I DIDN'T MEAN FOR ANY OF THIS TO HAPPEN.

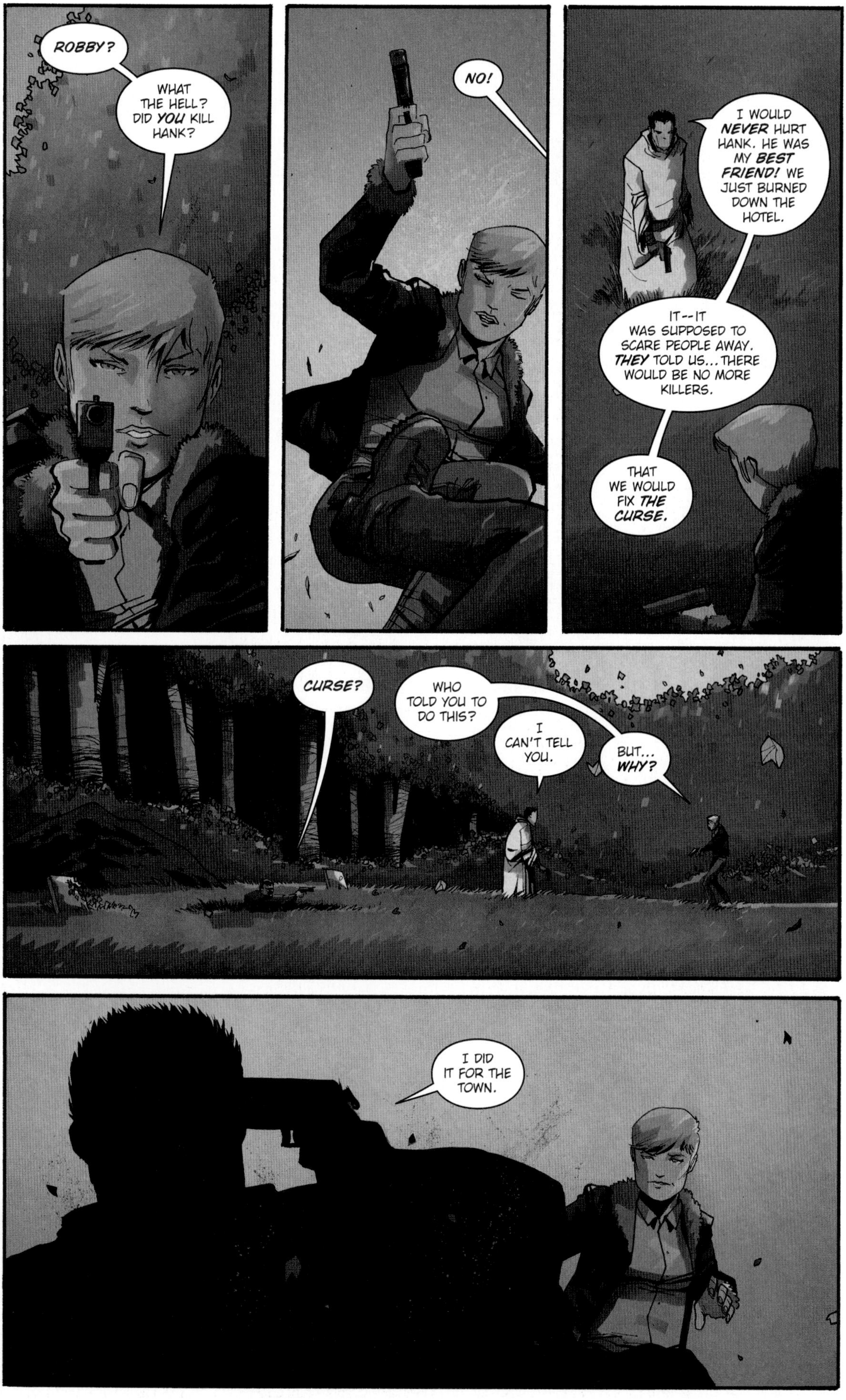
ROBBY?
WHAT THE HELL? DID YOU KILL HANK?
NO!
I WOULD NEVER HURT HANK. HE WAS MY BEST FRIEND! WE JUST BURNED DOWN THE HOTEL.
IT--IT WAS SUPPOSED TO SCARE PEOPLE AWAY. THEY TOLD US...THERE WOULD BE NO MORE KILLERS.
THAT WE WOULD FIX THE CURSE.
CURSE?
WHO TOLD YOU TO DO THIS?
I CAN'T TELL YOU.
BUT... WHY?
I DID IT FOR THE TOWN.

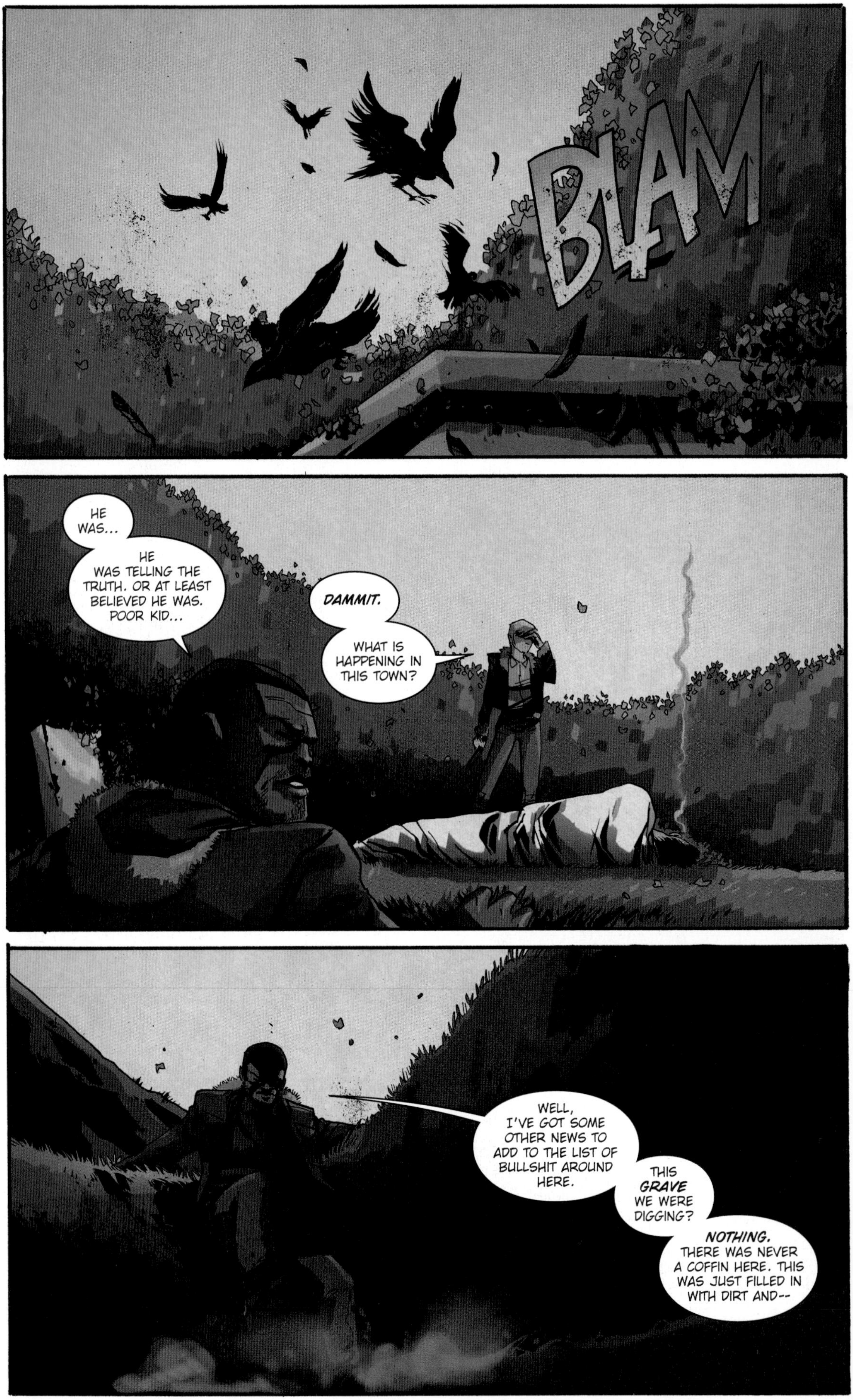
BLAM
HE WAS...
HE WAS TELLING THE TRUTH. OR AT LEAST BELIEVED HE WAS. POOR KID...
DAMMIT.
WHAT IS HAPPENING IN THIS TOWN?
WELL, I'VE GOT SOME OTHER NEWS TO ADD TO THE LIST OF BULLSHIT AROUND HERE.
THIS GRAVE WE WERE DIGGING?
NOTHING. THERE WAS NEVER A COFFIN HERE. THIS WAS JUST FILLED IN WITH DIRT AND--

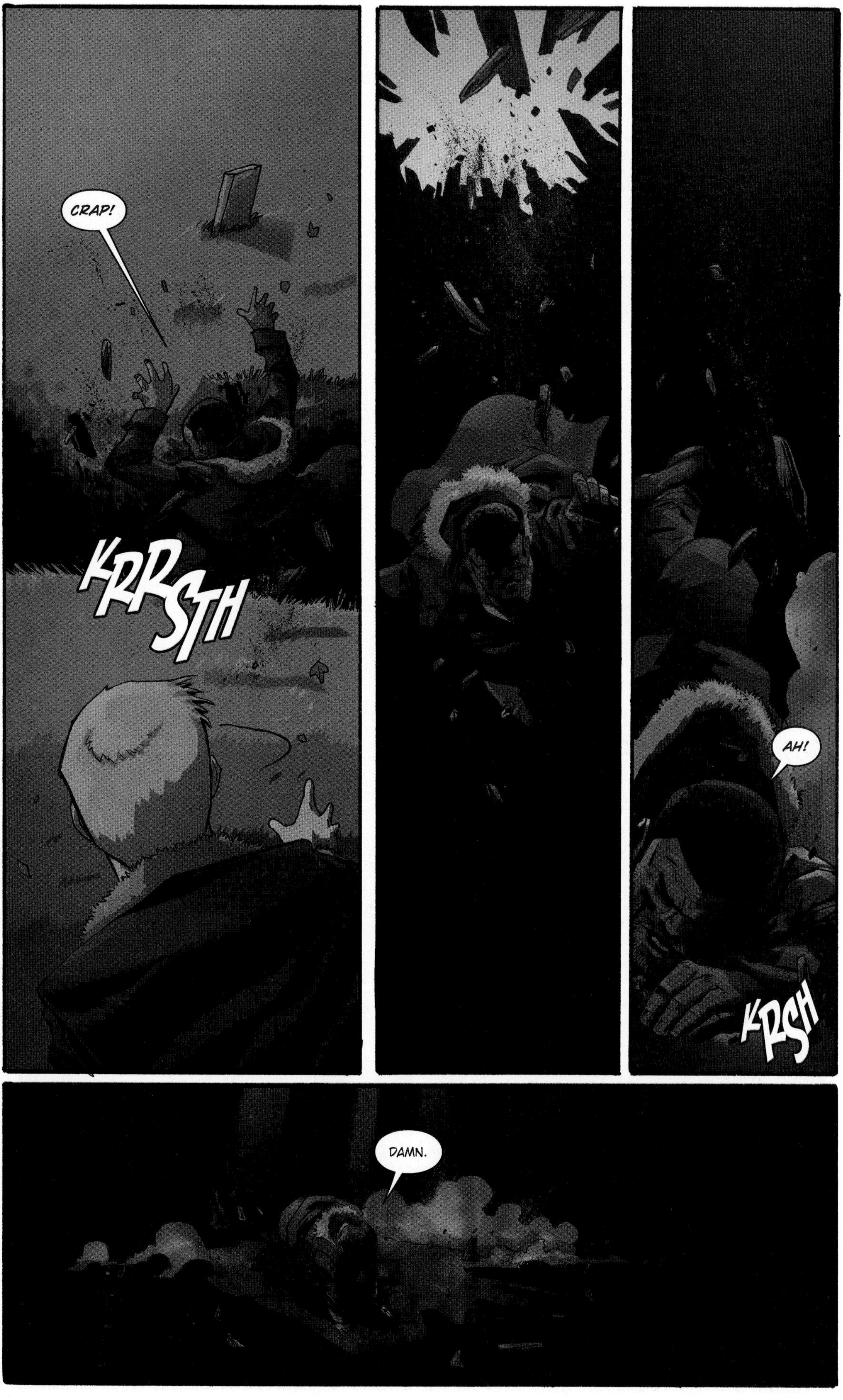
CRAP!
KRRSTH
AH!
KRSH
DAMN.

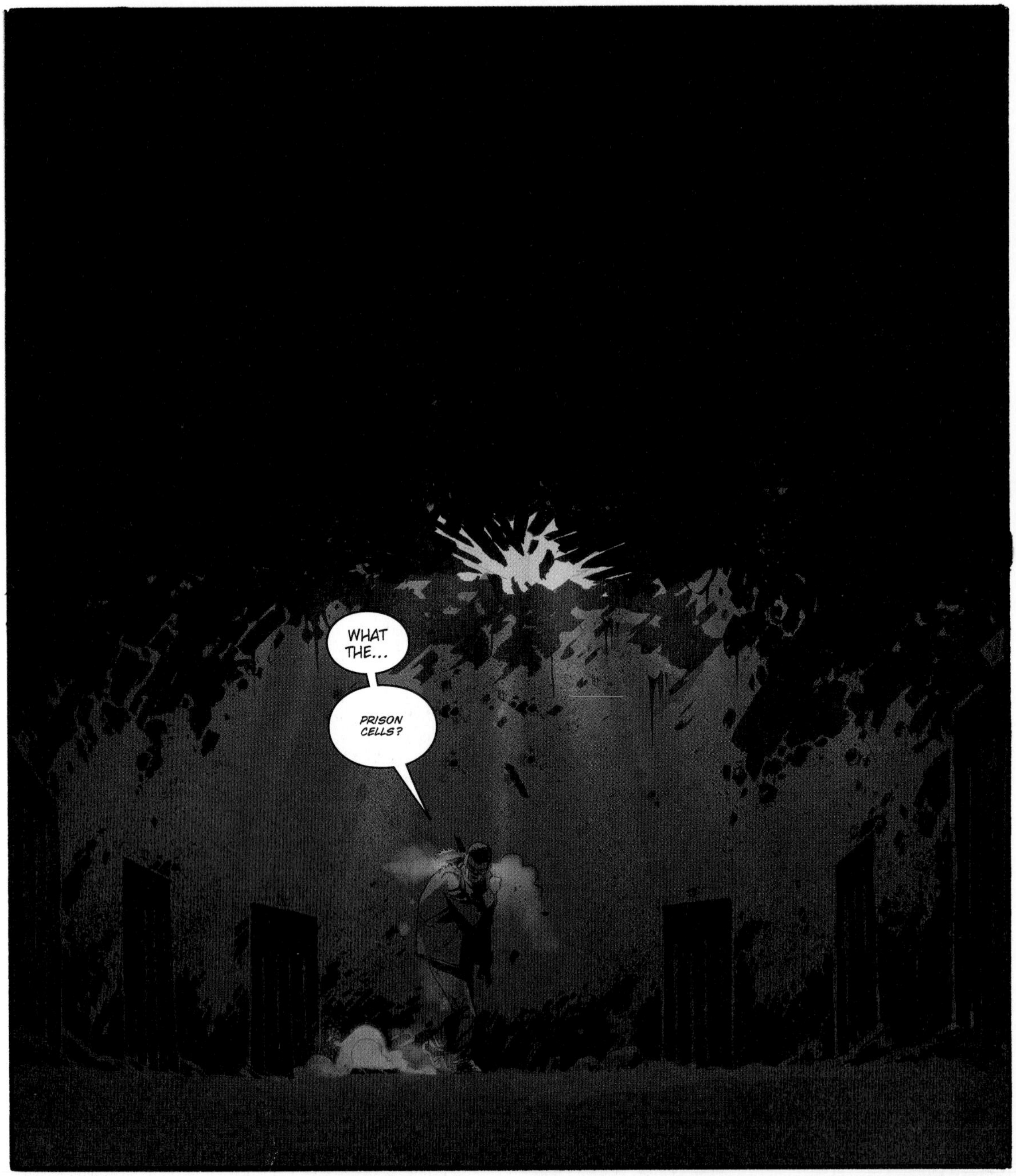
WHAT THE...
PRISON CELLS?

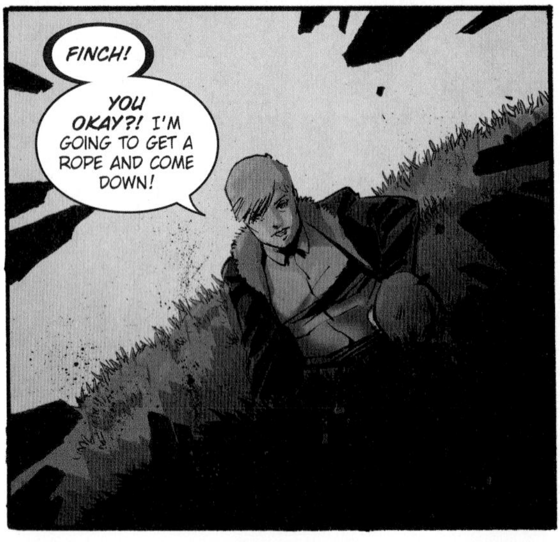
FINCH!
YOU OKAY?! I'M GOING TO GET A ROPE AND COME DOWN!

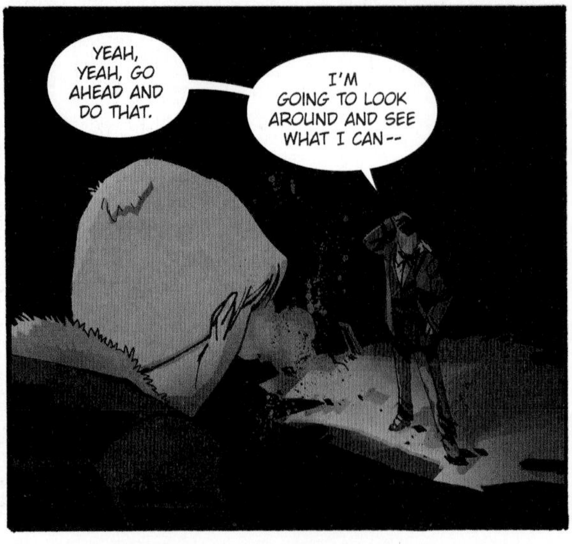
YEAH, YEAH, GO AHEAD AND DO THAT.
I'M GOING TO LOOK AROUND AND SEE WHAT I CAN--

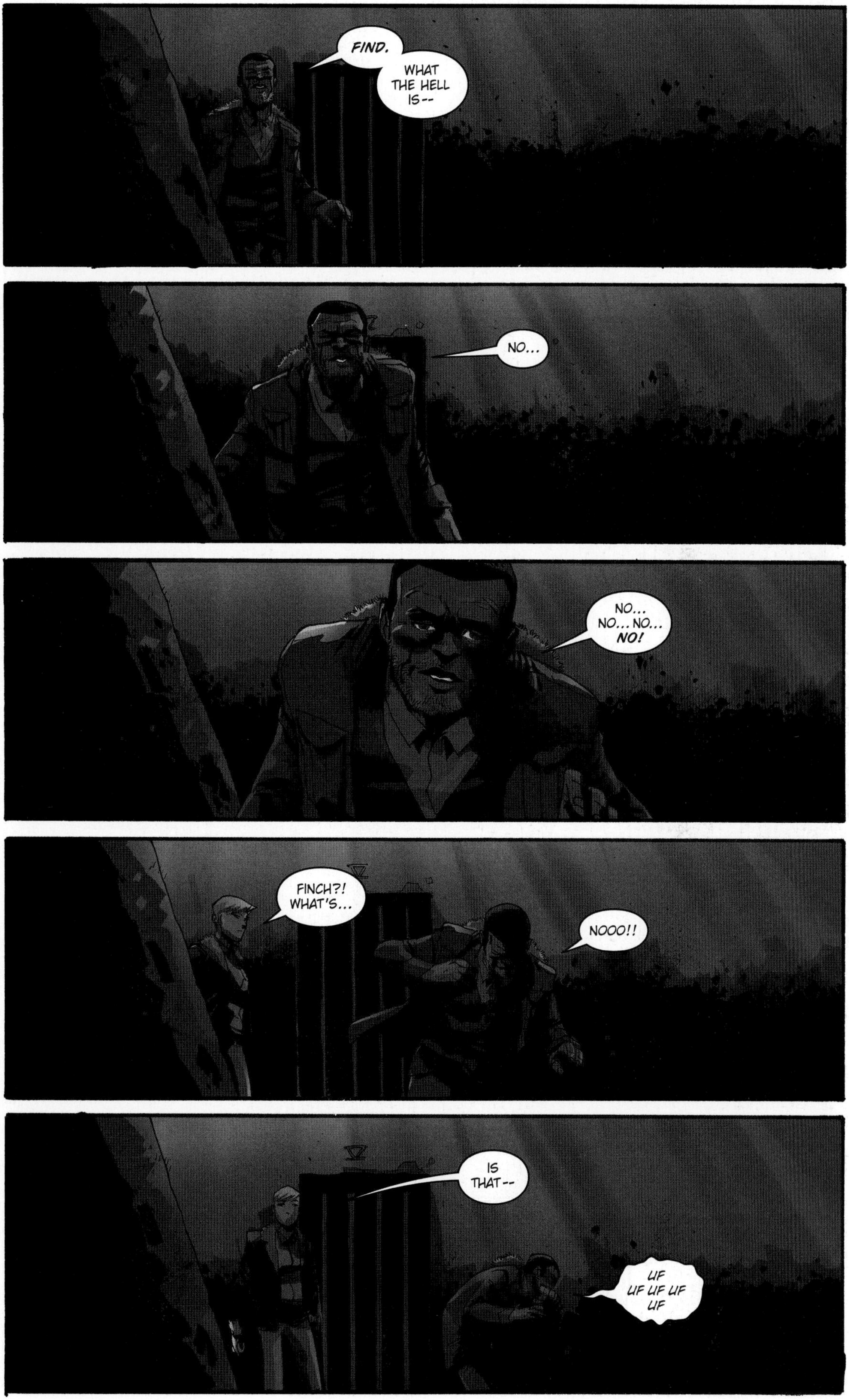
FIND.
WHAT THE HELL IS--
NO...
NO... NO... NO... NO!
FINCH?! WHAT'S...
NOOO!!
IS THAT--
UF UF UF UF UF

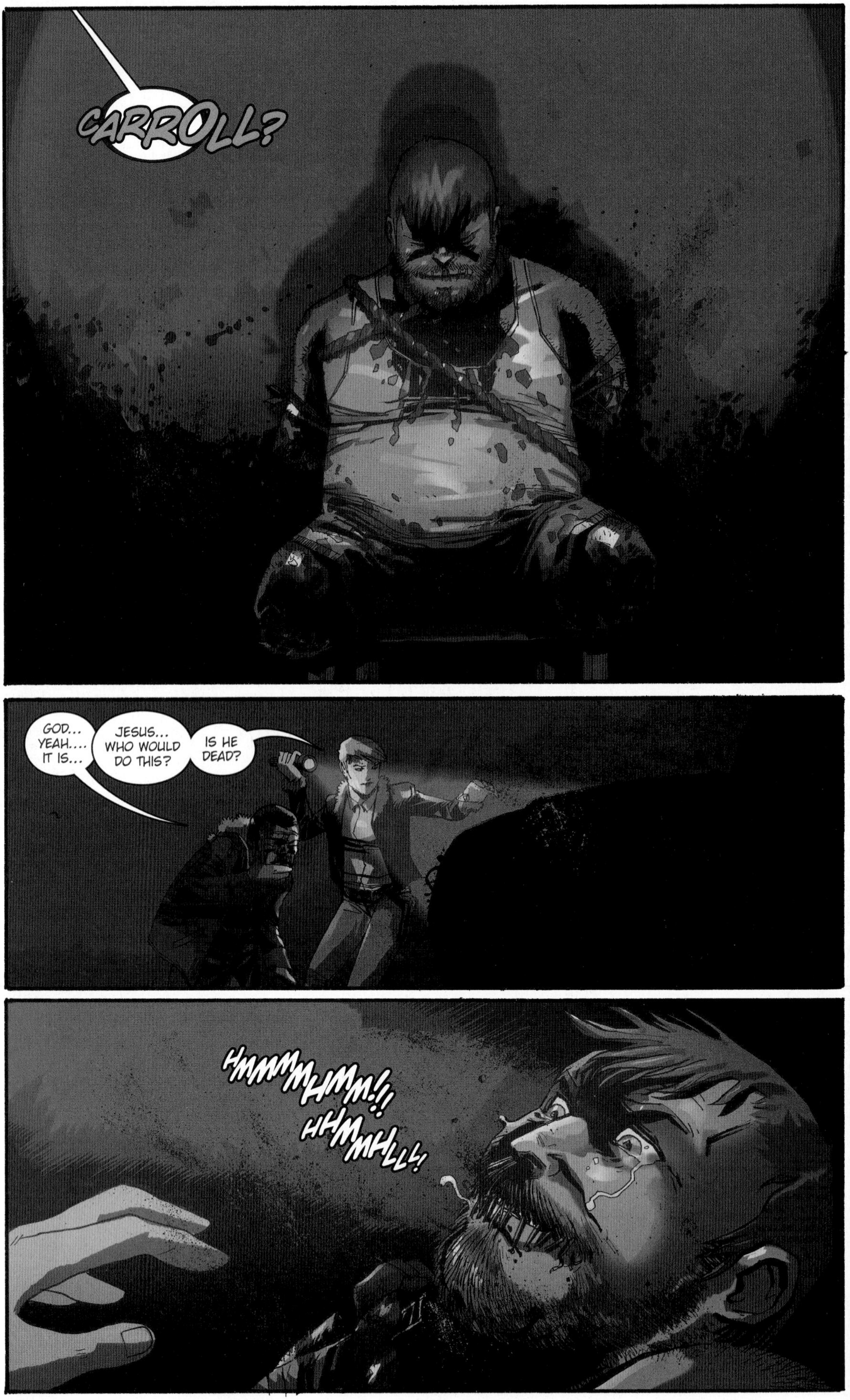
CARROLL?
GOD... YEAH.... IT IS...
JESUS... WHO WOULD DO THIS?
IS HE DEAD?
HMMMMHMM!!!
HHMMHLLL!

# ISSUE FIVE

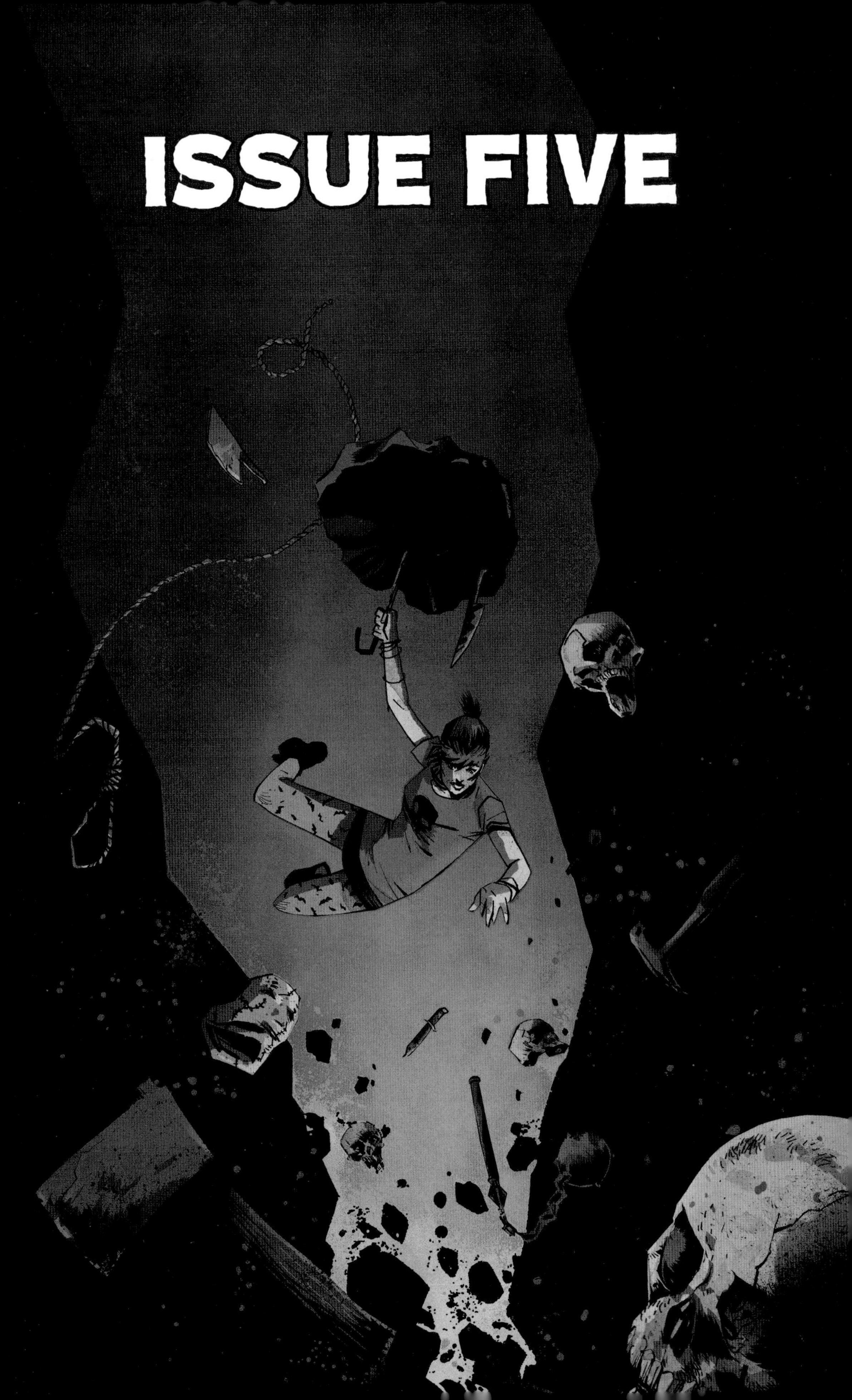

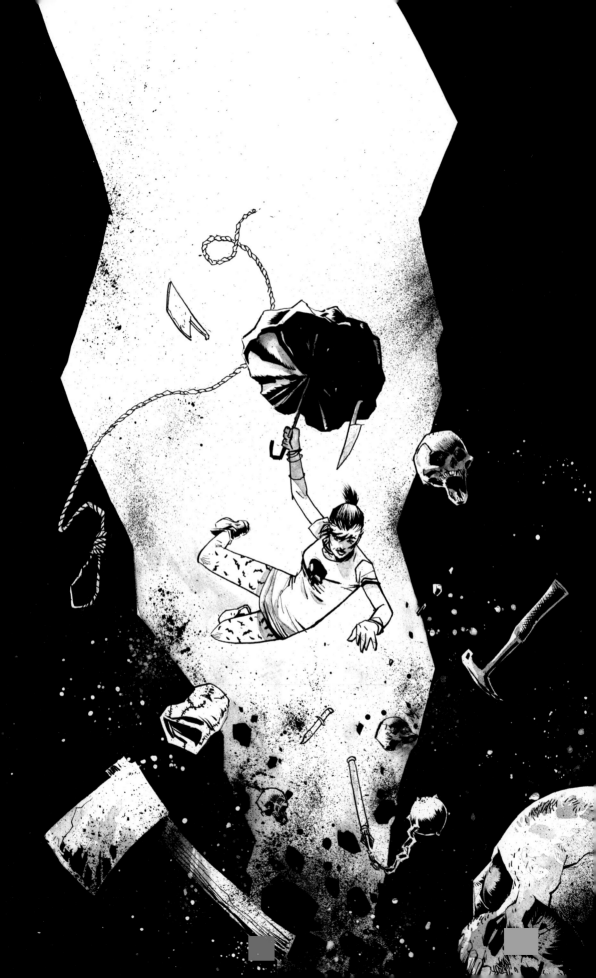

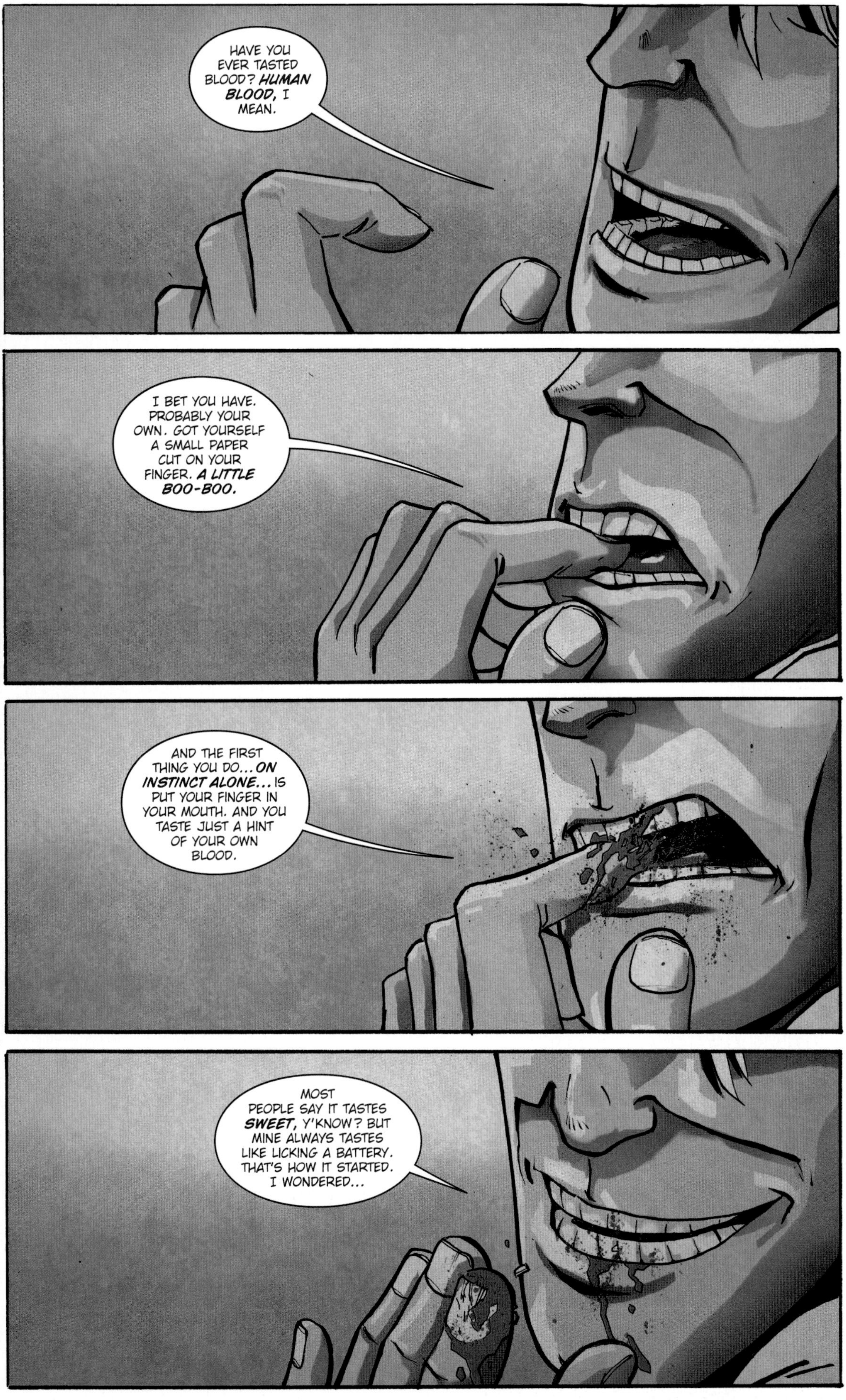
HAVE YOU EVER TASTED BLOOD? HUMAN BLOOD, I MEAN.
I BET YOU HAVE. PROBABLY YOUR OWN. GOT YOURSELF A SMALL PAPER CUT ON YOUR FINGER. A LITTLE BOO-BOO.
AND THE FIRST THING YOU DO... ON INSTINCT ALONE... IS PUT YOUR FINGER IN YOUR MOUTH. AND YOU TASTE JUST A HINT OF YOUR OWN BLOOD.
MOST PEOPLE SAY IT TASTES SWEET, Y'KNOW? BUT MINE ALWAYS TASTES LIKE LICKING A BATTERY. THAT'S HOW IT STARTED. I WONDERED...

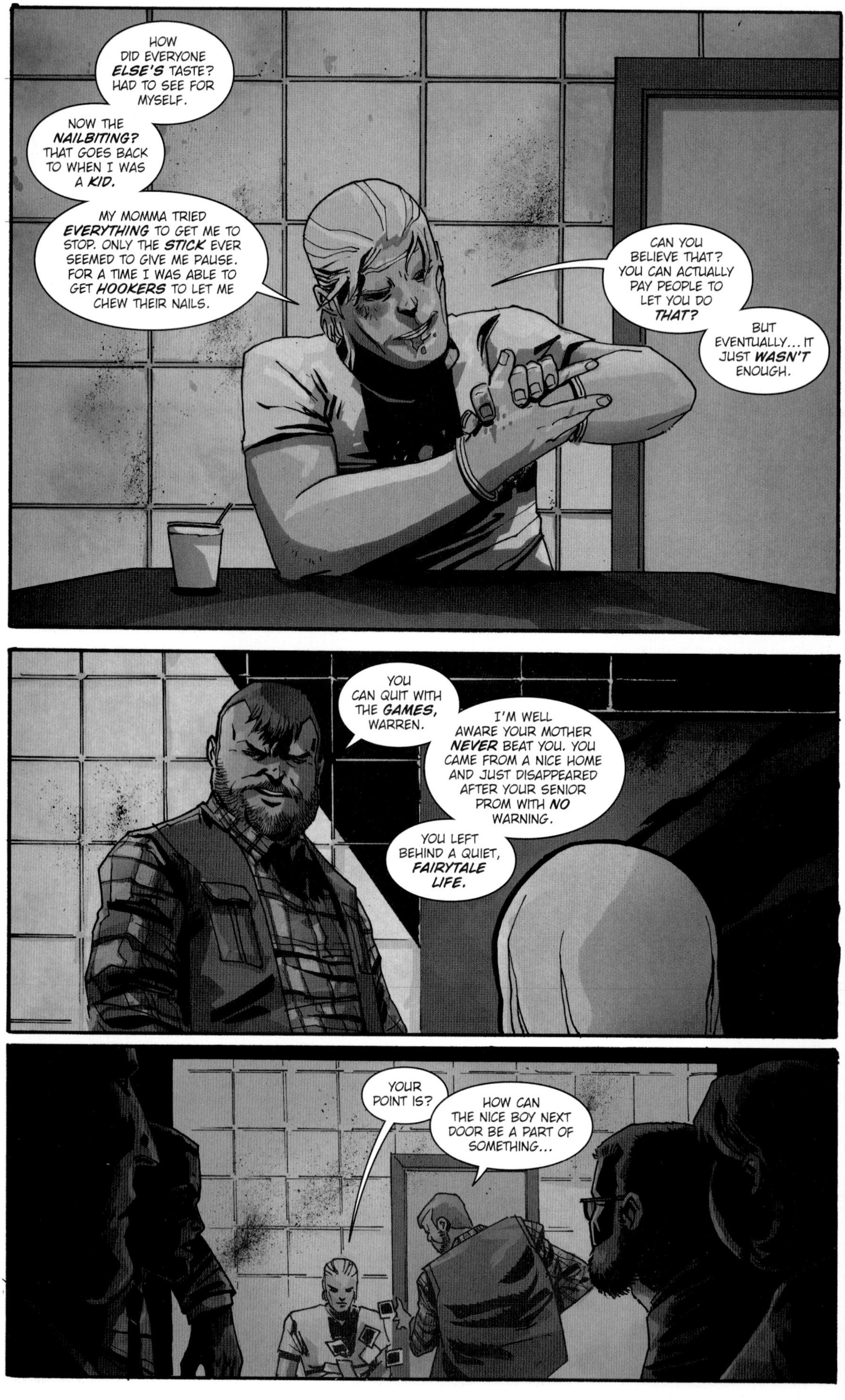
HOW DID EVERYONE ELSE'S TASTE? HAD TO SEE FOR MYSELF.
NOW THE NAILBITING? THAT GOES BACK TO WHEN I WAS A KID.
MY MOMMA TRIED EVERYTHING TO GET ME TO STOP. ONLY THE STICK EVER SEEMED TO GIVE ME PAUSE. FOR A TIME I WAS ABLE TO GET HOOKERS TO LET ME CHEW THEIR NAILS.
CAN YOU BELIEVE THAT? YOU CAN ACTUALLY PAY PEOPLE TO LET YOU DO THAT?
BUT EVENTUALLY... IT JUST WASN'T ENOUGH.
YOU CAN QUIT WITH THE GAMES, WARREN.
I'M WELL AWARE YOUR MOTHER NEVER BEAT YOU. YOU CAME FROM A NICE HOME AND JUST DISAPPEARED AFTER YOUR SENIOR PROM WITH NO WARNING.
YOU LEFT BEHIND A QUIET, FAIRYTALE LIFE.
YOUR POINT IS?
HOW CAN THE NICE BOY NEXT DOOR BE A PART OF SOMETHING...

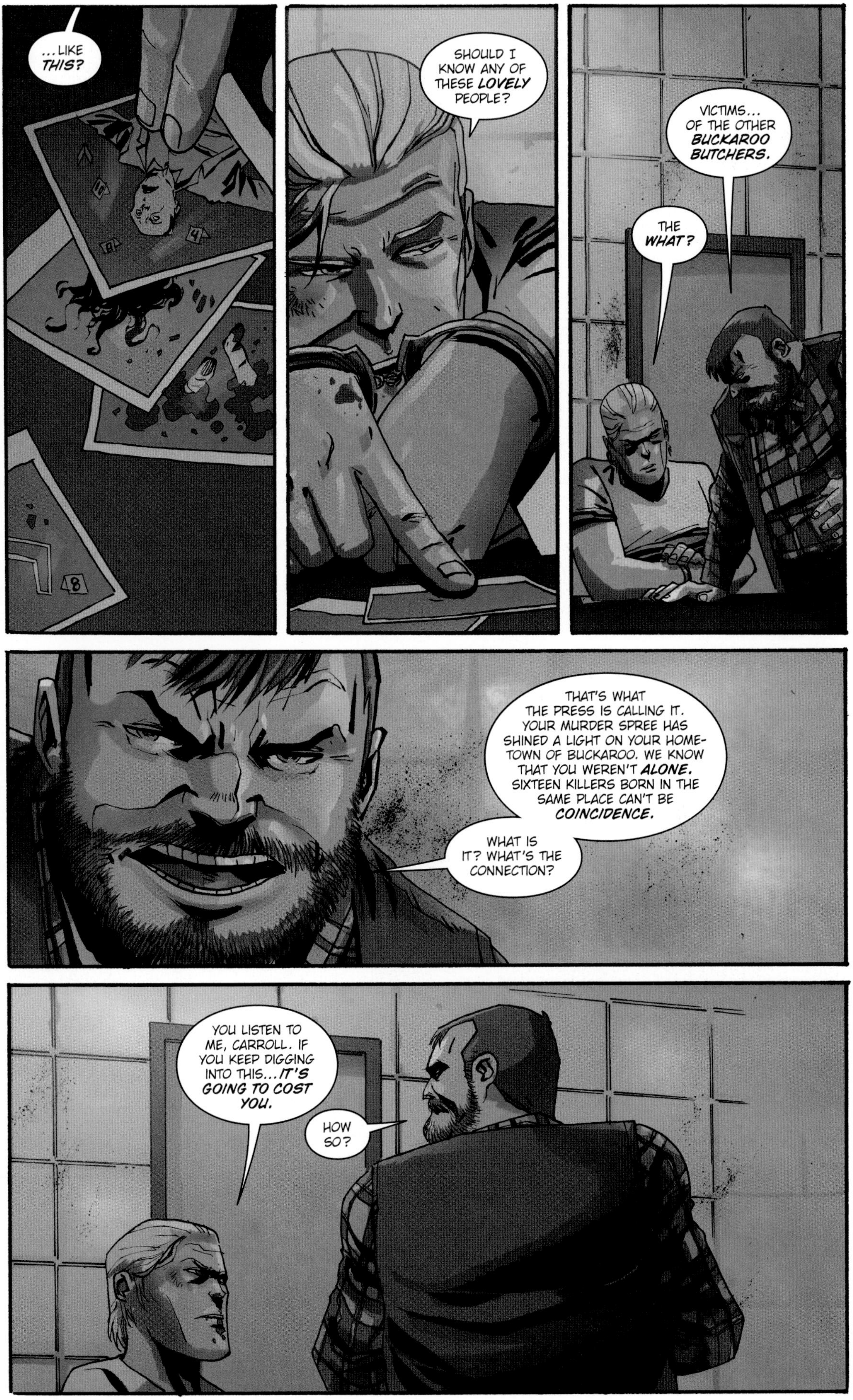
...LIKE THIS?
SHOULD I KNOW ANY OF THESE LOVELY PEOPLE?
VICTIMS... OF THE OTHER BUCKAROO BUTCHERS.
THE WHAT?
THAT'S WHAT THE PRESS IS CALLING IT. YOUR MURDER SPREE HAS SHINED A LIGHT ON YOUR HOME-TOWN OF BUCKAROO. WE KNOW THAT YOU WEREN'T ALONE. SIXTEEN KILLERS BORN IN THE SAME PLACE CAN'T BE COINCIDENCE.
WHAT IS IT? WHAT'S THE CONNECTION?
YOU LISTEN TO ME, CARROLL. IF YOU KEEP DIGGING INTO THIS... IT'S GOING TO COST YOU.
HOW SO?

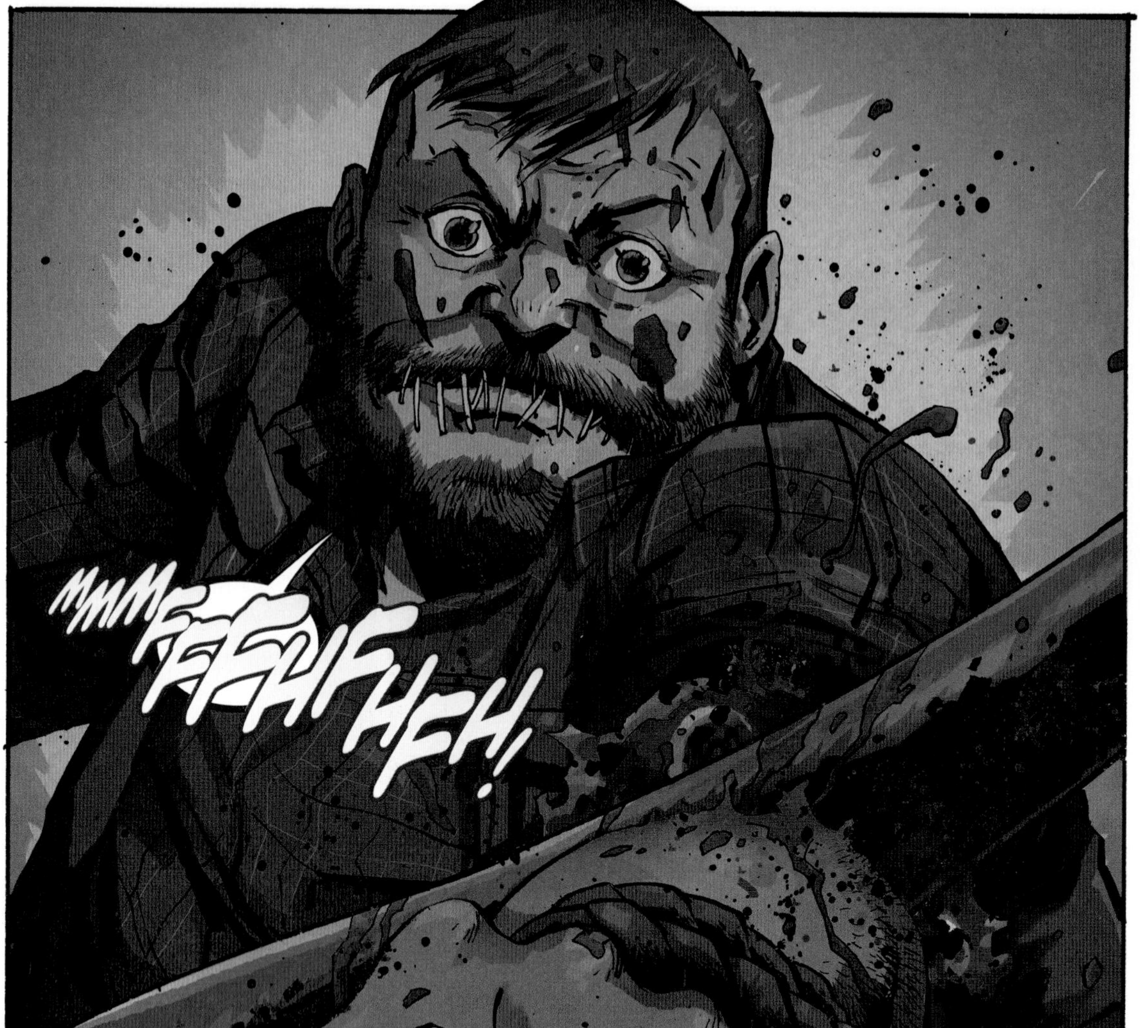
MMMFFFUFHFH!

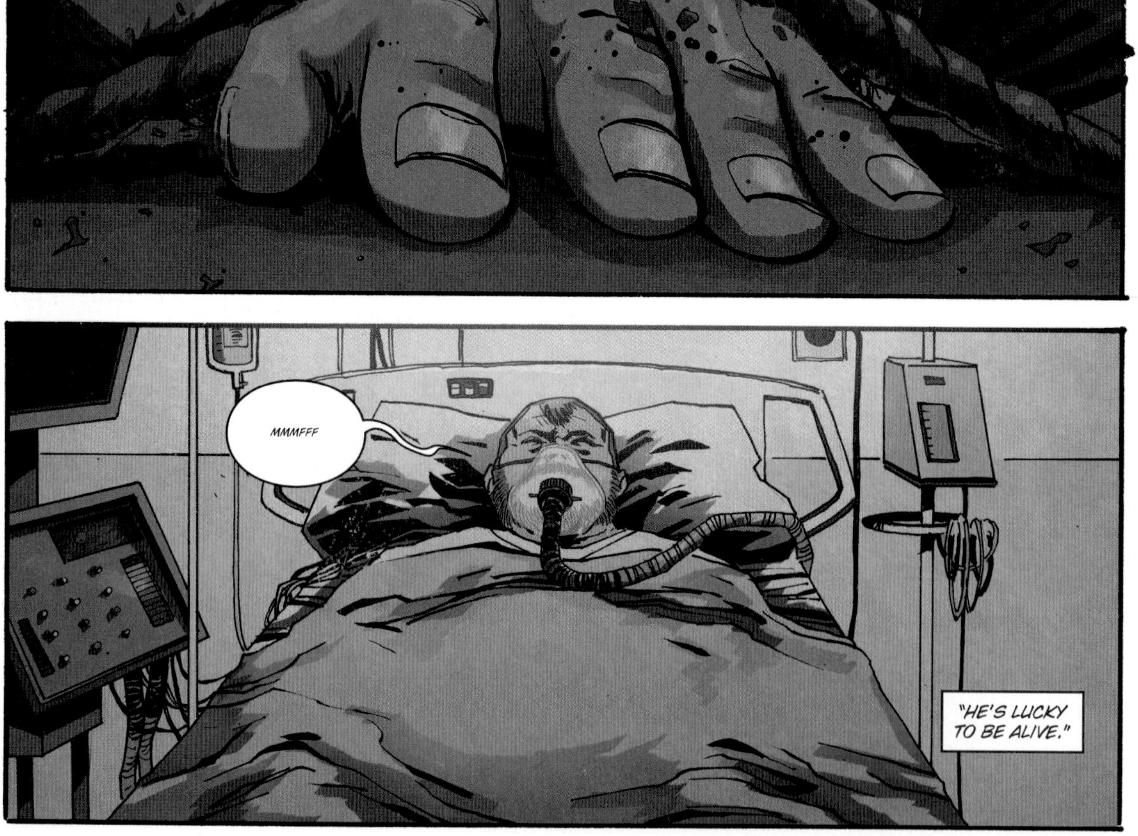
MMMFFF
"HE'S LUCKY TO BE ALIVE."

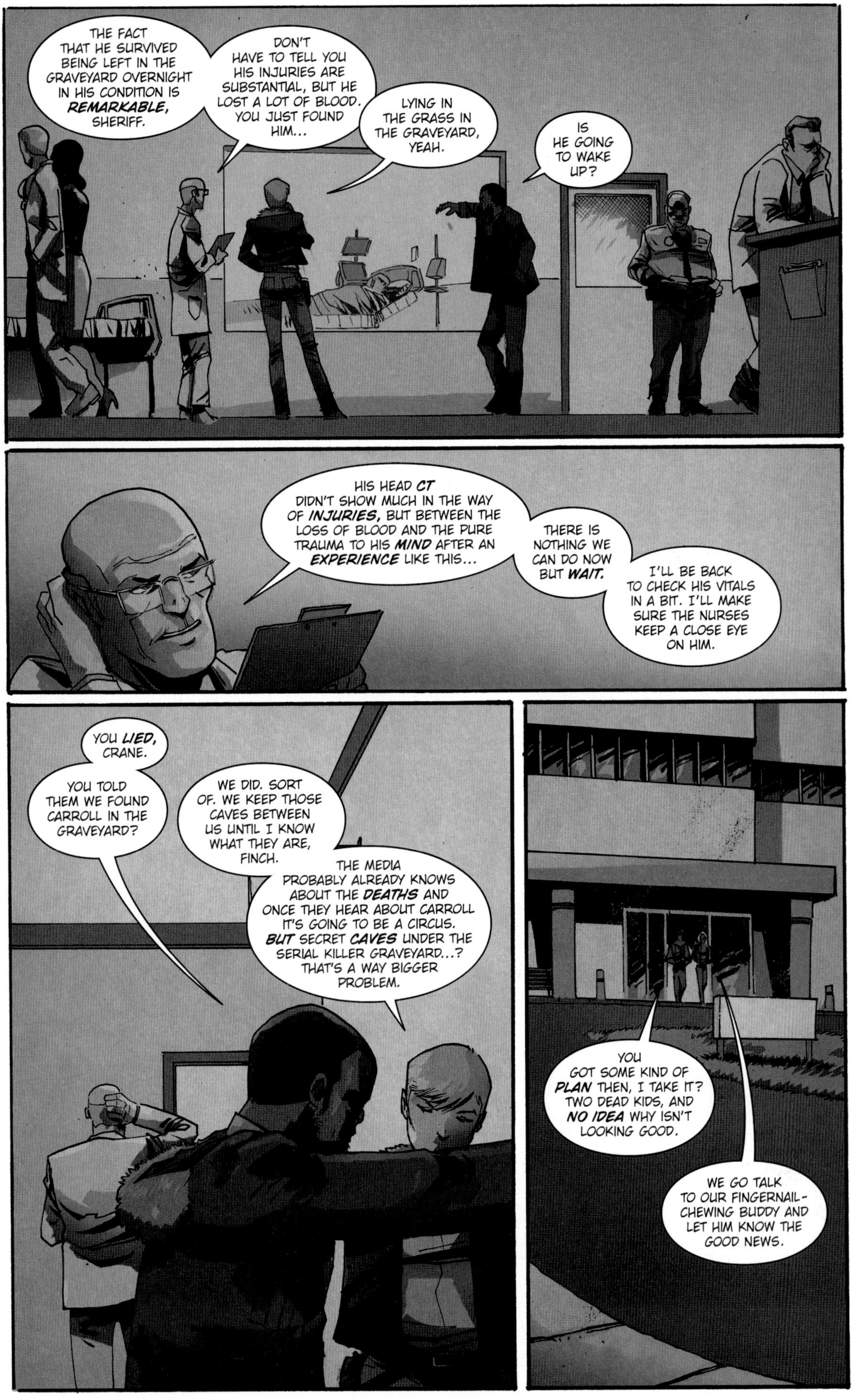
THE FACT THAT HE SURVIVED BEING LEFT IN THE GRAVEYARD OVERNIGHT IN HIS CONDITION IS REMARKABLE, SHERIFF.
DON'T HAVE TO TELL YOU HIS INJURIES ARE SUBSTANTIAL, BUT HE LOST A LOT OF BLOOD. YOU JUST FOUND HIM...
LYING IN THE GRASS IN THE GRAVEYARD, YEAH.
IS HE GOING TO WAKE UP?
HIS HEAD CT DIDN'T SHOW MUCH IN THE WAY OF INJURIES, BUT BETWEEN THE LOSS OF BLOOD AND THE PURE TRAUMA TO HIS MIND AFTER AN EXPERIENCE LIKE THIS...
THERE IS NOTHING WE CAN DO NOW BUT WAIT.
I'LL BE BACK TO CHECK HIS VITALS IN A BIT. I'LL MAKE SURE THE NURSES KEEP A CLOSE EYE ON HIM.
YOU LIED, CRANE.
YOU TOLD THEM WE FOUND CARROLL IN THE GRAVEYARD?
WE DID. SORT OF. WE KEEP THOSE CAVES BETWEEN US UNTIL I KNOW WHAT THEY ARE, FINCH.
THE MEDIA PROBABLY ALREADY KNOWS ABOUT THE DEATHS AND ONCE THEY HEAR ABOUT CARROLL IT'S GOING TO BE A CIRCUS. BUT SECRET CAVES UNDER THE SERIAL KILLER GRAVEYARD...? THAT'S A WAY BIGGER PROBLEM.
YOU GOT SOME KIND OF PLAN THEN, I TAKE IT? TWO DEAD KIDS, AND NO IDEA WHY ISN'T LOOKING GOOD.
WE GO TALK TO OUR FINGERNAIL-CHEWING BUDDY AND LET HIM KNOW THE GOOD NEWS.

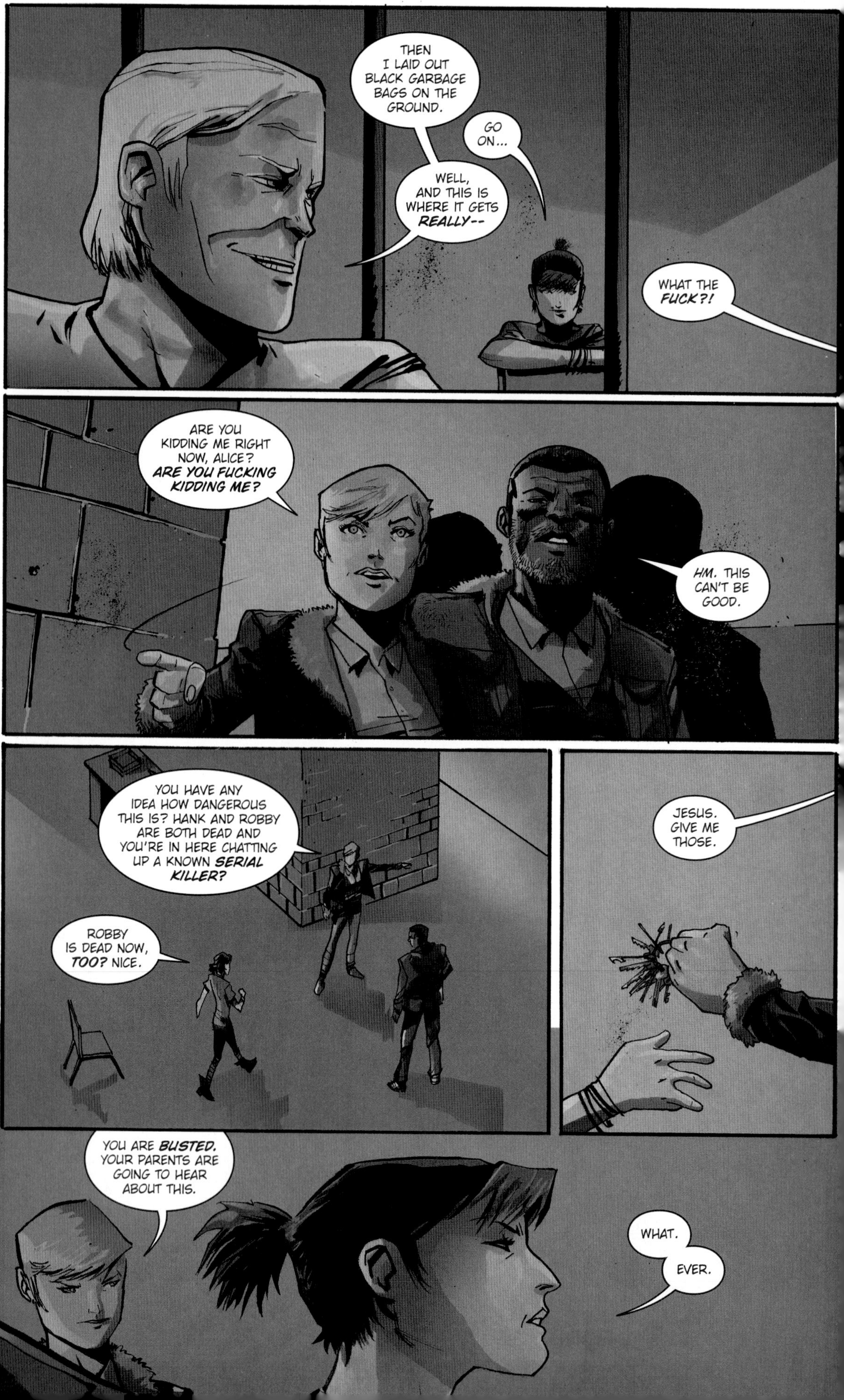
THEN I LAID OUT BLACK GARBAGE BAGS ON THE GROUND.
GO ON...
WELL, AND THIS IS WHERE IT GETS *REALLY*--
WHAT THE *FUCK?!*
ARE YOU KIDDING ME RIGHT NOW, ALICE? **ARE YOU FUCKING KIDDING ME?**
*HM.* THIS CAN'T BE GOOD.
YOU HAVE ANY IDEA HOW DANGEROUS THIS IS? HANK AND ROBBY ARE BOTH DEAD AND YOU'RE IN HERE CHATTING UP A KNOWN *SERIAL KILLER?*
ROBBY IS DEAD NOW, *TOO?* NICE.
JESUS. GIVE ME THOSE.
YOU ARE *BUSTED.* YOUR PARENTS ARE GOING TO HEAR ABOUT THIS.
WHAT.
EVER.

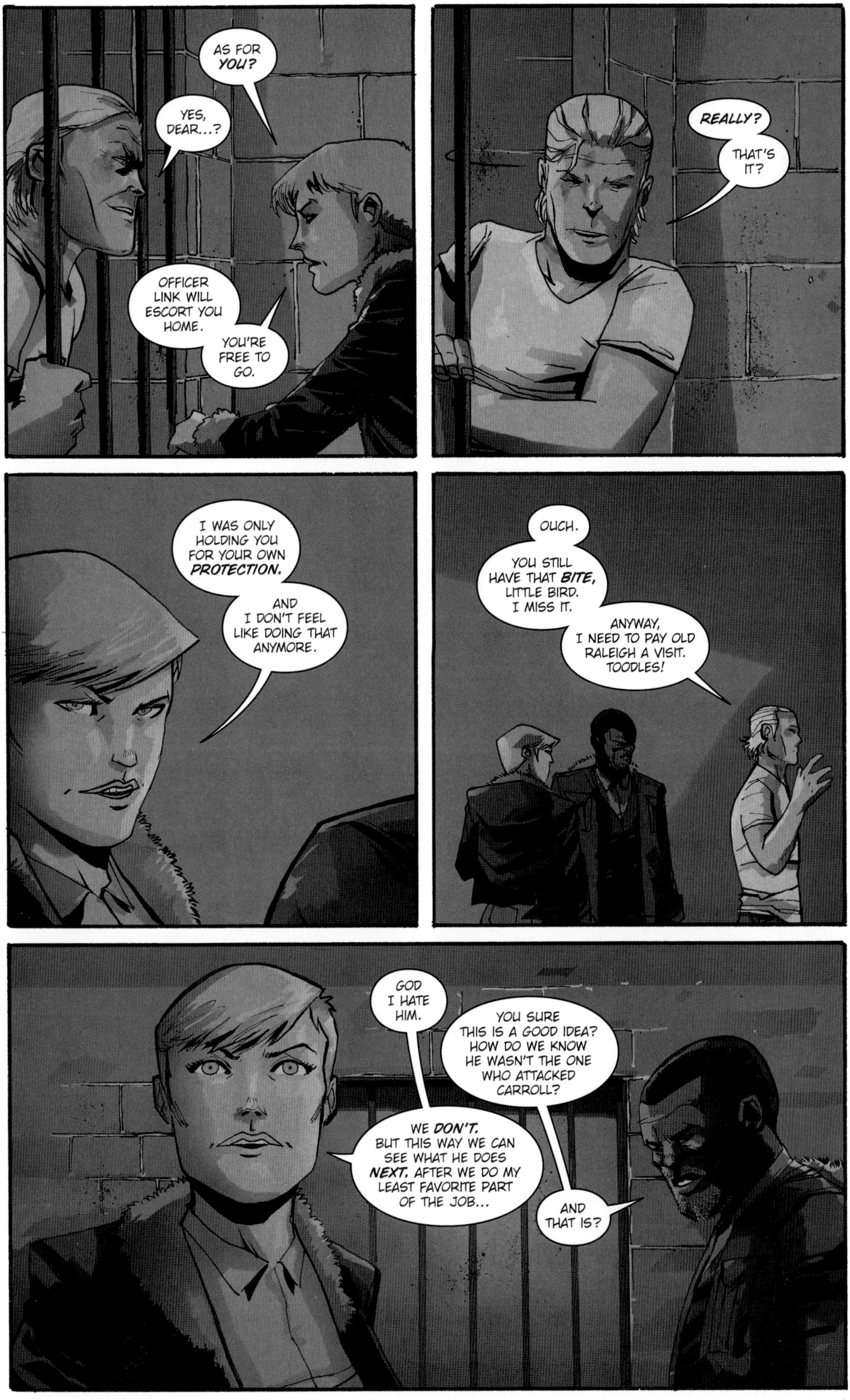
AS FOR YOU?
YES, DEAR...?
OFFICER LINK WILL ESCORT YOU HOME.
YOU'RE FREE TO GO.
REALLY?
THAT'S IT?
I WAS ONLY HOLDING YOU FOR YOUR OWN PROTECTION.
AND I DON'T FEEL LIKE DOING THAT ANYMORE.
OUCH.
YOU STILL HAVE THAT BITE, LITTLE BIRD. I MISS IT.
ANYWAY, I NEED TO PAY OLD RALEIGH A VISIT. TOODLES!
GOD I HATE HIM.
YOU SURE THIS IS A GOOD IDEA? HOW DO WE KNOW HE WASN'T THE ONE WHO ATTACKED CARROLL?
WE DON'T. BUT THIS WAY WE CAN SEE WHAT HE DOES NEXT. AFTER WE DO MY LEAST FAVORITE PART OF THE JOB...
AND THAT IS?

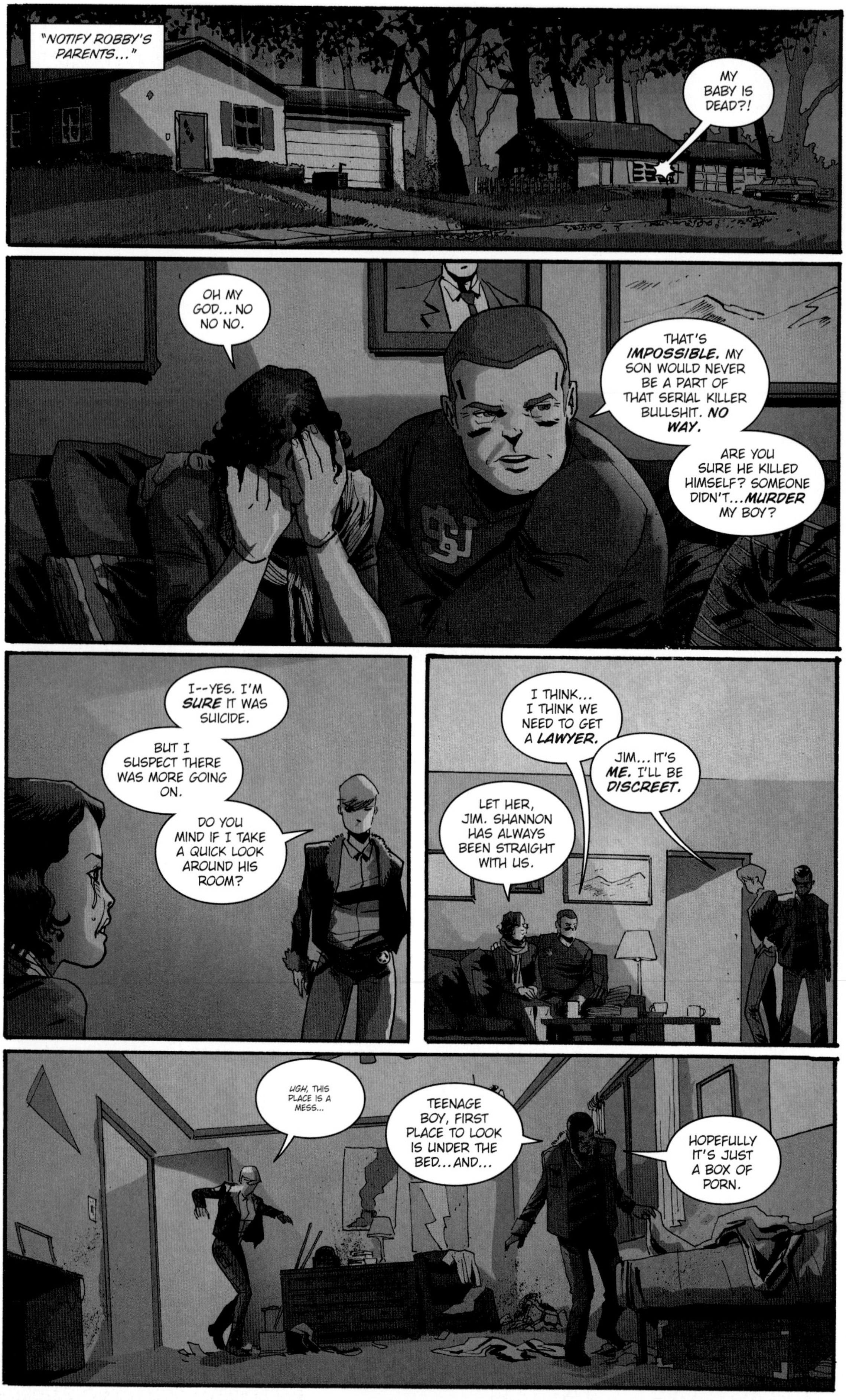
"NOTIFY ROBBY'S PARENTS..."
MY BABY IS DEAD?!
OH MY GOD... NO NO NO.
THAT'S IMPOSSIBLE. MY SON WOULD NEVER BE A PART OF THAT SERIAL KILLER BULLSHIT. NO WAY.
ARE YOU SURE HE KILLED HIMSELF? SOMEONE DIDN'T... MURDER MY BOY?
I--YES. I'M SURE IT WAS SUICIDE.
BUT I SUSPECT THERE WAS MORE GOING ON.
DO YOU MIND IF I TAKE A QUICK LOOK AROUND HIS ROOM?
I THINK... I THINK WE NEED TO GET A LAWYER.
JIM... IT'S ME. I'LL BE DISCREET.
LET HER, JIM. SHANNON HAS ALWAYS BEEN STRAIGHT WITH US.
UGH, THIS PLACE IS A MESS...
TEENAGE BOY, FIRST PLACE TO LOOK IS UNDER THE BED... AND...
HOPEFULLY IT'S JUST A BOX OF PORN.

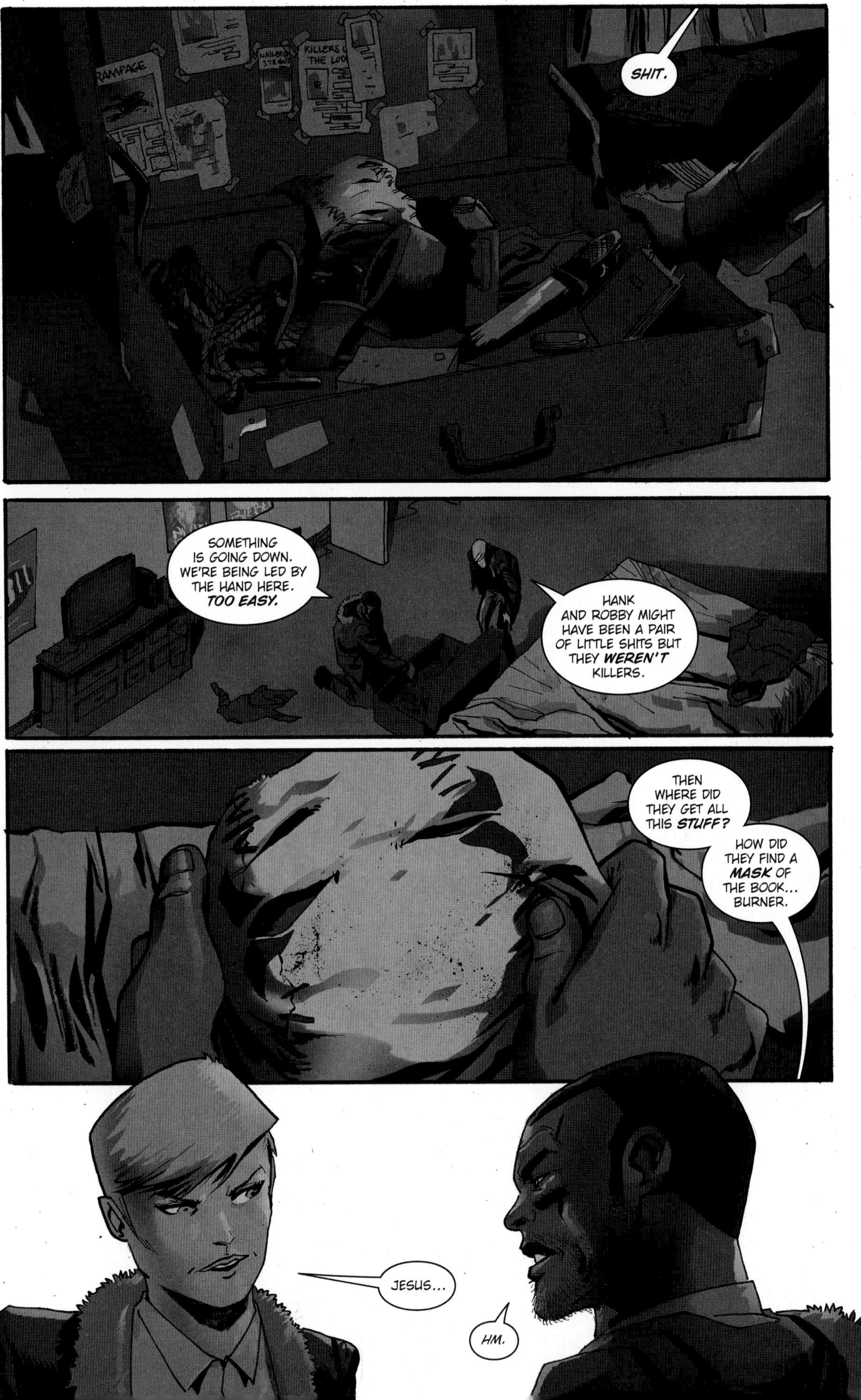
RAMPAGE
SHIT.
SOMETHING IS GOING DOWN. WE'RE BEING LED BY THE HAND HERE. TOO EASY.
HANK AND ROBBY MIGHT HAVE BEEN A PAIR OF LITTLE SHITS BUT THEY WEREN'T KILLERS.
THEN WHERE DID THEY GET ALL THIS STUFF?
HOW DID THEY FIND A MASK OF THE BOOK... BURNER.
JESUS...
HM.

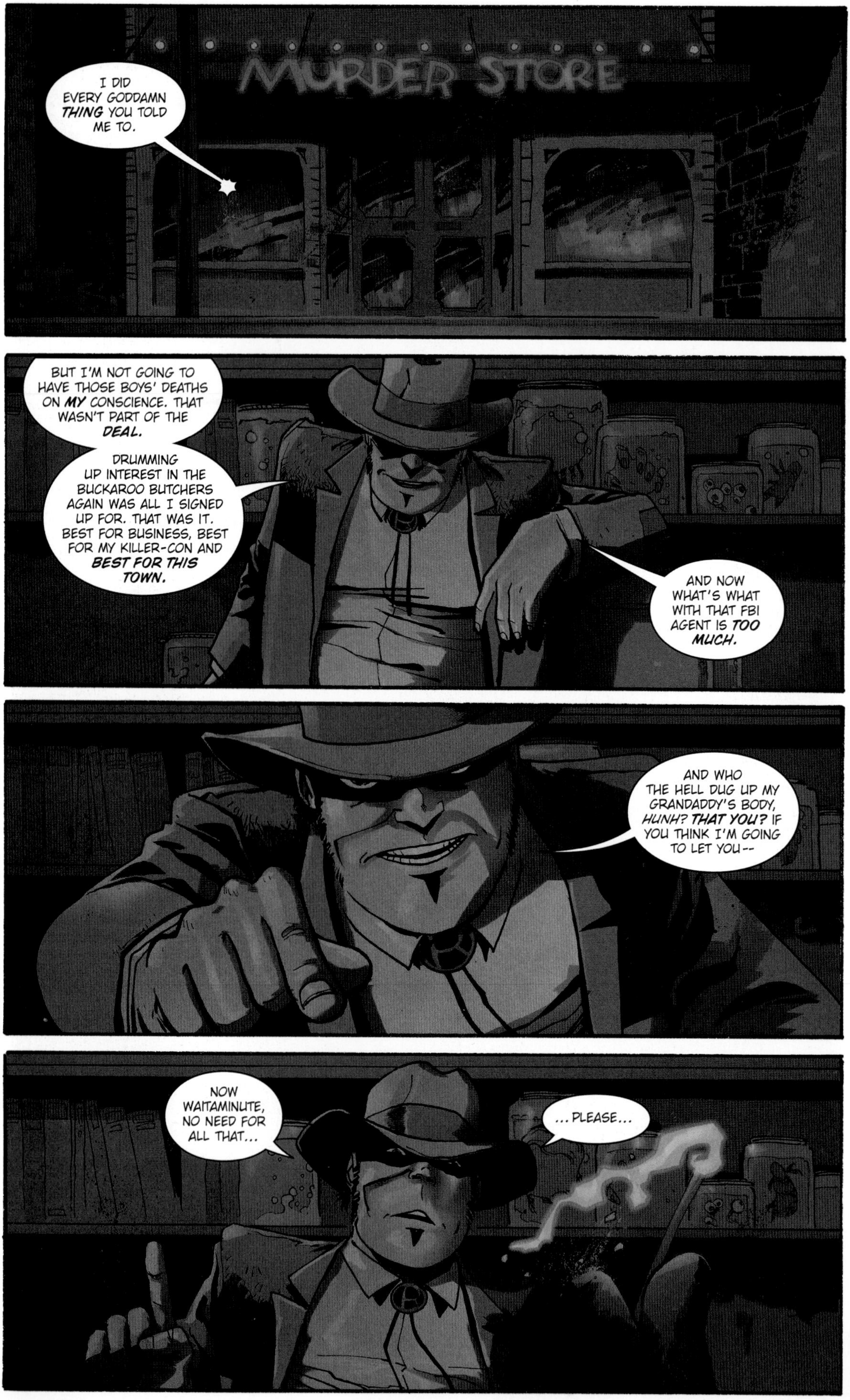
MURDER STORE
I DID EVERY GODDAMN THING YOU TOLD ME TO.
BUT I'M NOT GOING TO HAVE THOSE BOYS' DEATHS ON MY CONSCIENCE. THAT WASN'T PART OF THE DEAL.
DRUMMING UP INTEREST IN THE BUCKAROO BUTCHERS AGAIN WAS ALL I SIGNED UP FOR. THAT WAS IT. BEST FOR BUSINESS, BEST FOR MY KILLER-CON AND BEST FOR THIS TOWN.
AND NOW WHAT'S WHAT WITH THAT FBI AGENT IS TOO MUCH.
AND WHO THE HELL DUG UP MY GRANDADDY'S BODY, HUNH? THAT YOU? IF YOU THINK I'M GOING TO LET YOU--
NOW WAITAMINUTE, NO NEED FOR ALL THAT...
...PLEASE...

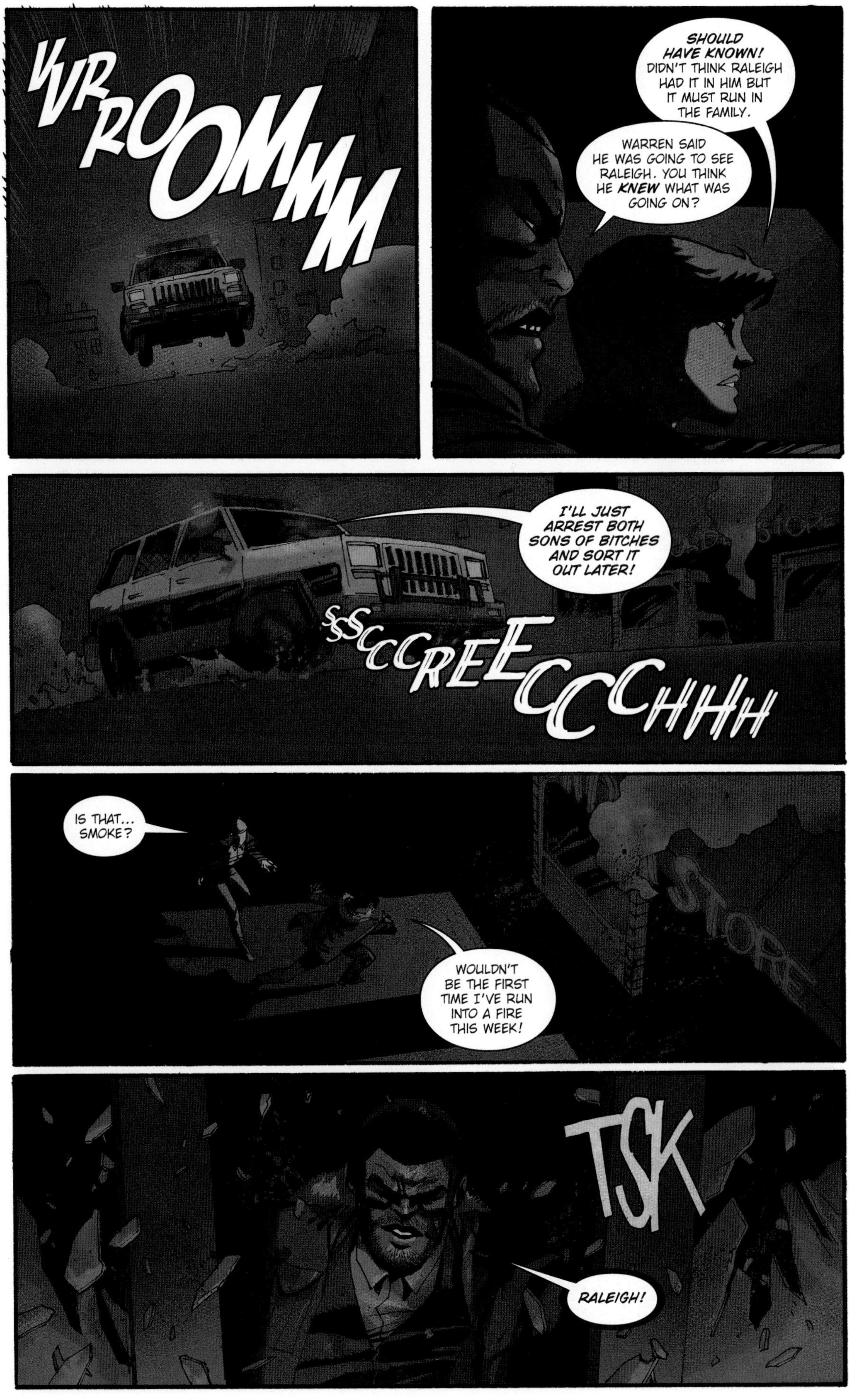
VVRROOMMMM
SHOULD HAVE KNOWN! DIDN'T THINK RALEIGH HAD IT IN HIM BUT IT MUST RUN IN THE FAMILY.
WARREN SAID HE WAS GOING TO SEE RALEIGH. YOU THINK HE KNEW WHAT WAS GOING ON?
I'LL JUST ARREST BOTH SONS OF BITCHES AND SORT IT OUT LATER!
SSSCCCREEECCCHHH
IS THAT... SMOKE?
STORE
WOULDN'T BE THE FIRST TIME I'VE RUN INTO A FIRE THIS WEEK!
TSK
RALEIGH!

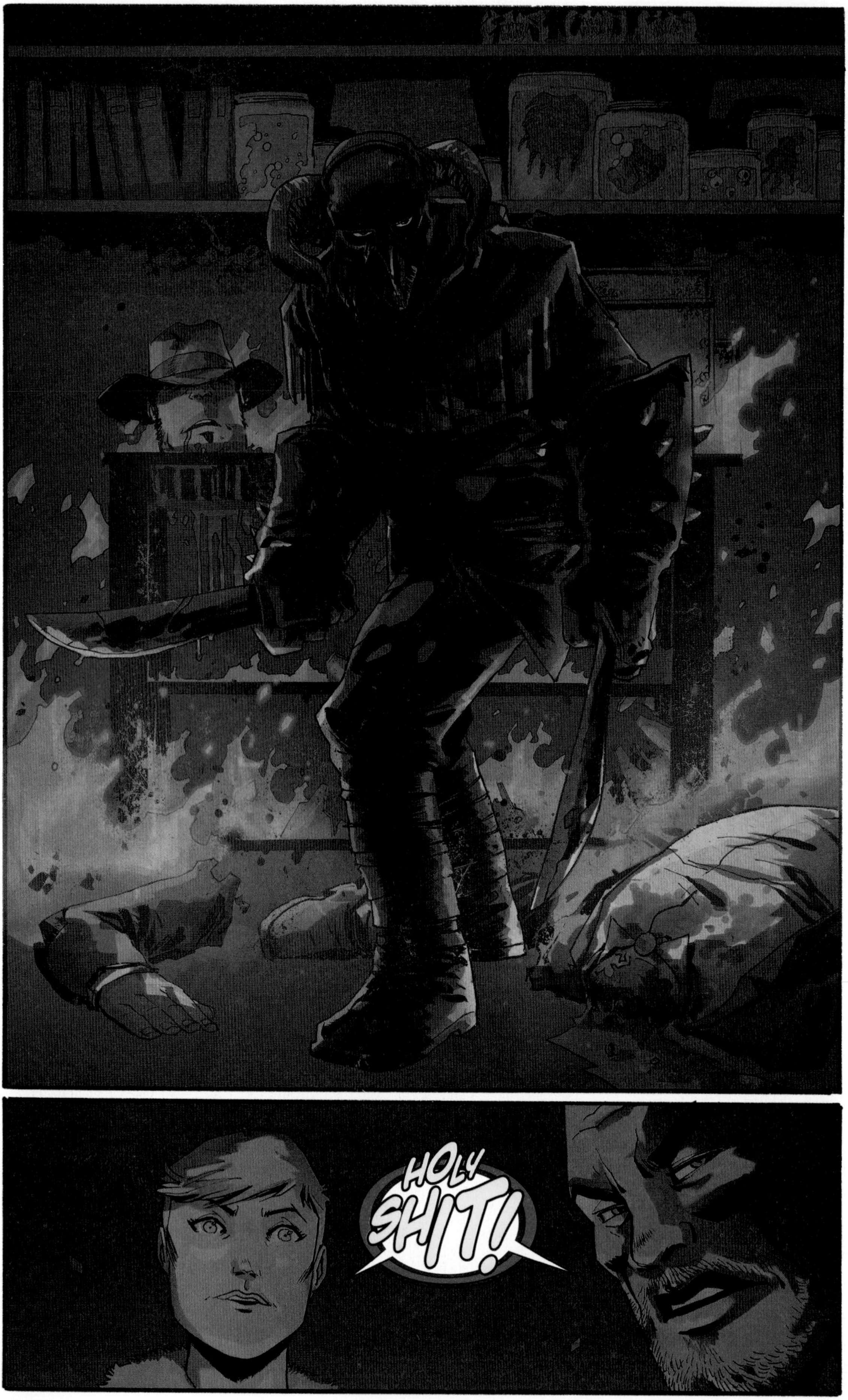
HOLY SHIT!

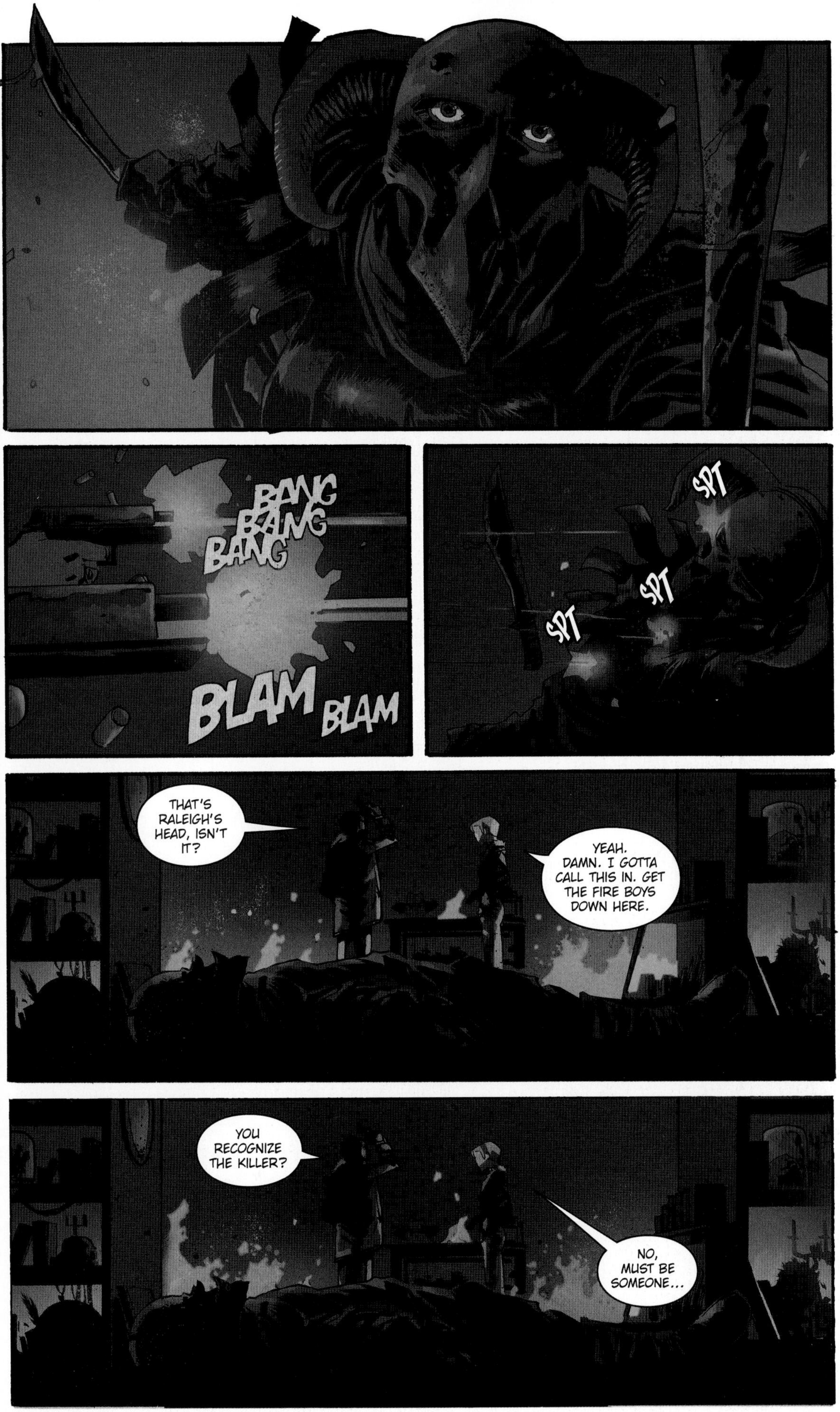
BANG
BANG
BANG
BLAM
BLAM
SPT
SPT
SPT
THAT'S RALEIGH'S HEAD, ISN'T IT?
YEAH. DAMN. I GOTTA CALL THIS IN. GET THE FIRE BOYS DOWN HERE.
YOU RECOGNIZE THE KILLER?
NO, MUST BE SOMEONE...

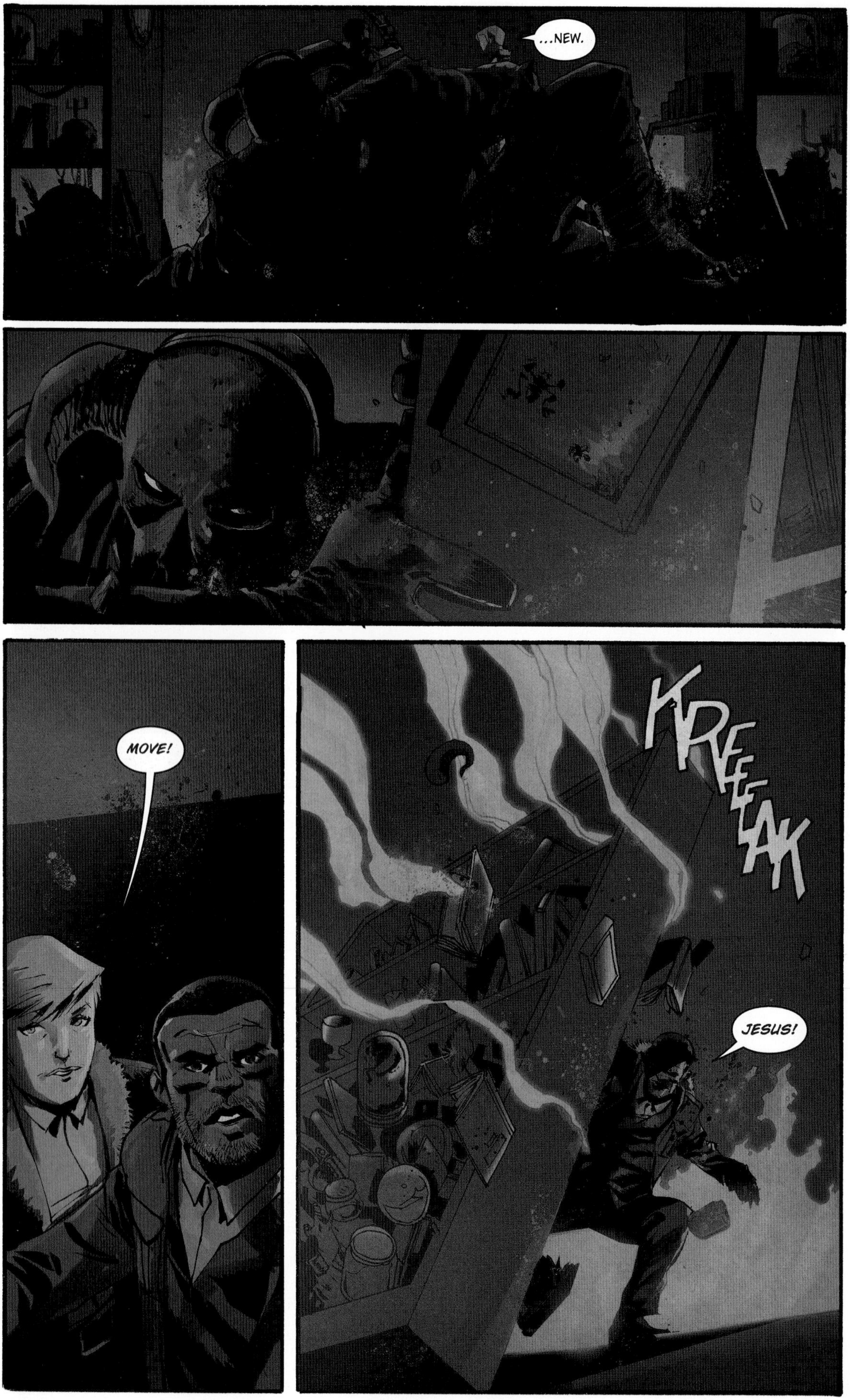
...NEW.
MOVE!
KREEEAK
JESUS!

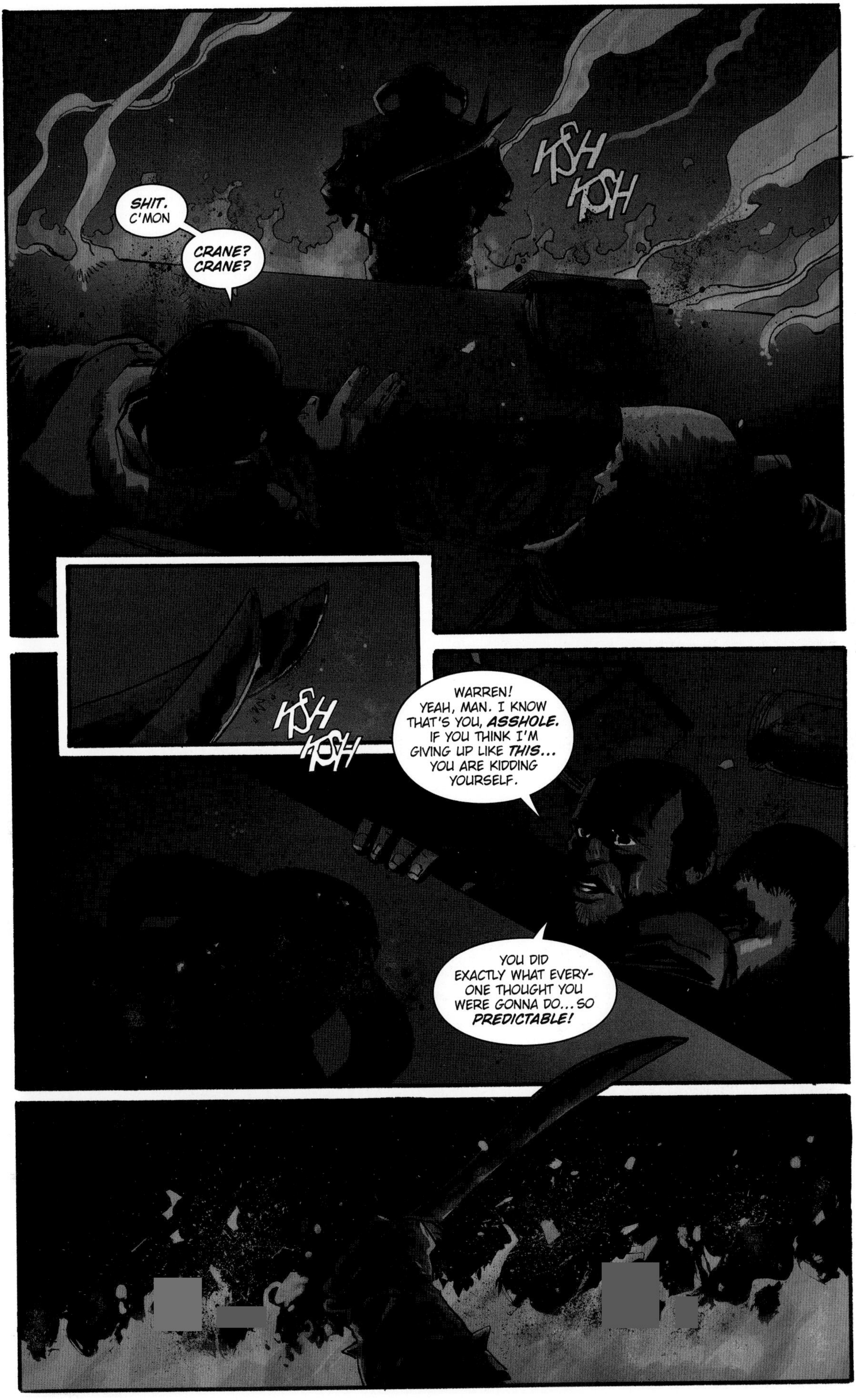
SHIT. C'MON
CRANE? CRANE?
KSH KSH
KSH KSH
WARREN! YEAH, MAN. I KNOW THAT'S YOU, ASSHOLE. IF YOU THINK I'M GIVING UP LIKE THIS... YOU ARE KIDDING YOURSELF.
YOU DID EXACTLY WHAT EVERY-ONE THOUGHT YOU WERE GONNA DO... SO PREDICTABLE!

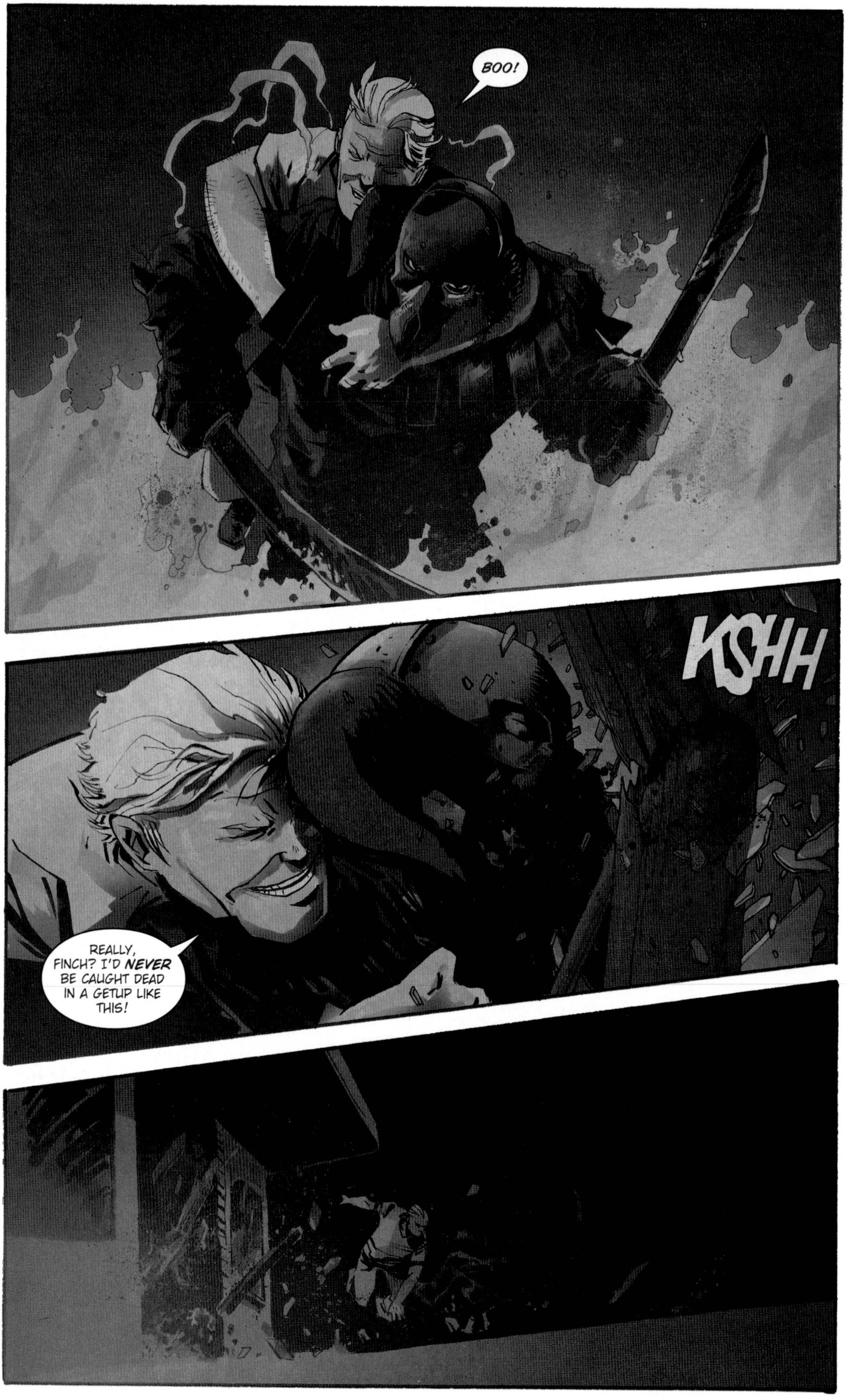
BOO!
KSHH
REALLY, FINCH? I'D NEVER BE CAUGHT DEAD IN A GETUP LIKE THIS!

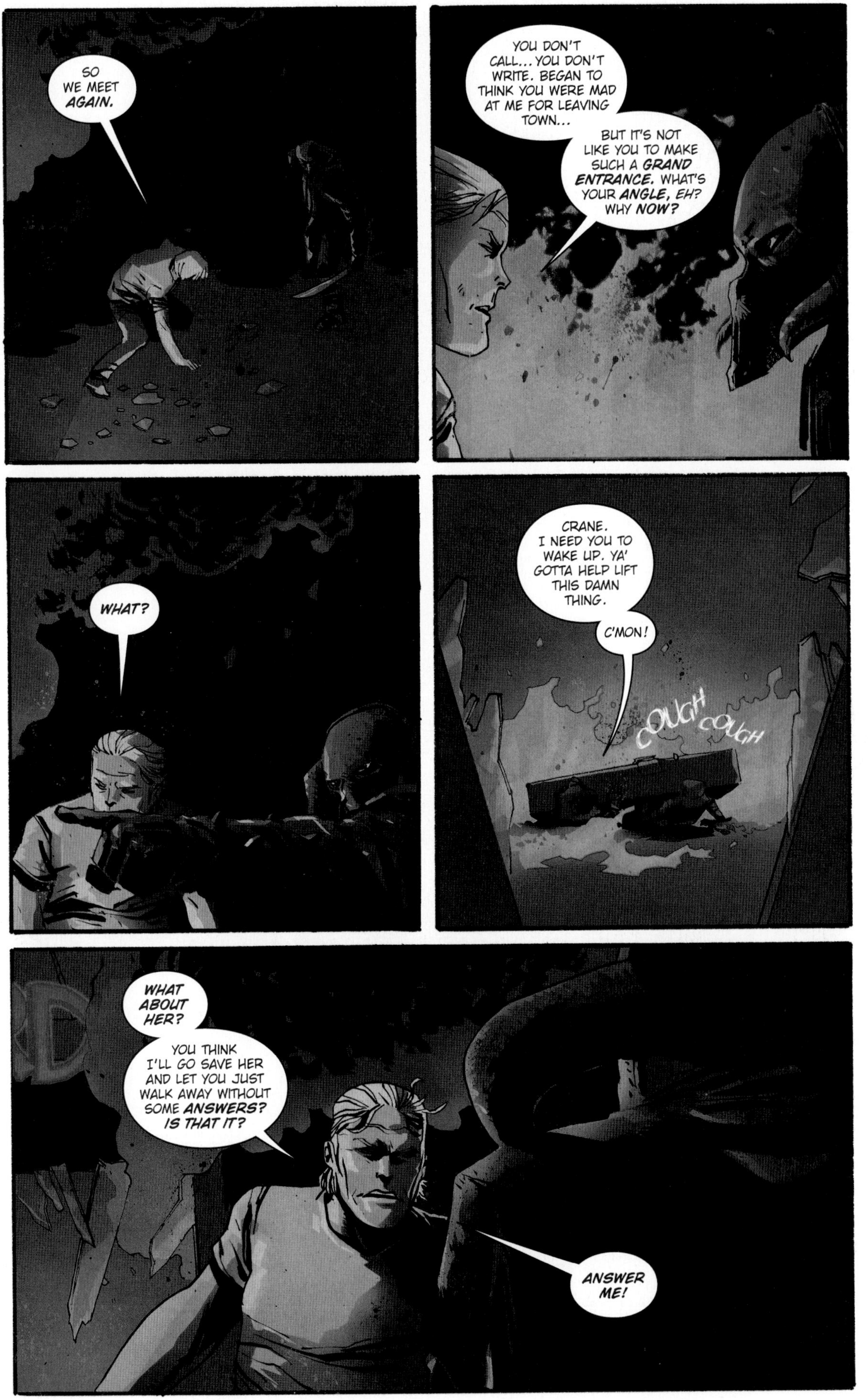
SO WE MEET **AGAIN.**
YOU DON'T CALL... YOU DON'T WRITE. BEGAN TO THINK YOU WERE MAD AT ME FOR LEAVING TOWN...
BUT IT'S NOT LIKE YOU TO MAKE SUCH A **GRAND ENTRANCE.** WHAT'S YOUR **ANGLE,** EH? WHY **NOW?**
**WHAT?**
CRANE. I NEED YOU TO WAKE UP. YA' GOTTA HELP LIFT THIS DAMN THING.
C'MON!
COUGH COUGH
**WHAT ABOUT HER?**
YOU THINK I'LL GO SAVE HER AND LET YOU JUST WALK AWAY WITHOUT SOME **ANSWERS? IS THAT IT?**
**ANSWER ME!**

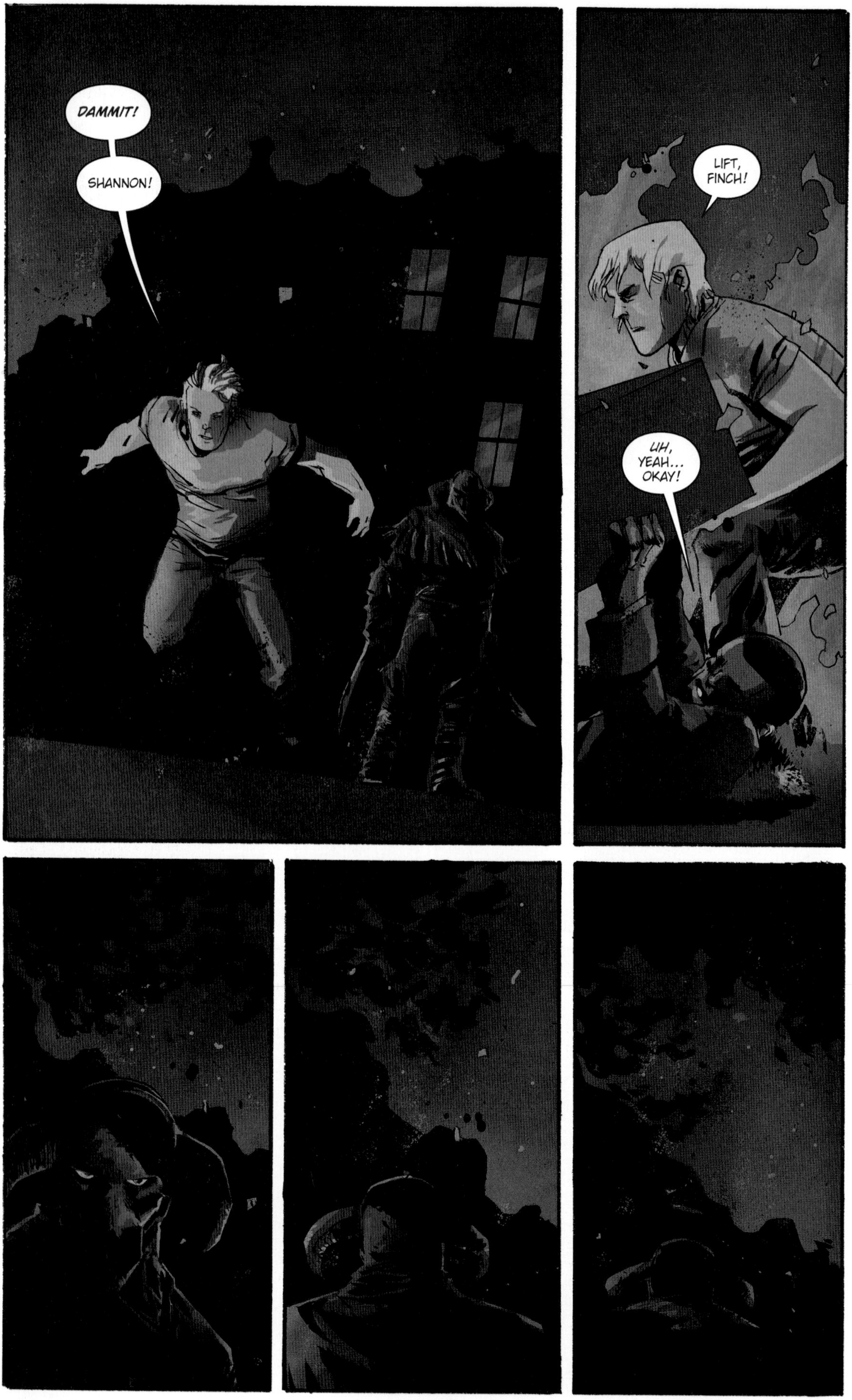
DAMMIT!
SHANNON!
LIFT, FINCH!
UH, YEAH... OKAY!

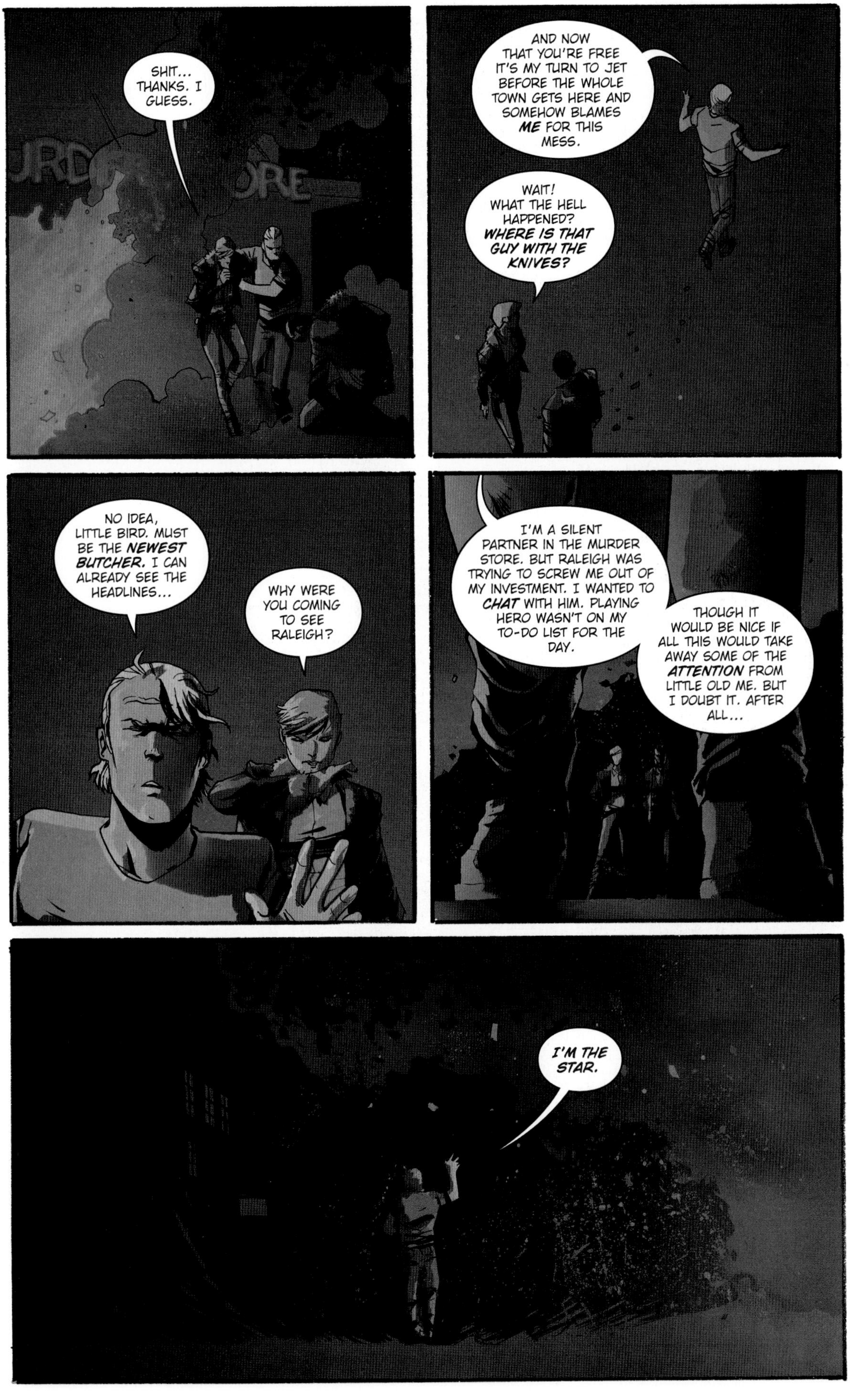
SHIT... THANKS. I GUESS.
AND NOW THAT YOU'RE FREE IT'S MY TURN TO JET BEFORE THE WHOLE TOWN GETS HERE AND SOMEHOW BLAMES ME FOR THIS MESS.
WAIT! WHAT THE HELL HAPPENED? WHERE IS THAT GUY WITH THE KNIVES?
NO IDEA, LITTLE BIRD. MUST BE THE NEWEST BUTCHER. I CAN ALREADY SEE THE HEADLINES...
WHY WERE YOU COMING TO SEE RALEIGH?
I'M A SILENT PARTNER IN THE MURDER STORE. BUT RALEIGH WAS TRYING TO SCREW ME OUT OF MY INVESTMENT. I WANTED TO CHAT WITH HIM. PLAYING HERO WASN'T ON MY TO-DO LIST FOR THE DAY.
THOUGH IT WOULD BE NICE IF ALL THIS WOULD TAKE AWAY SOME OF THE ATTENTION FROM LITTLE OLD ME. BUT I DOUBT IT. AFTER ALL...
I'M THE STAR.

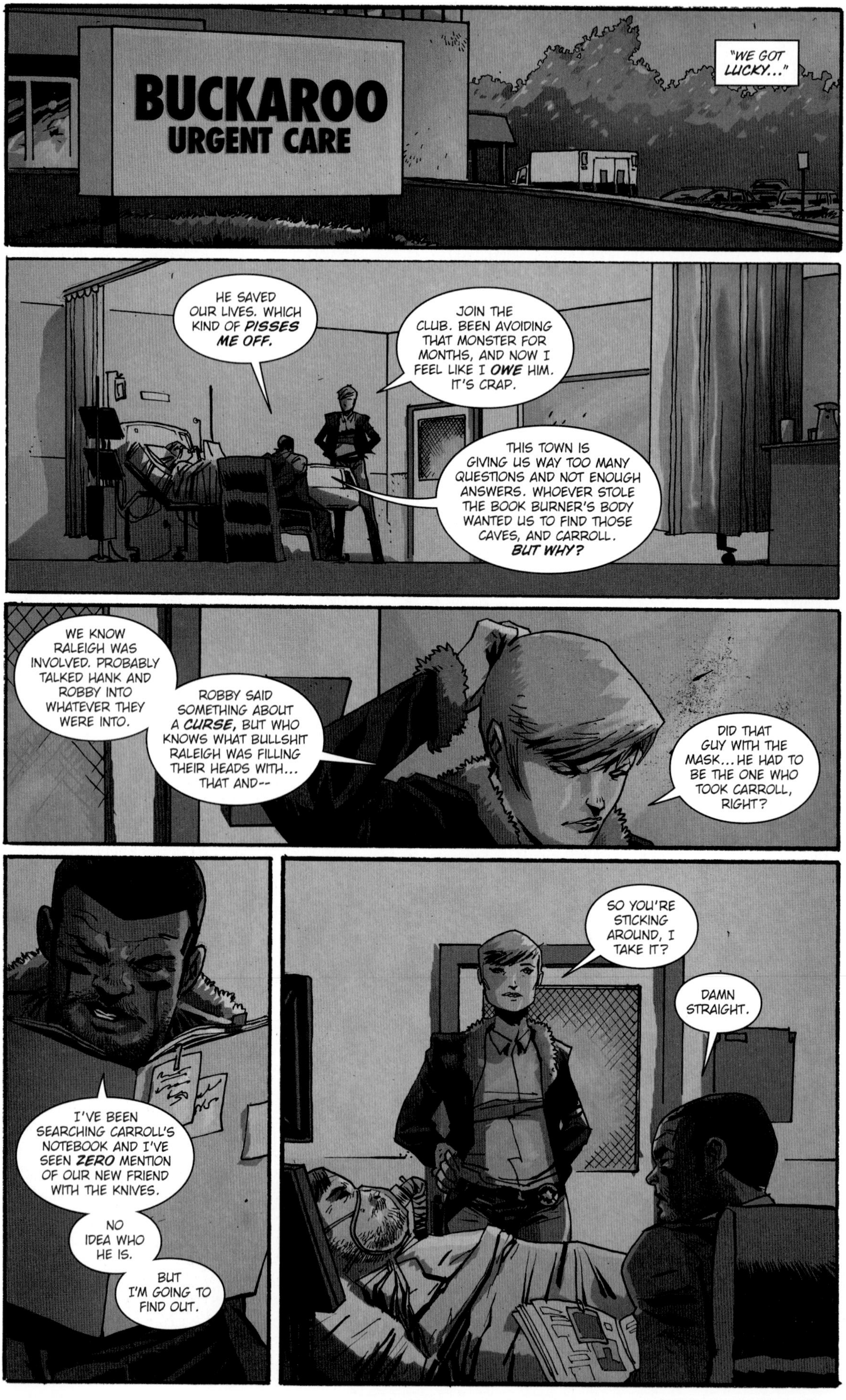
BUCKAROO URGENT CARE
"WE GOT LUCKY..."
HE SAVED OUR LIVES. WHICH KIND OF PISSES ME OFF.
JOIN THE CLUB. BEEN AVOIDING THAT MONSTER FOR MONTHS, AND NOW I FEEL LIKE I OWE HIM. IT'S CRAP.
THIS TOWN IS GIVING US WAY TOO MANY QUESTIONS AND NOT ENOUGH ANSWERS. WHOEVER STOLE THE BOOK BURNER'S BODY WANTED US TO FIND THOSE CAVES, AND CARROLL. BUT WHY?
WE KNOW RALEIGH WAS INVOLVED. PROBABLY TALKED HANK AND ROBBY INTO WHATEVER THEY WERE INTO.
ROBBY SAID SOMETHING ABOUT A CURSE, BUT WHO KNOWS WHAT BULLSHIT RALEIGH WAS FILLING THEIR HEADS WITH... THAT AND--
DID THAT GUY WITH THE MASK... HE HAD TO BE THE ONE WHO TOOK CARROLL, RIGHT?
I'VE BEEN SEARCHING CARROLL'S NOTEBOOK AND I'VE SEEN ZERO MENTION OF OUR NEW FRIEND WITH THE KNIVES.
NO IDEA WHO HE IS.
BUT I'M GOING TO FIND OUT.
SO YOU'RE STICKING AROUND, I TAKE IT?
DAMN STRAIGHT.

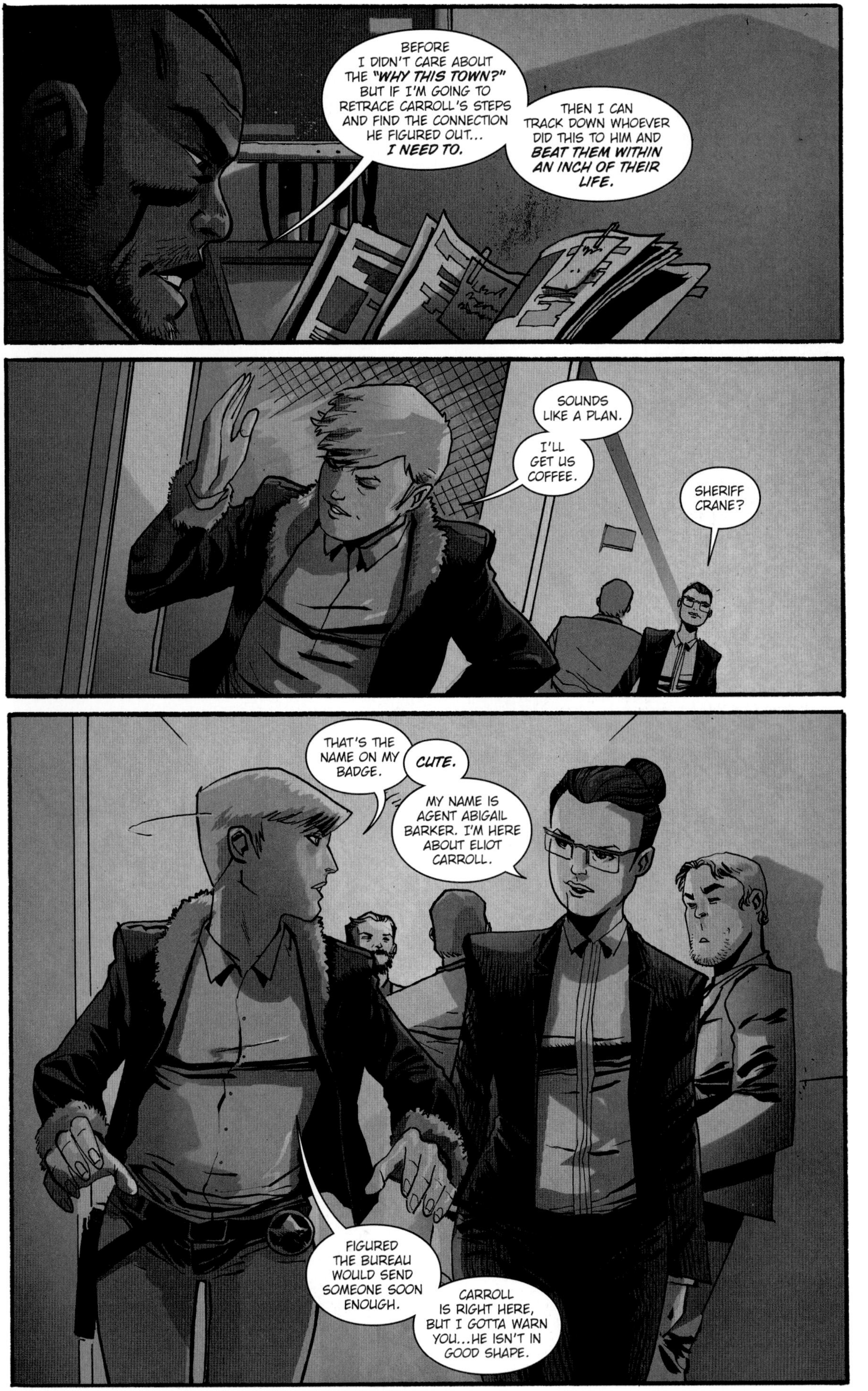
BEFORE I DIDN'T CARE ABOUT THE *"WHY THIS TOWN?"* BUT IF I'M GOING TO RETRACE CARROLL'S STEPS AND FIND THE CONNECTION HE FIGURED OUT... ***I NEED TO.***
THEN I CAN TRACK DOWN WHOEVER DID THIS TO HIM AND ***BEAT THEM WITHIN AN INCH OF THEIR LIFE.***
SOUNDS LIKE A PLAN.
I'LL GET US COFFEE.
SHERIFF CRANE?
THAT'S THE NAME ON MY BADGE.
***CUTE.***
MY NAME IS AGENT ABIGAIL BARKER. I'M HERE ABOUT ELIOT CARROLL.
FIGURED THE BUREAU WOULD SEND SOMEONE SOON ENOUGH.
CARROLL IS RIGHT HERE, BUT I GOTTA WARN YOU...HE ISN'T IN GOOD SHAPE.

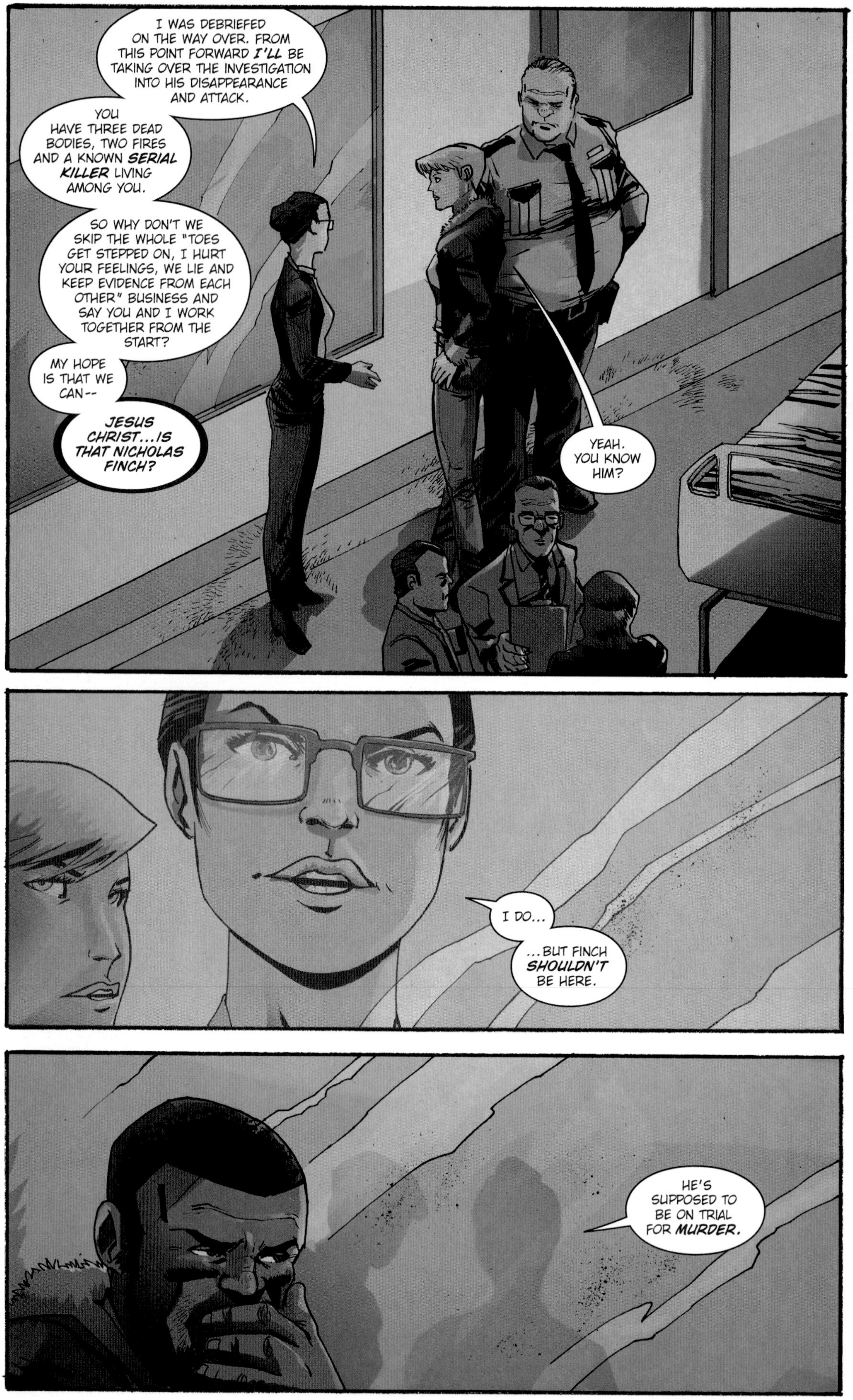
I WAS DEBRIEFED ON THE WAY OVER. FROM THIS POINT FORWARD *I'LL* BE TAKING OVER THE INVESTIGATION INTO HIS DISAPPEARANCE AND ATTACK.
YOU HAVE THREE DEAD BODIES, TWO FIRES AND A KNOWN *SERIAL KILLER* LIVING AMONG YOU.
SO WHY DON'T WE SKIP THE WHOLE "TOES GET STEPPED ON, I HURT YOUR FEELINGS, WE LIE AND KEEP EVIDENCE FROM EACH OTHER" BUSINESS AND SAY YOU AND I WORK TOGETHER FROM THE START?
MY HOPE IS THAT WE CAN--
*JESUS CHRIST...IS THAT NICHOLAS FINCH?*
YEAH. YOU KNOW HIM?
I DO...
...BUT FINCH *SHOULDN'T* BE HERE.
HE'S SUPPOSED TO BE ON TRIAL FOR *MURDER.*

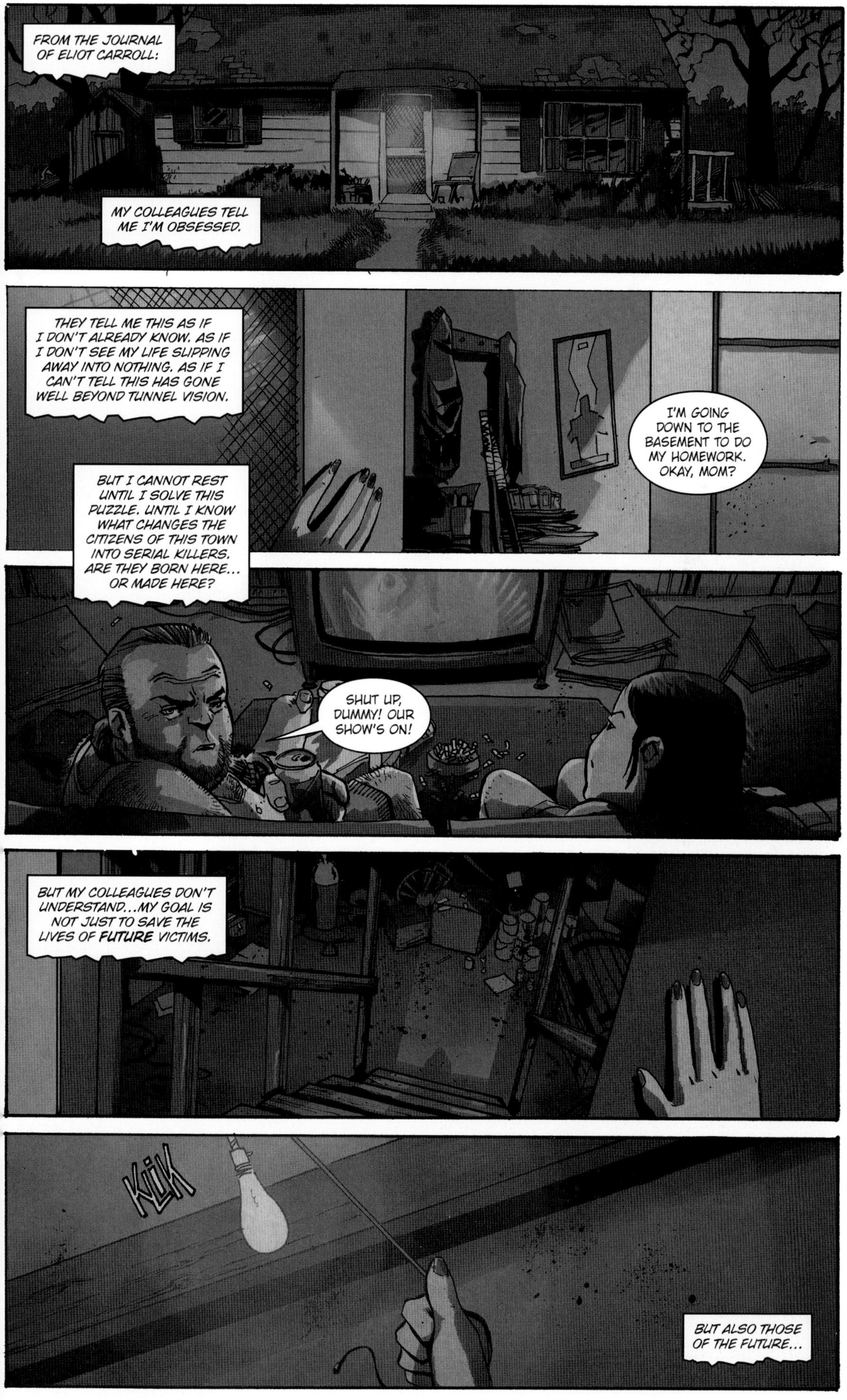
FROM THE JOURNAL OF ELIOT CARROLL:
MY COLLEAGUES TELL ME I'M OBSESSED.
THEY TELL ME THIS AS IF I DON'T ALREADY KNOW. AS IF I DON'T SEE MY LIFE SLIPPING AWAY INTO NOTHING. AS IF I CAN'T TELL THIS HAS GONE WELL BEYOND TUNNEL VISION.
I'M GOING DOWN TO THE BASEMENT TO DO MY HOMEWORK. OKAY, MOM?
BUT I CANNOT REST UNTIL I SOLVE THIS PUZZLE. UNTIL I KNOW WHAT CHANGES THE CITIZENS OF THIS TOWN INTO SERIAL KILLERS. ARE THEY BORN HERE... OR MADE HERE?
SHUT UP, DUMMY! OUR SHOW'S ON!
BUT MY COLLEAGUES DON'T UNDERSTAND...MY GOAL IS NOT JUST TO SAVE THE LIVES OF **FUTURE** VICTIMS.
KLIK
BUT ALSO THOSE OF THE FUTURE...

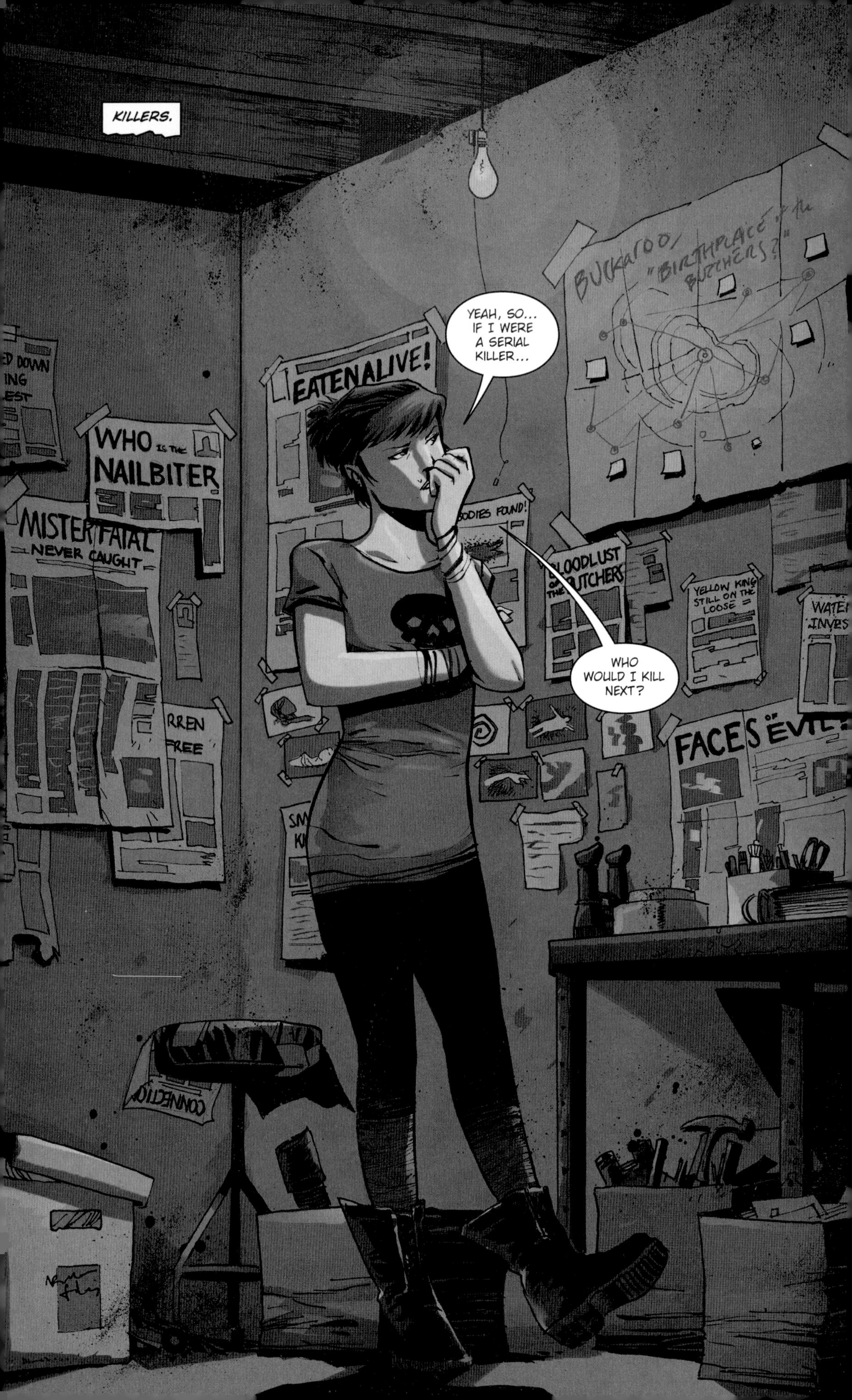
KILLERS.
YEAH, SO... IF I WERE A SERIAL KILLER...
WHO WOULD I KILL NEXT?
BUCKAROO, "BIRTHPLACE of the BUTCHERS?"
EATEN ALIVE!
WHO IS THE NAILBITER
MISTER FATAL NEVER CAUGHT
BODIES FOUND!
BLOODLUST OF THE BUTCHERS
YELLOW KING STILL ON THE LOOSE
FACES OF EVIL

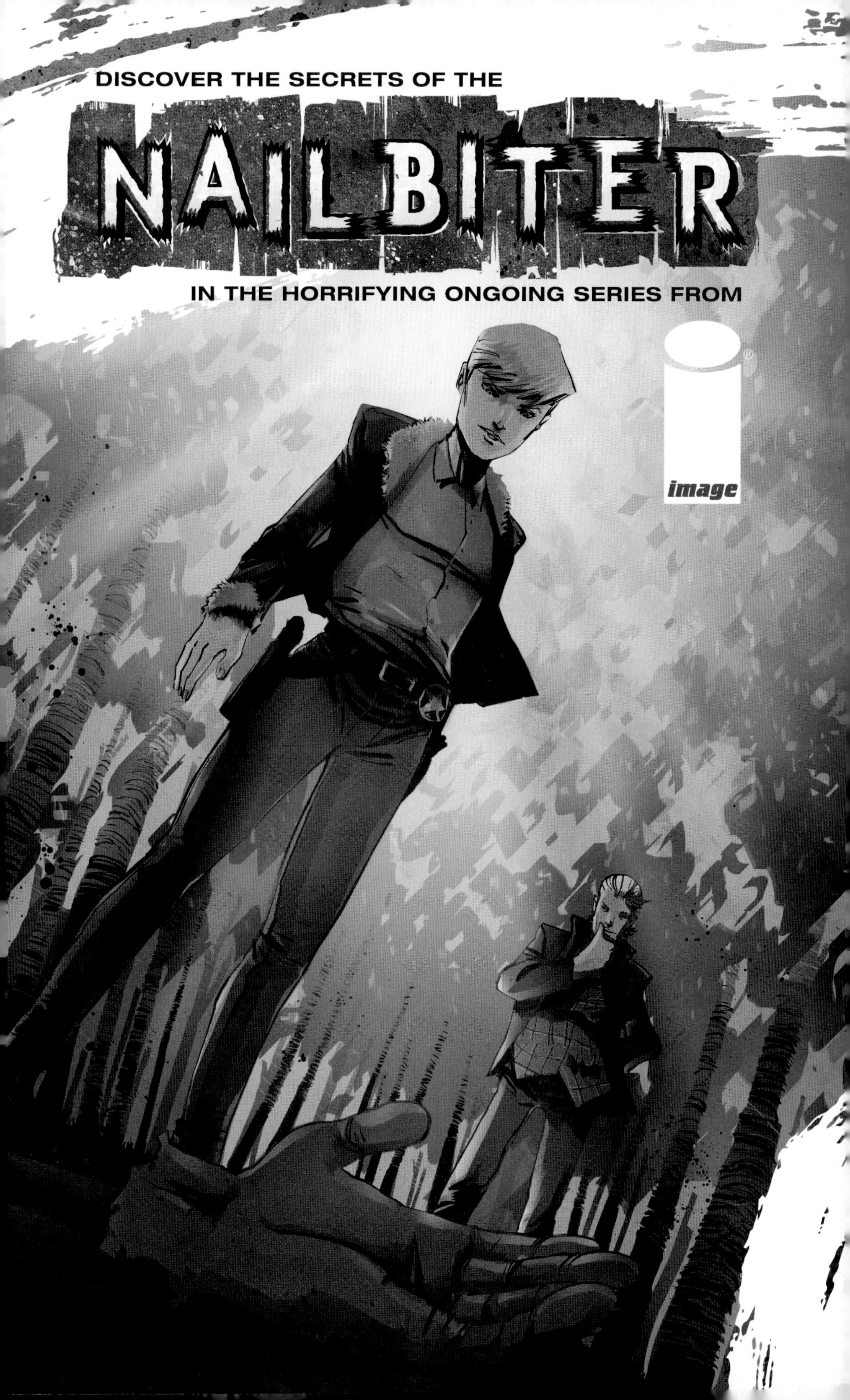
DISCOVER THE SECRETS OF THE
NAILBITER
IN THE HORRIFYING ONGOING SERIES FROM
image

# COVER GALLERY

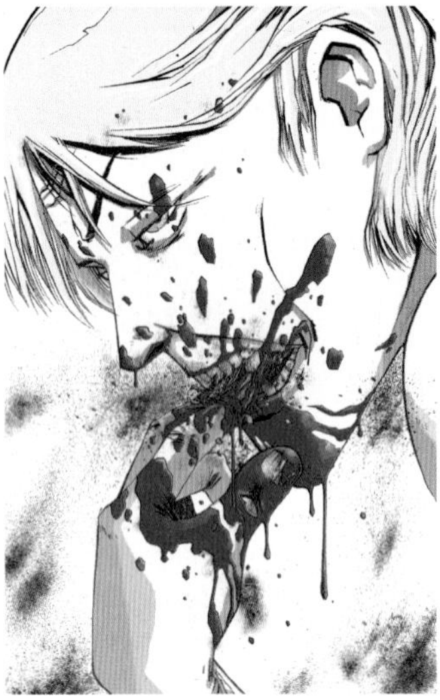

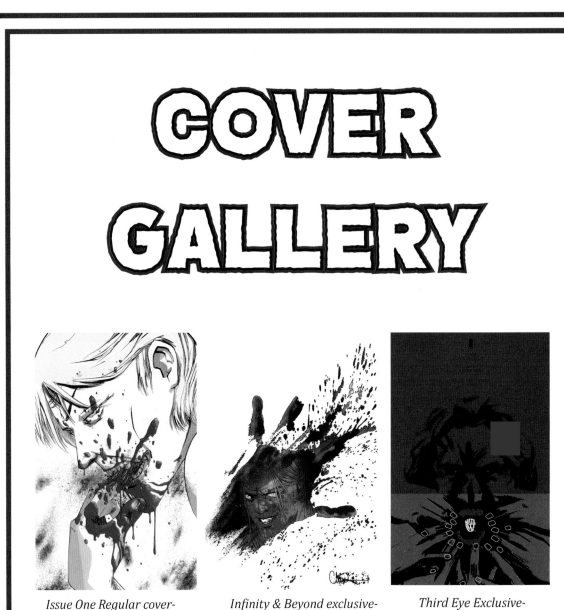

*Issue One Regular cover-
Mike Henderson*

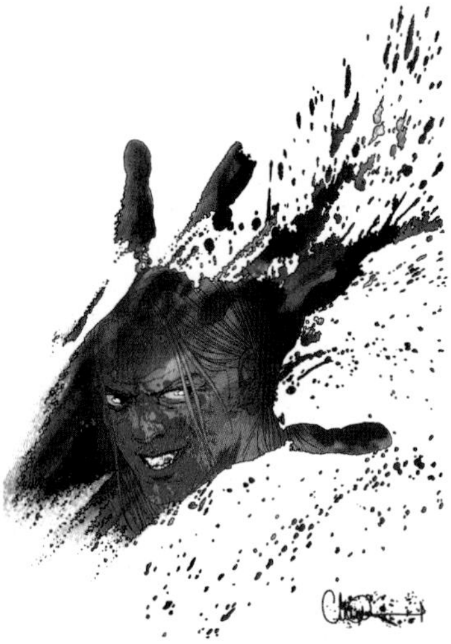

*Infinity & Beyond exclusive-
Charlie Adlard*

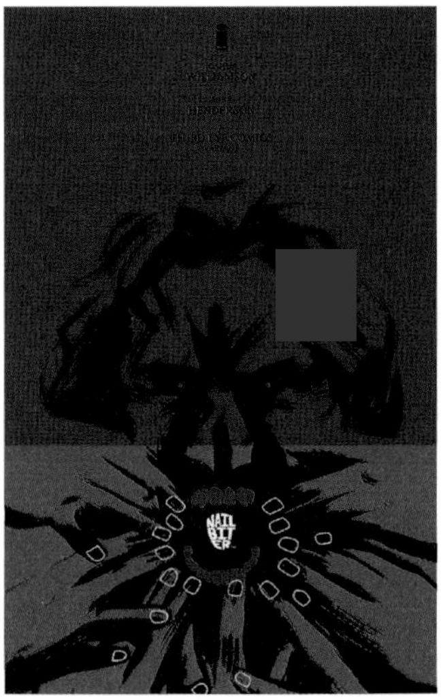

*Third Eye Exclusive-
Chip Zdarsky*

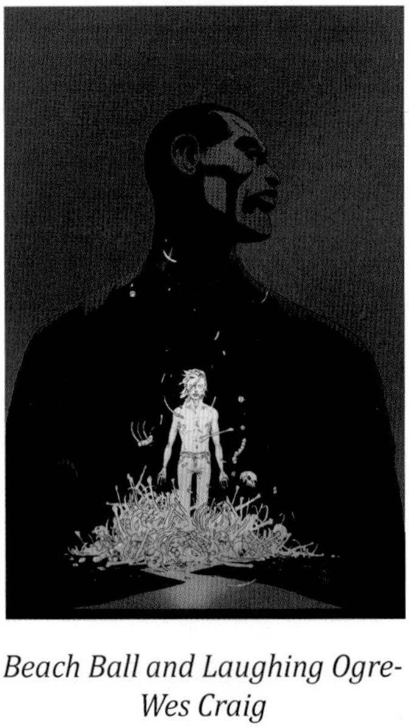

*Beach Ball and Laughing Ogre-
Wes Craig*

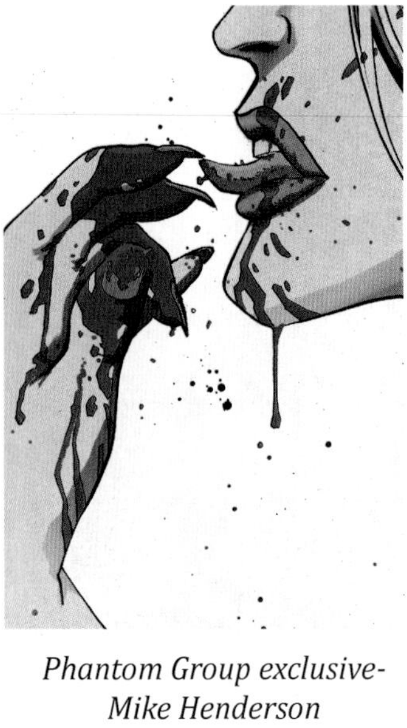

*Phantom Group exclusive-
Mike Henderson*

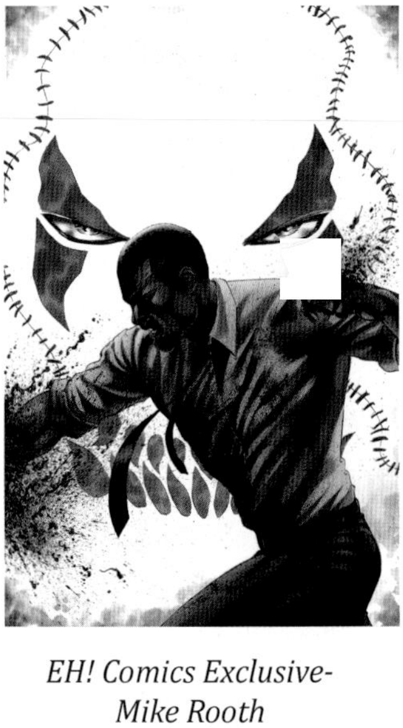

*EH! Comics Exclusive-
Mike Rooth*

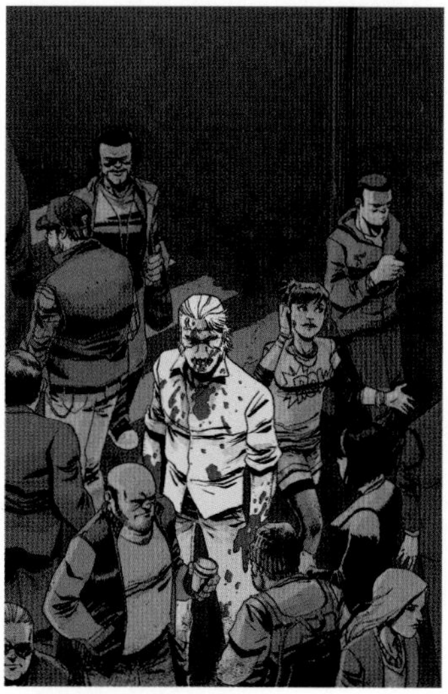

*Issue Two 2nd print*

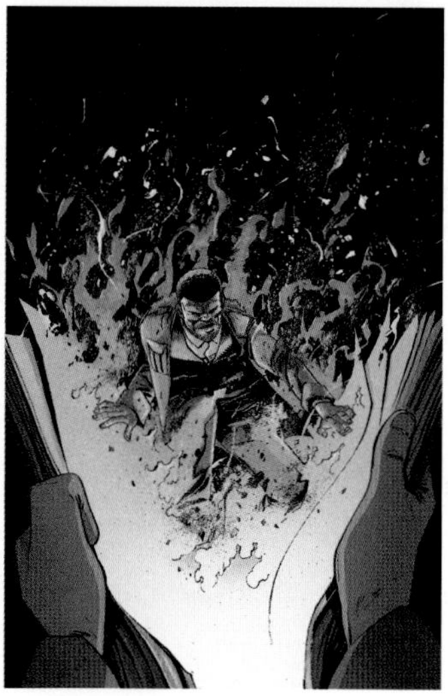

*Issue Two cover*

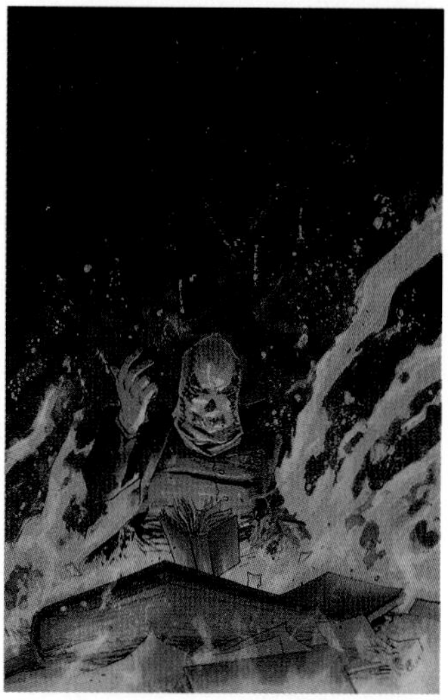

*Issue Two 2nd print*

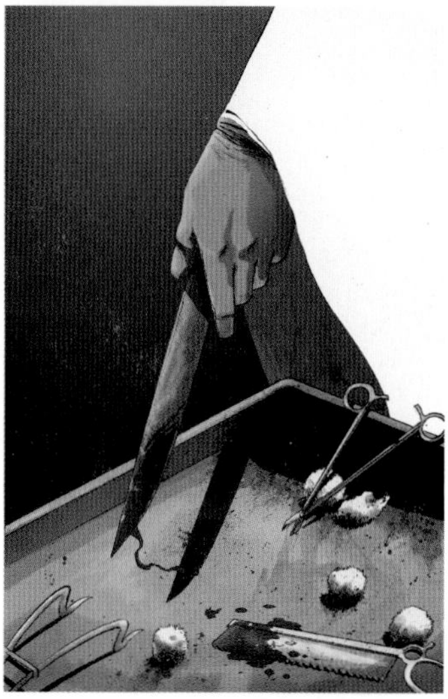

*Issue Three cover*

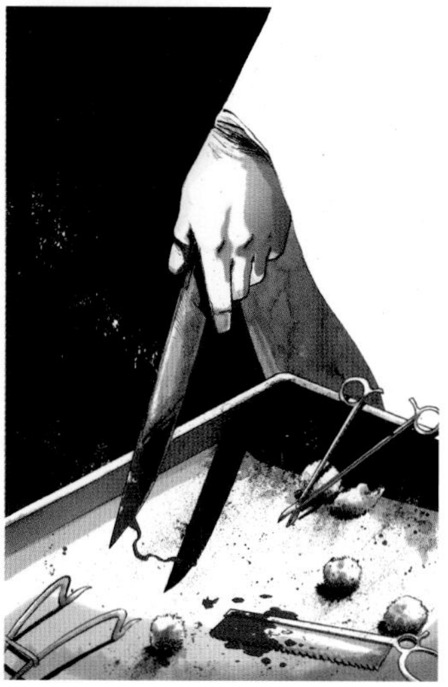

*Issue Three 2nd print*

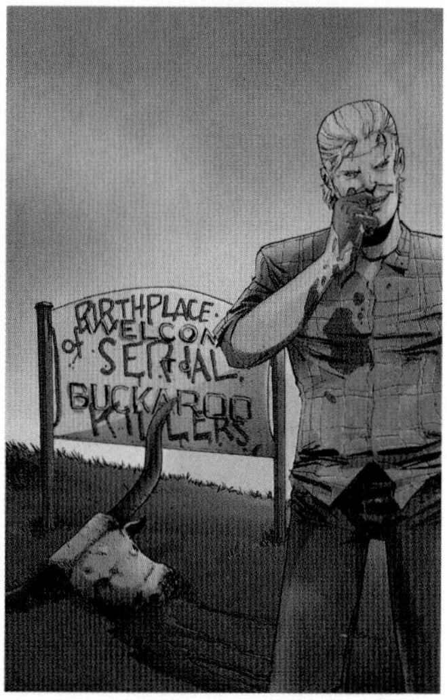
SERIAL
BUCKAROO
KILLERS

*Issue Three SDCC exclusive*

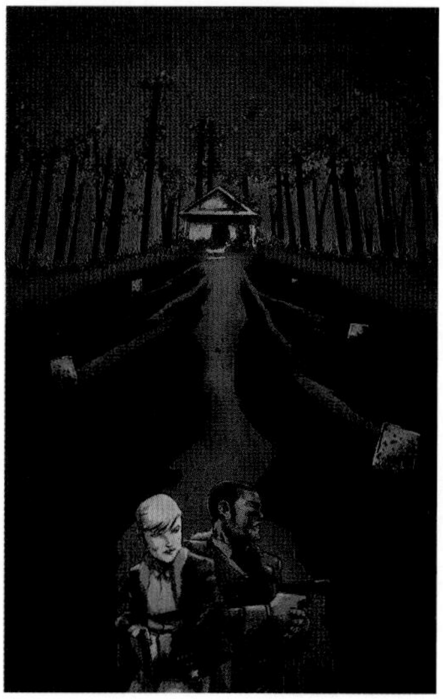

*Issue Four cover*

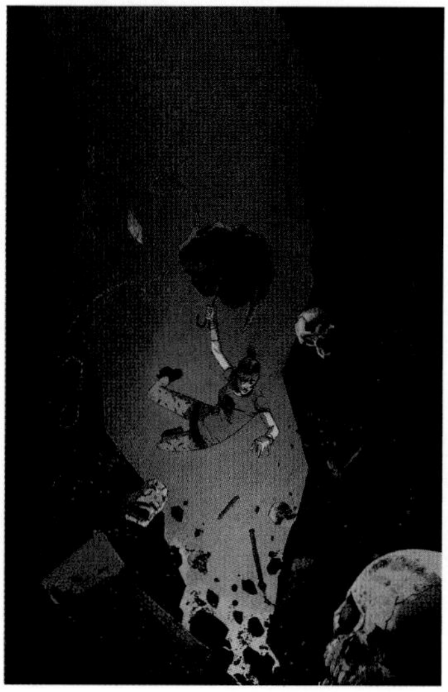

*Issue Five cover*

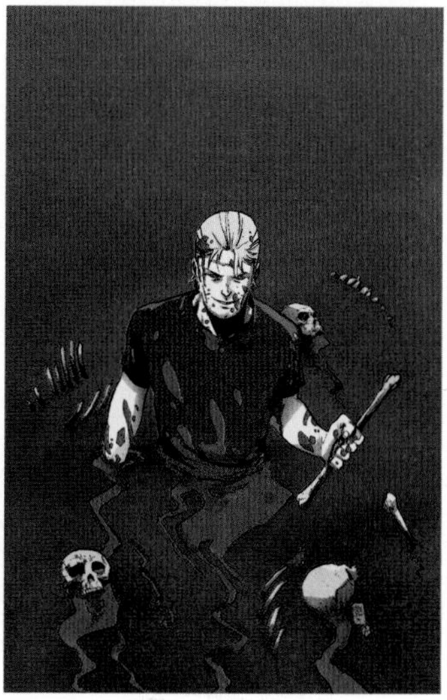

*Issue Five RonCon Exclusive*

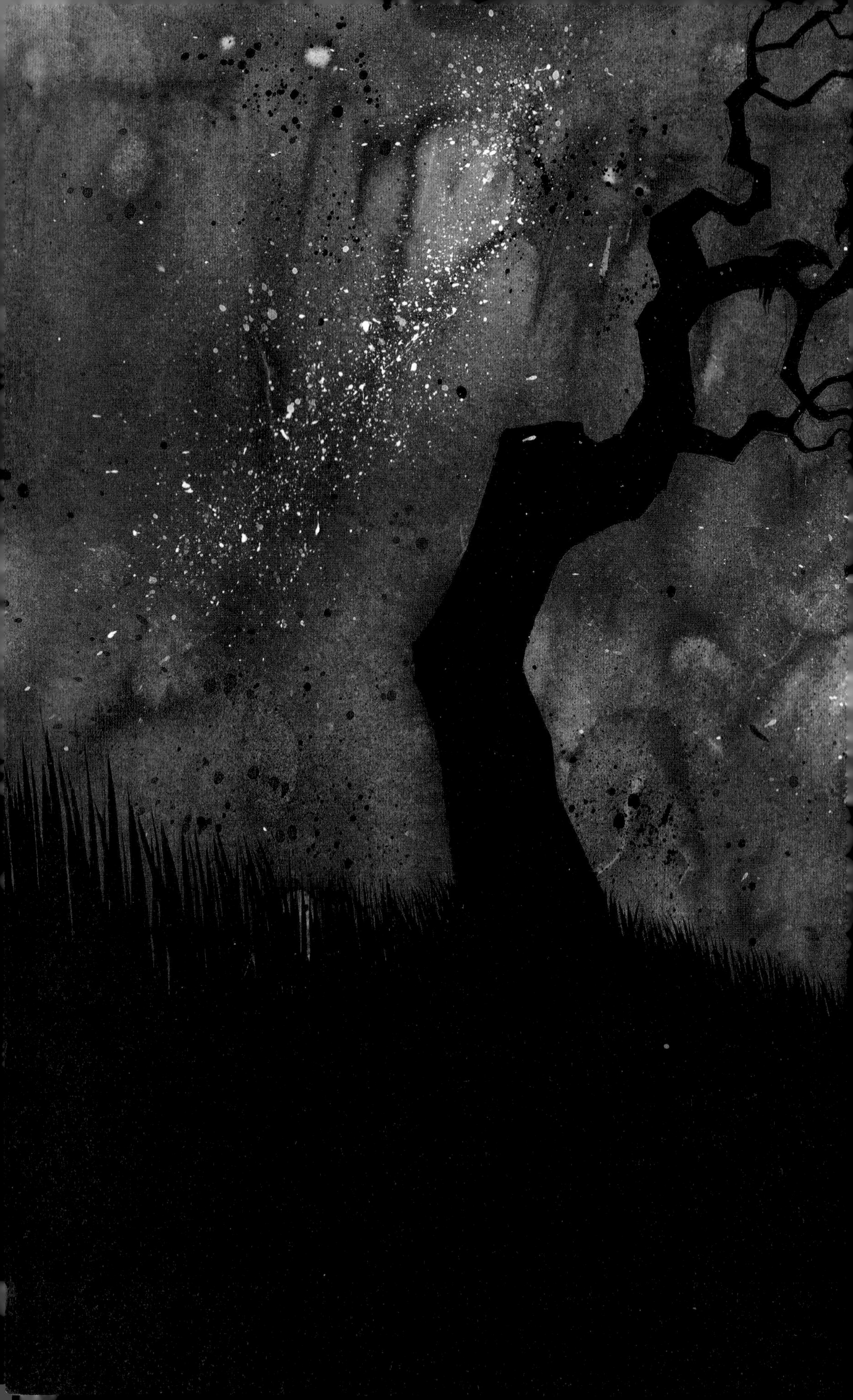

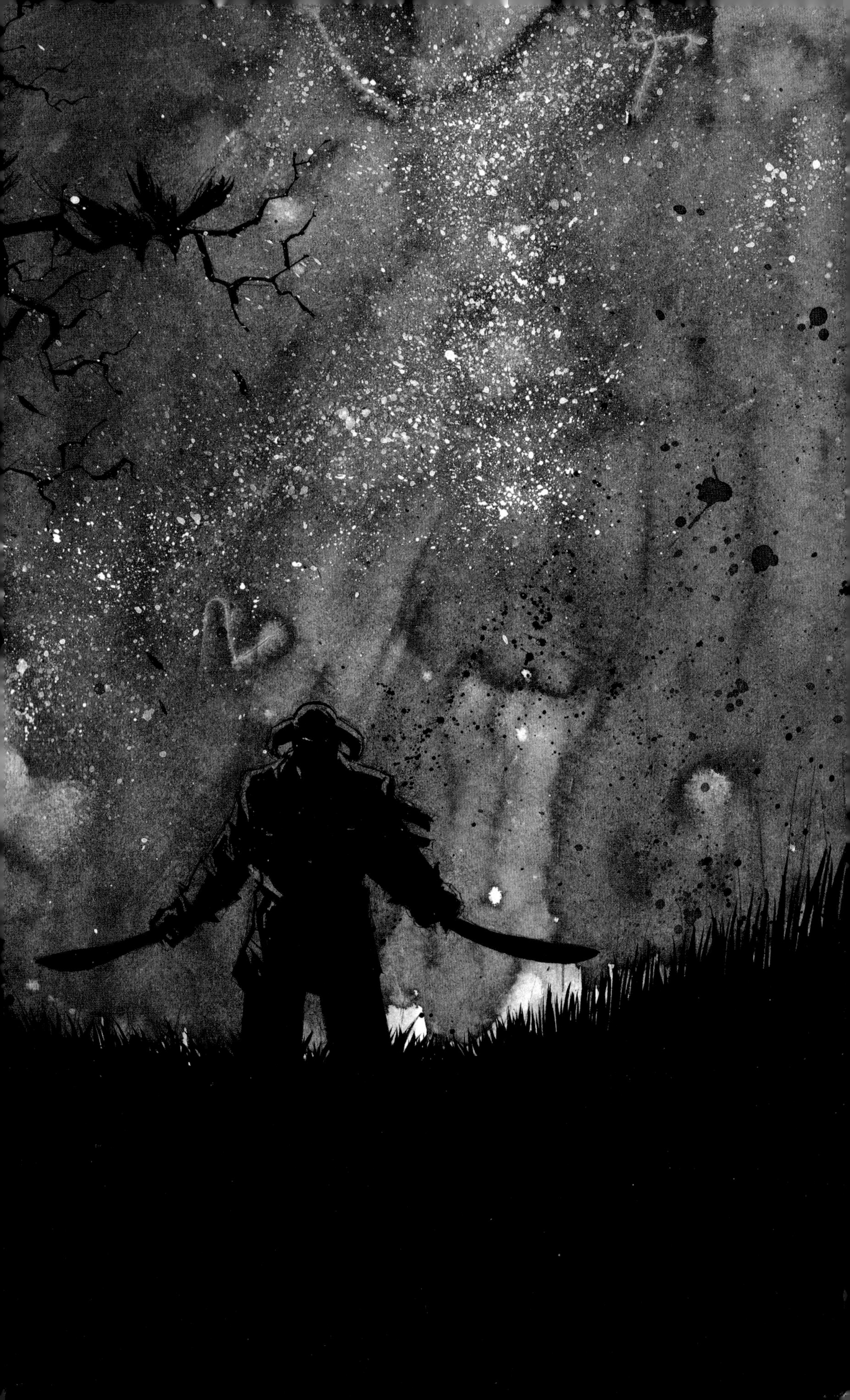

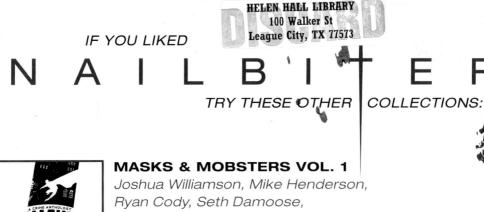

*IF YOU LIKED*

# N A I L B I T E R

*TRY THESE OTHER COLLECTIONS:*

A CRIME ANTHOLOGY
MASKS & MOBSTERS
JOSHUA WILLIAMSON · MIKE HENDERSON

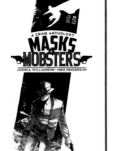

**MASKS & MOBSTERS VOL. 1**

*Joshua Williamson, Mike Henderson, Ryan Cody, Seth Damoose, Justin Greenwood, Jason Copland*

**128 PAGES HARDCOVER**
**ISBN: 978-1607067658**

**GHOSTED VOL. 1**

*Joshua Williamson, Goran Sudzuka & Miroslav Mrva*

**144 PAGES SOFTCOVER**
**ISBN: 978-1607068365**

JOSHUA WILLIAMSON · GORAN SUDZUKA · MIROSLAV MRVA
GHOSTED
VOLUME ONE · HAUNTED HEIST

JOSHUA WILLIAMSON · DAVIDE GIANFELICE · MIROSLAV MRVA
GHOSTED
VOLUME TWO · BOOKS OF THE DEAD

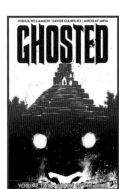

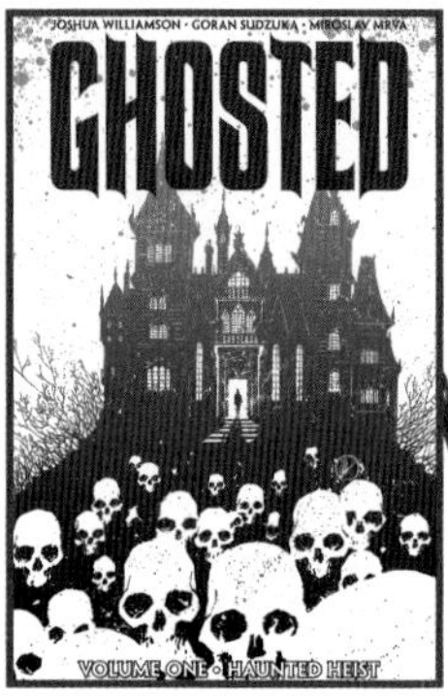

**GHOSTED VOL. 2**

*Joshua Williamson, Davide Gianfelice & Miroslav Mrva*

**120 PAGES SOFTCOVER**
**ISBN: 978-1632150462**

**GHOSTED VOL. 3**

*Joshua Williamson, Goran Sudzuka, Davide Gianfelice, Miroslav Mrva*

**120 PAGES SOFTCOVER**
**ISBN: 978-1632150516**

WILLIAMSON · GIANFELICE · SUDZUKA · MRVA
GHOSTED
VOLUME THREE · DEATH WISH

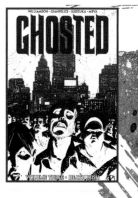

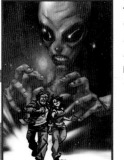

**XENOHOLICS**

*Joshua Williamson & Seth Damoose*

**126 PAGES SOFTCOVER**
**ISBN: 978-1607065579**

**DEAR DRACULA**

*Joshua Williamson & Vicente "Vinny" Navarrete*

**48 PAGES HARDCOVER**
**ISBN: 978-1582409702**

DEAR DRACULA
JOSHUA WILLIAMSON
VICENTE "VINNY" NAVARRETE

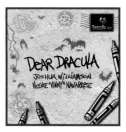

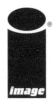

PLEASE VISIT: **IMAGECOMICS.COM** for more information.
To find your local comic shop call **1-888-comicbook** or visit **www.comicshop.us**